LEADERSHIP REIMAGINED

Leadership Reimagined

The Impacts of Continuous Improvement
& Respect for People

Brian deFonteny

Only the humble are capable of shifting from traditional management to Servant leadership behaviors once they learn about Lean. The rest cling mightily to their caveman ways.

Library of Congress Control Number: 2019912786
ISBN: 978-0-578-55249-1

Many events contained herein have been recreated from memory of actual events in the author's life, though some have been supplemented for illustrative purposes. When necessary, names and details of individuals have been changed to respect privacy, and certain individuals may be composites.

Cover Design: Angie at Pro_ebookcovers
Drawings: Mohammedbinzain, Alextes
Photos: Odejacob, Bokskapet
For help above and beyond: Ivan Ortiz
Special thanks to Tanmay Vora at QAspire.com for the use of What Rebels Want

Dedication

As this book was coming to fruition, I contemplated to whom I might dedicate it. With no intentionally generated list of contenders in my head, an epiphany came to me one day with crystal clarity. One of the thousands of students I've had the distinct honor to guide along my Lean journey said to me during a Green Belt class in Tulsa, Oklahoma, *"Why would anyone NOT want to be Lean minded?"* I continue to ponder the question daily – as I have since my journey began—and simply responded to Jon Nelson with, *"because habits, even bad ones are very difficult to replace."*

Jon was a brilliant, likable, selfless young engineer in his late 20s with incredible leadership potential, but tragically lost his life in an automobile accident in July 2017, just four months after asking me this question. I will never forget the inspiration Jon bestowed on me and others with his hunger for absorbing more Lean concepts and application techniques. He wholly accepted the power of the Lean business system as the only logical alternative to traditional management. Jon was, without a doubt, a converted Lean change agent. He got it quickly. Some never do. I am convinced Jon would have enjoyed the stories and broken processes I now share with the rest of the world. I am a better person for having known Jon Nelson. We mere mortals are fortunate for being exposed to others capable of inspiring us beyond our current interpretation of the world around us. Now if we can only take the time to listen and recognize there are always better ways of doing everything, even after we discover them.

"If your actions inspire others to Dream more, Do more and Become more, you are a Leader." - Dolly Parton

Acknowledgement

When a human being completes an endeavor in life, of any magnitude large or small, they should pause for a moment and recognize they didn't do it alone. It is simply not possible. Other people were required for various elements. And so was the case with this book. It could not have reached fruition without the significant contributions of editing, sanity checking, formatting, and overall support from my wife, Cheri. Her literary skills far exceed mine and I was abundantly grateful to have her as an objective participant to help me throughout the process.

Table of Contents

10 Things I've Learned on My Lean Journey
(And Fully Believe from the Core of My Being)

1. The label "Leader" is not automatically bestowed upon those with assigned authority, title, or rank, and definitely not from longevity in a formal managerial role. It must be earned.
2. Lean leadership, when culturally inserted as the mandated behavior to extinguish traditional management, can take any company from mediocre to wildly successful.
3. Every employee on planet Earth deserves to be treated with respect, including not only common decency, but also respect as it applies to the work they are asked to do and the cultural environment they are asked to do it in.
4. Every person has at least one forte, but broken selection processes fail to identify it, while other broken processes fail to intentionally help it manifest and grow.
5. If you are not an avid Gemba walker, you are clueless about the hurdles your employees are fighting within processes you are trying to manage.
6. If you lack humility <u>and</u> the ability to view direct reports as your customers and the most important players in the value stream (**far** more important than you as the formal manager), your process of progressing from manager to leader will never manifest.
7. If you do not fully understand the concept of Voice of the Customer (VOC), don't measure it, or fail to seek updates to it, then plan to be far less successful than your competitors who do.
8. People in positions of formal authority are either leaders or managers, and the latter can only be permanently transformed if they possess humility and a genuine desire (the want) to shift.

9. If you are not continuously (*daily*) trying to improve your capability to instill higher levels of empowerment and engagement in the employees reporting to you, you should change your process or relinquish your role of formal authority.

10. If you are unfamiliar with the incredible power of the Lean Business System, you are living in the dark ages. Fortunately, you are still on the right side of the dirt and have time to transform.

The Genesis of My Lean Journey

"All the world is my school and all humanity is my teacher." - George Whitman

CAUTION: If you are entirely content with the results of your leadership style, then you probably will not need to read this book. But, keep in mind, 'completely content' should equal:

- Your empowerment actions are driving intense levels of loyalty and passion within the people you lead
- Your company is experiencing wild success with zero re-work
- Quality levels are precisely where they should be with no safety issues ever
- Customers are beating down your doors for your product or service because you far exceed your competitors' capabilities
- Customers (internal and external) never have to wait on anything
- Your employees are dramatically engaged, can't wait to get to work each day, and are energized with a mission of making processes better based on documented customer requirements

If this description is your current reality, this book's content will be redundant to you, and while it might amuse you to read how I've seen leadership conducted so effectively by some and so pathetically ineffectively by others, it probably will not educate you further. However, if your company has not yet reached the cultural excellence I've described above, I invite you to explore the enlightenment I have experienced on my personal Lean journey, which started in 2000. It includes the good, the bad, and, most educational to me, the butt ugly.

I often wondered what motivates a person to write a book. So many authors and influencers have captured my interest over the years on the topic of Lean, leadership, employee engagement, and process improvement in general. Lean makes total sense to me, and it has for a very long time. How any business could not take the time to learn and practice Lean is beyond logical comprehension. After retiring from a government career of 35 years and taking a job in the natural gas industry, coming to work was a joy. I couldn't wait to get there. When Sunday night rolled around, I'd think to myself, *I get to go to work tomorrow!* How many people are this excited about their job these days? Poll your employees and get a count. Then deduct the ones who said yes but are proficient at sarcasm or lying through their teeth because they think it's the answer you wanted to hear. It's likely a smaller number than you thought.

My euphoria was a long time coming, and, unfortunately, it did not remain a constant companion on my journey. When I finally retired from my corporate gig, I admitted to myself that I didn't have the energy to start again unless some company was fully receptive to process improvement done properly. I would need a company with leadership willing to admit they didn't have all the answers to creating amazing engagement in the workforce and their processes were something short of spectacular. This would be a monumental achievement, and I needed something to fill the gap in the event it didn't manifest quickly, or at all. Regardless, I still felt compelled to share the things I'd learned with some audience who would, perhaps, appreciate and learn from it.

And so, I began to document the experiences I've had along the way since my journey started with the hope it can inspire others to shift from just a manager to a Leader. These labels are not even close to synonymous. My journey includes the insanity, the joy, the wins, the losses, the horrible bosses and the great ones, the insightful Gemba walks, the wonderful people, the pathetically broken processes that defy all logic known to mankind, the rapid improvement events (RIEs) souring north, the ones plunging to the south, the managers who, after attending some of my training, humbly admitted they were not inspiring their employees or treating them with sufficient respect, and everything contributing to my 100% buy-in of the Lean business system. If the word Gemba is brand new to you, I will very briefly describe the activity here, but I devote an entire chapter to Gemba walking. Feel free to read it first then return to this point. A Gemba is a place where the actual work is being accomplished by an employee, and a Gemba Walk is the activity of someone observing the task first-hand to understand the process flow, discover hurdles for employees, then assisting in removing these wasteful hurdles frustrating people burdened with them. Gemba walking is a profound form of empowerment most managers are missing out on, but a staple of the Lean leader.

I've stepped in many potholes along my nearly twenty-year journey, and I now take pleasure in pointing them out to the unaware so they can avoid them. If Black Belts (and other process improvement specialists) are not mapping the minefield they have previously walked through and guiding others as their #1 mission, they do not understand their role as process improvement practitioners. We should be change agents at heart, not just data crunchers and chart builders to depict common and special cause variability in process X. Transforming the culture in a direction which teaches the masses to fish—both formal and informal leaders alike—is why we should get out of bed in the morning. Of course, some are "doers" (conducting projects themselves) to a notable extent, but the majority of their activity should be in influencing others and shifting behaviors in the company. This is the process and the destination of real continuous improvement + respect for people.

And this is why I now invite you on this journey with me. If you are a leader of people - formally or informally - officially involved in process improvement in your organization, or an employee searching for ways to provide the best customer experience possible, I hope that you will engage in some introspective analysis, take some wisdom away from my experiences, and implement changes into your own workplace environment. If this is the case, we will both have benefited from the endeavor of this book.

"All great changes are preceded by chaos." – Deepak Chopra

What is Lean? The Big Picture

"We cannot become what we want to be by remaining what we are." –Max DePree

Critical Elements of Lean

So, what is Lean, anyway? I like to begin my classes by asking this question, just to get a baseline of student understanding. One day, in a class full of primarily frontline workers who only needed to learn the absolute basics, an employee in Texas proudly raised his hand.

"Yes, sir, I'm familiar with Lean." Excellent. I was genuinely interested in his perception.

Without pause, a morsel of sarcasm, or lack of conviction, this young man said, "It's all about getting rid of employees, so a company can get the job done with the least number of people possible."

My heart sank. How in the name of holy hell could this completely incorrect assumption make its way into anyone's head? In fact, it was the flawed process of communicating this information effectively to 6000+ employees scattered across the country, and I was a part of the broken process. Message received!

I quickly explained nothing could be further from the truth, and gave the class a succinct definition of what Lean really is: First determining what your customer needs (the product/service, the quality level required, the timeline important to them, the cost they are willing to pay, etc.), then striving to design a process to meet these requirements in the most efficient manner possible.

I let them know this meant reducing waste in the form of defects, delays, over-processing, and other things the customer had no interest in paying for but was generally subjected to in most processes. And lastly, I assured them if a particular process could be subsequently done with fewer people, the extra workers in a Lean environment are shifted to another process truly needing more people – they are not discarded like extra chairs or desks. Excess capacity is within the awareness of leadership, and people might move to another process, but not out the door. Canning employees is disrespectful, and it starts when a company hires more people than needed in the first place. More bodies get thrown at wasteful processes to keep up, instead of reducing wasteful activity.

Unfortunately, my explanation was exponentially more difficult in the current environment we were enduring at the time. The company had just laid off about 700+ employees in reaction to an oil/gas price downturn. Here I was telling the masses Lean was not about getting rid of bodies, and the company had done precisely this. The hypocrisy was ringing in my own ears, but I strived nonetheless to help them understand.

Back to a definition of what Lean is. You will no doubt be exposed to any number of variations, but this is how I interpret the concept I eat, sleep, live, breathe, teach, coach, and now write about. It is both complicated and simplistic at the same time. Buckle up. The magic of the Big Picture is about to be revealed.

Lean is a business mentality of providing a product or service with minimal waste from the customer's perspective.

Let this wash over you for a bit. It may seem utterly intuitive on the first pass, but there are mountains of elements buried within it. If you consider Lean a tool, a program, or something sounding like touchy-feely fluff, you could not be more mistaken. I cringe when I hear people define Lean as a tool. Six Sigma is a tool. Taking a statistical approach to determining the path to reducing process variation is a noble endeavor, but it doesn't even come close to the business mentality I strive to explain here. Sophisticated spreadsheets, charts, process maps, A3s, and fancy electronic gadgets or software to capture critical business information are tools, but they fall dramatically short of cultural behaviors necessary to make employees excited about coming to work and wanting to continuously improve the processes they work in, all based on customer requirements. Understanding this difference is critical to grasping what Lean is all about. You need to key in on the *business mentality* language to understand it.

If by chance you have ever experienced frustrating service from a restaurant, store, or any type of business, then you will immediately connect with the dismal considerations given to the most critical contributor in any value stream – the ***customer!*** Without a customer, any product or service on earth has a bleak future. The customer wanting a product or a service has a certain expectation of quality and timeliness in mind. The disconnect begins when the provider fails to keep this on a front burner. Assumption and ignorance both play a big part, along with doing wasteful things just because this is how they have always been done. *It's been good enough for the past 50 years we've been in business, so why change now?* This is the mantra of the non-Lean mind.

Now let's add in another corrosive element—the self-serving, traditional manager who is supposed to be guiding this Charlie Foxtrot (military code for something less-than-stellar) of a process to provide the service or product to customers. They are clueless how to fully empower employees, how to get them engaged and excited about the job, so, armed with their management training from the University of Cavemen (UC), they replicate dysfunctional command and control methods. My-Way-or-The-Highway is embroidered on he back of their varsity jackets. Perhaps you have worked for one (or more) of these individuals in your career at some point. They tell people what to do and how to do it, but when you make a mistake, you are berated as though you intentionally produced the defect, delay, or safety issue. The instructions you are given are vague or incomplete, the tools to perform the task inadequate, the subjective feedback batched, and the support to be successful withheld (or poorly dispensed) all because of ignorance within the broken managerial process these individuals embrace. It's a formula for most of the undesirable outcomes companies experience today. Surely there is a better way.

Indeed, there is.

To repeat: Lean is a business mentality of providing a product or service with minimal waste from the *customer's* perspective.

Let's spend some time on the word *waste*. Is it like a defective product or delay in delivery? Well, yes, it can be, but it's time you expand your understanding of what waste is in the Lean vernacular. If Lean is a brand-new concept to you, this explanation will no doubt strike a chord, perhaps even anger you. You will rebel, resist, or maybe label this concept complete BS. It's a normal reaction, but I encourage you to please hang with me. Until you can recognize/accept tasks as waste, they will remain in place and continue to minimize your levels of success.

First, you have to recognize what your customers need and are willing to pay for. Let's assume you sell and install tires on cars. Your customers need new tires installed on their car; this is their requirement and what they are willing to pay for. Now let's explore the mountains of waste you insist they wade through to get those new tires on their car. It's about 95% of the entire process.

They come into your store and have to wait for an available salesperson to help them (waste). Then the employee finally is "helping" the customer but has to struggle with the computer because they are either poorly trained (waste) or because the software is not processing quickly (waste). In either case, the customer has to wait some more (waste). Now suppose the tires they want are unavailable because the process you use to project consumption is flawed, making inventory listed on their computer unreliable (waste), and you spend time describing an alternative tire (waste). This is not the tire the customer wanted, but they are settling because your current process is not accommodating their needs. After this defect occurs, chances are high you do nothing to investigate and prevent it from happening again. Now the car has to be transported inside the shop (waste), assuming the mechanic is even aware it's in queue. He/she fills out paperwork (waste), pulls the car onto the lift (waste), raises the car (waste), gathers up his tools (waste), removes lug nuts (waste), puts them down somewhere (waste), takes the wheel/tire assembly off the vehicle (waste), rolls it over to mount it on the machine which breaks the tire loose from the wheel (waste), and then finally is physically removing the old tire (valued added). Whew! We haven't even gotten anywhere close to the post-tire change steps the customer will have to endure. And by the way, the customer is paying for all this insanity because you bury it in the final price to cover your overhead. Imagine their demeanor if you itemized every step with separate fees on the bill. Fill out paperwork, $15.89, transport car to lift, $22.55, etc. Counter workers would need body armor, earplugs, and full-face shields.

Let's pause here to address your objections to all these items being waste. You may have heard the term "value added" to describe a step which the external customer is **willing** to pay for. The vast majority of steps in any process exist not because the customer says they want all this minutia; they exist because a process has been designed without significant analysis to reduce or eliminate them. Process waste creeps in and remains forever unless recognized and challenged.

Looking at the steps themselves, allow me to explain why they are waste. Waste is any task (*in isolation of all other tasks*) not physically changing the form, fit, or function of the service/product the customer wants. The customer waiting for an available salesperson is waste because your process is not robust enough to immediately engage with the customer, or to clearly educate them on options before arriving at the store. If you think your website is getting this done, just ask the customers to verify or clarify perceptions. You might argue you can't have more employees because of the cost, but you are presumptively concluding more people will resolve this issue. Reduce the wasteful activity bestowed on the employees, and they will be better able to quickly engage with the customer. Flow will increase and cycle times will decrease.

Driving the car into the shop – *How can this be waste? It is where we do the work!* Well, recognize it's your process design dictating the vehicle be moved into the shop. You are only moving the car, nothing physically changed related to what the customer needs—old tires removed and new tires installed on the wheels. I can imagine every parking spot outside having a lift. Now, this might be cost prohibitive for the establishment, but the example supports the assertion of moving the car as valueless to the customer.

Now we raise the car on the lift. *Surely this is value-added.* Nope. Again, nothing has changed yet according to what the customer wants. You might argue if you don't raise the car, you can't remove the tire/wheel assembly. But notice your objection to the waste label here is combining steps. You need to critique each step in isolation of all other steps. Raising the car, by itself, in isolation of all other steps coming after it, does *not* change the form, fit, or function of what the customer wants. We could raise the car up and down a dozen times in a row and still not have affected the status of the tires on the wheels. It's waste, and waste equals the opportunity to increase the flow of your process by reducing steps of no value. Imagine using a tool to remove the tire from the rim while it is still on the car. They actually exist. The more steps you add in, the greater the chance for the flow to reach sloth speed. The customer wants their tires changed, and this step in isolation has done nothing to change the status of tires on the car. I know, it seems nit-picky, but when you shift your perspective to attacking all these wasteful steps and manage to reduce or eliminate some of them, your process just got more attractive to customers (in the form of quicker flow) than your caveman competitors down the street. Given equal quality of the product/service, a customer will choose the better customer experience. You will also become the less expensive provider because cost reduction comes from waste reduction. When you pass these savings onto the customer, your competitors will not be able to keep up.

Using this new lens of labeling steps value-added (an action which by itself actually changes form, fit, or function of what the customer wants, and one he/she is willing to pay for if given an itemized bill) or non-value added (everything else), you will begin to see the enormous opportunity to improve your processes. Gathering tools, filling out paperwork, ordering material, putting product on the shelf, getting it back off the shelf, inspecting anything, moving things around, holding meetings, forcing people to wait in lines—it's all waste to your external customer. Ignore it by arguing you *have* to do it and you risk obsolescence as a provider. Currently, you force the customer to pay for all the wasteful activity, but given an alternative provider who reduced some of it, or eliminated some of it altogether, your customers might run from your burdensome, costly madness. As a consumer, wouldn't you? Unfortunately, there are only a small fraction of Lean-minded businesses out there, but should you choose this path, your competitors are in serious trouble. That is, of course, assuming you embrace Lean properly. Fake Lean is alive and well in the cultures located at dysfunction junction. This is a whole other soapbox topic I intend to address.

While Lean may seem a straight-forward concept (and in many ways it is), it is so much more than its simple definition, and I have barely scratched the surface. Continue to keep an open mind as we travel through my explanation of how to take your business (and your leadership style) from moderately tolerable to wildly successful. I don't believe anyone intentionally wants to suck as a boss. The initial step of transformation is just to imagine the alternatives.

"Your assumptions are your windows on the world. Scrub them off every once in a while, or the light won't come in." – Alan Alda

Voice of the Customer (VOC)

"We had clients that wanted kitchens, and we were selling them pots and pans." - Eric Murphy

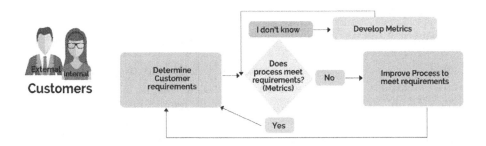

Central to my message is a fundamental mantra. There is only one correct place to start a process design or improvement initiative—with the customer. I define this player in the value stream as a person, organization, or other group of people who consume your product or service in part or whole. This will include both internal and external customers. Consequently, supervisors are not customers to employees because they are not consuming the product/service, something many of them will not appreciate hearing. They may hand out assignments, but they don't actually consume the outcome of it. Customers consume products and services from countless suppliers. Some of their broken processes I find entertaining at times, and at other times dramatically painful. I'm sure many of you will relate. Those of you sustaining the dysfunctional customer services I describe will no doubt find yourself trying to defend them with thoughts/comments like, *Well the reason we do that is_____*, or, *We have to do that because_____*, or, my all-time favorite, *We've always done it that way.* You have to marvel at these defensive postures because they embrace the status quo. Instead of defending the madness, please just listen to your customer – the person who, if absent or insufficient in volume, will become the catalyst for your company vaporizing. Their needs are called Voice-of-the-Customer (VOC). It doesn't matter if you are trying to document, design, improve, analyze, or just communicate your process to a new employee. Start anywhere else, and you are on the path to traditional, cave-man approaches to running a business or behaving in the role of "Leader." I put this word in quotes to make a point. Anyone can be a manager, but it takes special insight to be a Leader. I've known many managers in my lifetime, but very few leaders. A leader ensures all his/her employees are fully aware of downstream customer requirements, has translated them into performance indicators so workers are aware of the extent the requirements are being met every time the process turns on, and empowers everyone to continuously make improvements which will result in a better customer experience and easier methodology for the workers to accomplish same. Can you make the same claim about your current state managerial process? Would your employees agree with your assessment?

Much more will come on VOC because of its foundational criticality to Lean, so consider this just a first pass. I do want to share a story I found particularly entertaining related to VOC. My Lean journey has been filled with them.

Side Story – While traveling for business one day, I was forced to transfer from my original and always preferred carrier, Southwest Airlines, to another one. Without citing the name of this other carrier, suffice it to say they had an extreme reaction to a customer in 2017. I was traveling on this airline a few months after the significant public relations incident, and by chance, a pilot (in uniform) was seated next to me. We struck up a conversation to pass the time, and at some point, I said to him, "You guys have sure had your hands full with public relation nightmares lately, huh?" In retrospect, I wish I had asked him about his favorite football team, or the weather at our destination city. Apparently, this was the trigger that set him off. He demonstratively responded to me with, "I'm so sick of hearing about customer complaints about every damn thing under the sun. . ." He continued with comments too shocking to even cite here, but you get the idea. This was one frustrated and confused employee.

It took every fiber of my being not to launch into my elevator speech about the importance of VOC, and without customers, he had no job, etc., etc. Obviously, he wouldn't have appreciated my thoughts, so I decided it was time to bury my head in a book and allow him to remain comfortable in his deluded world. I didn't want to get dragged out the exit door just to help him understand the importance of VOC! Just kidding, but it was indeed a clear indication to me their culture was not customer based the way Southwest Airlines is. Not that Southwest is perfect by any means—they have process breakdowns too—but they have a cultural element of continuous improvement to customer service and respect for employees. I admire this in any company. Herb Kelleher created a unique environment. If you are making customers conform to your broken process instead of listening to their feedback and altering your processes accordingly to their requirements, then you are on the wrong and well-traveled path. Employee behavior is a function of the culture where they exist. Allow a negative culture to develop, and caustic results will be likely. Then traditional managers will blame the employees. The Lean business system addresses all of this madness.

To give you an idea of what a stellar VOC process looks like, I cite Menlo, a software provider in Ann Arbor, Michigan, that has taken VOC (in my opinion) to an art form. I'll summarize their approach so you might compare it to status-quo processes.

Imagine you wish to purchase software to do something, anything. The options include buying something generic off the shelf or contracting a software provider to custom build what you need. With the latter choice, you tell the designer what you want, they build it, and then the frustration of shortcomings typically begin to surface. Either way, you are living with inadequacies not meeting your specific requirements, or perhaps spending a bazillion man-hours trying to repeatedly tweak it. And let's not leave out the formal training to use this broken tool. Gotta have that. After all the adaptations (and re-training of users to understand the changes), the damn thing is still frustrating users. Employees fight it, and customers live with the waste ensuing from its usage. Finally, someone makes the command decision to discard system X and purchase system Y, then three years later you replace it with system Z. Maybe you even keep/use all three systems at once and deal with the waste from non-standard approaches. Unfortunately, though you tried to customize and avoid generic options, you have merely traded one inadequate system for another. The pain continues because a **_critical_** element was missing at the far left of the value stream to acquire software—the VOC element.

The Menlo process is **_not_**. . . Sit down with us, puke out your requirements/wants/needs, we write code, you buy it, you tell us it sucks, we re-work it a few dozen times, you continuously train your employees to use it, and we patch it for eternity as bugs impede your flow. Nope! Not their process. Instead of this traditional series of steps with guaranteed re-work and confusion to users, they employ folks with the title of High-Tech Anthropologists (HTA). These people will hang out in your work environment to understand exactly what your process looks like, the obstacles you encounter, the conditions you work in, the specificity of your needs, the pain you suffer through conducting your service or producing your product so they can fully capture what the software needs to do for YOU. They are not creating a generic tool for the masses. They want to make your process easier, not harder. Therefore, your oral description alone is pathetically inadequate from their perspective – Menlo wants to know far more before they start writing code. They want to deeply understand your conditions, well beyond a few conference room meetings or phone calls. They also don't build the whole thing and throw it over the wall. Instead, they create small sections and allow you to piecemeal evaluate it before continuing. Why build the whole car only to find out you don't like the length of the frame I gave you? It's a totally collaborative process, and the final product requires no owners' manual, and no training for users to be entirely successful. Right out of the box you get an intuitive product the user can benefit from immediately. How often has this occurred with software you purchased? Twenty percent of the time? Ever? How many human beings navigate PowerPoint without some training to learn all the hidden tricks of manipulating slides? Menlo embraces the power of VOC, and their culture is unlike most you have experienced. I cite them often when I teach the Lean concepts related to VOC.

Of course, I significantly condensed their process here, but the book *Joy, Inc.* by Richard Sheridan will explain their culture at length. I highly encourage you to read it. Not only does Menlo provide a superior product, but their treatment of employees encapsulates what servant leadership is all about. When a person in authority behaves like a servant, their highest priority role becomes supplying what employees need to be successful. I recommended the book to a friend of mine, and he was so inspired he considered uprooting his family to go work for them. Like any employee, he wants to be appreciated, respected, properly utilized, and valued in the eyes of his employer. Menlo is obsessed with the mission of making the workplace a joyous experience for the employee, and this, in turn, generates engagement to satisfy VOC. Sounds crazy, right? *Joyous?* What's up with that? Since when was work ever a joyous experience? You suffer through eight hours of disgruntled encounters with management and co-workers then go home to rest up for another round tomorrow, right? Read the book and get the full effect. You won't regret the time you spent digesting their unique culture. At a minimum, it will give you fresh insight on how VOC is captured and utilized.

"You've got to start with the customer experience and work backward toward the technology – not the other way around." – Steve Jobs

Processes That Annoy This Customer

"Your most unhappy customers are your greatest source of learning." Bill Gates

Before I go into more detail about my Lean journey and some of the people who helped educate me on how and how not to do things, I'd like to describe a few broken process conditions. Perhaps you may have encountered them yourself, but my intent is to comment on why they persist, and how Lean leadership can transform them into stellar alternatives to be proud of.

1. Automated phone menus/recordings

You call some business seeking help with some product or service they already have or will potentially provide to you. You have questions, specific questions, and you are immediately met with a mountain of non-applicable drivel from the recorded voice. *"Thank you for calling Customers Generally Annoy Us Incorporated. We value your business but are currently experiencing a large influx of other annoying calls and must, therefore, begin wasting your time. . ."* And it goes on from there. Cue the hold music and unleash some sailor language.

Is this any way to treat a valued customer? Obviously, I shouldn't have used the adjective 'valued.' Readers may recall a time when you called a company, and an actual human being answered the phone. You explained what you wanted, and this person acted to satisfy your request because they really **did** value you as a customer. They didn't come back at you with, *"I'm sorry sir, I don't actually resolve questions or problems. My job is to email someone else and they will get back to you when they are done torturing the 50 customers waiting in front of you."* Or worse yet, they give you another number, so you can hang up and call back, only to have the pleasure of telling your story all over again to a different person (including a repeat of the menu option experience). Or they transfer you electronically so you can experience the recorded advertisement citing the fantastic products and services they provide while you continue to wait. No doubt this is why you called in the first place.

Getting the right person to satisfy your inquiry on the first attempt is highly unlikely, but the companies designing these less-than-stellar processes are either clueless about customer service or are driven to cut the service to the bone to compensate for the rest of their unaddressed wasteful activities. I say we collect some data. At the beginning of the automated menu, we give customers an option to press 1 if they wish to continue with the recorded options or press 2 if they want a human being to speak with **immediately** – without scratchy elevator music or unsolicited advertisement to distract them during a wait. Then we build a simple bar chart to see what the preference of customers is (VOC) and make process changes accordingly to improve the customer experience. Wouldn't *this* be a novel approach? This is how a Lean mind critiques everything. Increasing the flow by reducing waste based on VOC. In time, it becomes muscle memory. Waste becomes impossible not to see. We all endure broken processes, and many of us have completely habituated to the madness. It's the norm, and we're conditioned to expect it.

Justifiers of the automated menu will tell you it's cheaper and more efficient than having human beings answering phones, humans who are knowledgeable enough to understand your questions and then empowered to resolve it without a chain of mother-may-I emails to supervisors for permission, or handoffs to other employees because everyone specializes. Perhaps you can convince me on first glance the menu mess is less expensive than real people, but what is the cost of customers exiting your value stream forever because you annoyed the living hell out of them? Does this make it into your decision matrix? Perhaps one defense is it helps get the customer to the right person for their issue. I would ask why it's necessary to have so many specialists. Can you not cross-train employees to answer a variety of questions the customer might have? The more specialists you have, the longer the cycle time you inflict on your customers when the specialist is not available. I argue you have designed the process to accommodate yourself, not the customer. This is completely backward. Make customers wait long enough or cut the quality to a threshold they can no longer endure, and you will lose them forever. This, of course, assumes there is a provider with a better process than yours, led by supervisors continually improving the customer experience with the insight from the people doing the actual work. If all providers' processes suck equally, you might be in luck.

I could buy brand X, sixty grit toilet paper because it's seventy-five percent cheaper than the product with a smiling bear on the wrapper, but the customer experience might not justify the initial savings. Quality matters, and if you are not listening to your customers before you slash service to save a few bucks, you are on the wrong path. In short order, a creative competitor embracing Lean might annihilate you.

Should you desire to have what I call the ultimate example of frustration with menu systems, I challenge you to call the 800 number to the Internal Revenue Service. Whew! Assuming any of the listed options match your need correctly (this was not the case for me), and you press a number, you then get another list of options, then more after your next click, and after the next click, and so on. Mind-numbing in the sheer volume of choices alone. They just keep coming. I was unable to reach a human being despite my repeated attempts. The menu options were not even in the ballpark of the information I was seeking, and I eventually just gave up, picking things I thought might be close enough. Success was not the final outcome. You just have to make the call yourself to get the full experience. My point here – this is NOT the way to design a process if you care about the customer experience. Successful navigation through a process should be intuitive and easy for customers, not equivalent to a root canal in the dark.

When I teach Lean classes and talk about the design of processes, I always pound home one objective. **Design your process to accommodate the customers instead of forcing your customers to accommodate YOUR wasteful process!** If the producer/supplier doesn't get this foundational concept, then they are doing things backward and are probably ripe for exposure to the Lean message—or a significant negative impact, whichever comes first. Kodak comes to mind. Get the picture?

I especially enjoy the in-queue game when they tell you how long you can expect to wait before being connected to a human being – assuming this is even a possible option. *"Please remain on the line. You are now number 27 in the queue, and your wait time will be approximately ninety minutes."* Perhaps this is a nudge to hang up and stop bothering this busy company. Interesting how they took the time to do the math, but not the time to capture voice-of-the-customer and then improve their process. Now I will say, some have incorporated an improvement to this completely non-valued added process. They instruct you to press a number allowing you to hang up but retain your place in the queue. When these overburdened employees finally get around to your spot in the line, they will call you back. Still a broken process no customer is willing to pay for but better than the ones insisting you endure a loop of unwanted advertisements and lousy music. I wonder how many man-hours in meetings were expended picking the music and getting it to play and stop at just the right point when this precious time could have been better spent designing a way to avoid the need for it altogether. I wonder if the customer experience was a critical element of the system design? Just a thought.

Bottom line, if you are making your customers endure frustration – at all, **ever** – your process is currently broken and incapable of meeting their needs to some extent. You are also disrespecting your customers. You can admit it and try to reduce the performance gap, or you can return to your cave and convince yourself your customers are content with the current process. This is not to say you will eliminate it entirely, but do you think you could reduce it at all? And then, do you think you could reduce it some more? If you believe this is not possible, go experience the drive-through at Chick-fil-A. Watch what happens if the line of cars builds beyond a certain threshold. This company knows what customer service and process improvement are all about. How many other fast food chains routinely say (and even sound like they mean), "It's my pleasure?" How many of them are keenly aware lines are slowing down then immediately insert another process to reduce the wait? Waiting is still going on, but less of it. That's the idea. What you can't currently eliminate, you continually reduce. Imagine the customers (and sales) you lose because of people get frustrated in your burdensome lines. Perhaps you are too busy to imagine anything beyond the next crisis waiting its turn to be inadequately dealt with, or ignored altogether. Has traditional management ill-prepared you to deal with chaos, and you now accept it as the norm?

2. Employees clueless about the product/service and unwilling to help a customer

You go into a store and ask about a service or gizmo, and the person has a deer-in-the-headlights look. Maybe you only want to know where it is. You're hoping someone will help out and lead you to its location. Perhaps they will even inquire if you have further questions they can assist with. An owner would, but a poorly trained, disengaged employee views this as just a job and at best points you in the general direction of where the item might be, assuming they even have it. Translation: *"Customer, can you not see I'm busy putting excess inventory on this shelf? Why are you interrupting me so close to my break?"*

It seems like stores continually fill these revolving-door positions with warm bodies then do virtually nothing to train, empower, or inspire them. Nor do these employees' managers (I withhold the label of 'Leader' until it is earned) convey and actively model the behavior conducive to generating fantastic customer experiences. Why would they? No one showed them how to do it when they started out. Hand the poor chap a nametag, head them in the direction of the boxes full of crap to be put on shelves, remind them when breaks and lunch take place, tell them to stay gainfully employed (I just love this term), and hope for the best. Hard to beat this onboarding process. Graduates of UC are in charge here, and their process of empowering human beings is dismal.

Doesn't really set the employee up for success, does it? No wonder they display apathy, disloyalty, and eventually leave when the place down the street offers a bit more money, larger employee discounts, or longer breaks. Perhaps employers see no value in training someone likely to leave in short order. I can appreciate this argument, but their countermeasure of beefed-up advertising for new employees or shorter cycle times to hire them is not addressing the root cause. Regardless, the end result is a lousy place to work and a broken process for the customers you desperately need to sustain your business.

About a gazillion years ago (before cell phones, microwave ovens, and computers), you could enter the plumbing department at the local hardware store and be confident the person waiting on you had actual plumbing experience. They would listen to your leaky toilet dilemma and offer viable options to resolve it. They knew what this fitting was for, this O-ring, that valve, and procedures to install things. Now stores pile products on shelves and the customer wades in unassisted hoping to find whatever it is they might need. I won't even get into the lack of a human being to answer questions about online products. That jacked up process is beyond frustrating. Assuming you are in a brick and mortar store, this is typically the scenario. *When you are ready Mr. Customer, I'm fully trained on how to take your payment and bag your selections, but don't ask me what this stuff is for or how to install it, because I've never done it myself or been trained to answer your questions. In fact, this place hasn't even given me the correct name tag yet, so please stop calling me Bubba. He got fired yesterday.*

I know I'm showing my age here, and one might argue it is unreasonable to ask a store clerk to possess how-to experience or the what-this-thing-is knowledge. It would force stores to hire subject matter experts, and then pay them more than the limited ability cashier. Mr. Store Owner would argue his budget couldn't sustain such a model, and he has to reduce costs everywhere just to stay open. But this is a strategy of mere survival, not growth by continuous improvement, and only the non-Lean mind embraces and replicates it. UC grads remain resistant to change because viable options elude or threaten them. Some just are not willing to explore a better way. Much too busy. Imagine that.

If the process does not instill a sense of confidence and actual value from the perspective of your customer, will these cost-cutting initiatives keep the customer coming back? Maybe, maybe not. But the mentality of Lean says to start with what your customer needs (VOC), then design your processes to most efficiently accommodate it. This doesn't mean you give them everything under the sun – highly experienced clerks, quality products, elaborate visual displays, etc. – and not expect a fair price in return. Customers are willing to pay for quality, if indeed quality is what they seek, and VOC will help you establish these thresholds. The dime store imported items also have their place because there is a customer base asking for precisely these low-end products. They might not expect much customer service on the low-quality article and realize this is partly why the price is so low. I'm just strenuously advocating knowing what YOUR customer deems essential and then designing your process to accommodate it in the most efficient manner you can, with the assistance of the employees performing the work. Anything less degrades the customer (and employee) experience, and given a competitor with something better to offer, they will both head for the exit. If your customers expect the clerk to understand plumbing fixtures, you need to make it happen or risk losing repeat business. And please stop guessing what your customer expects. **Ask them**! It's called voice of the customer (VOC) for a reason. Not only does it give you valuable information, but it says something powerful back to the customer. *I care about what you need/want in my products and services and will strive to provide it every time. I might fail occasionally, but those become opportunities to learn why my process broke down, and I will try to prevent re-occurrence – because I want you to come back.*

Side Story - Have to share an experience I had at the local box store.

Being an avid fan of chocolate milk, my shopping routine was never complete until a half gallon of the good stuff (not skim, and not the generic brand) was placed in my cart. The only problem here is the product was notoriously missing from the refrigerator shelf on Sunday mornings – my time-of-choice to shop. Now for folks preferring the skim version or the brand X chocolate milk, you would be in luck. They always had plenty of these. Not for me, though. I wanted the real thing, but nearly every time it was absent. Realizing there was the remotest of possibilities some less-than-engaged employee failed to move available inventory onto the refrigerator shelves, I would often try to round up someone to check in the back. And behold the magic, there was usually some available. It became a routine, but the broken process persisted. No milk on the shelf, corral an employee busy loading other crap on shelves nearby, beg for assistance, get milk. I just got used to it. However, on one occasion, this band-aid process of mine met with a different outcome. Standing at the glass doors feeling my standard level of disappointment, an employee just happened to be walking by. Insert begging step onto the process map here. "Excuse me, could you please look back there and see if you have any half-gallons of the full-strength chocolate milk for me?"

Without a twinge of guilt or pause in his gait, this employee with a walkie-talkie on his belt responded with, "Sorry dude, I don't work in this department," and continued on his merry way.

I don't work in this department? Really? You have a walkie-talkie and could instantly get another employee to come help the customer, but you offer nothing but the "not-my-job-syndrome" answer? And how could you walk away from a customer with such a simple request to accommodate? All these thoughts and more were running through my mind, but the complete lack of regard for a customer was just too much to accept on this particular Sunday morning. I had to tell someone, so as usual when I encountered a badly broken process in this store-of-pain, I texted my buddy Larry Fisher so he could share the madness too. Larry, in turn, would relate my stories in the Green Belt classes he taught for the Air Force. I guess when you do the analysis, I was his supplier of examples and he was MY customer. The shelf of new examples in this store would never be empty. You might wonder why I would frequent this provider, and the reality is their prices are unbeatable. The tolerance of poor service, in this case, is offset by my desire to save money. Lest you think bargain prices is a justifiable excuse, imagine if a competitor had excellent service (chocolate milk always available to the customer) and was charging the same. Would customers shift? You decide.

Again, recognize this employee simply exists in a culture void of modeled behavior to influence him in a different, intentional direction. Telling a manager would only have resulted in this person getting in trouble, and zero change to the process or culture would have emerged. Beat up the employee, and at best, you will get one person to behave differently – for a while. Beat up the <u>process</u> and clearly set expectations of how customers will be treated with simplistic visual indicators on when to replace the chocolate milk, then model this behavior as the leader (versus a *do-as-I-say-not-as-I-do* world), and you slowly and intentionally develop the desirable culture. Need an example of how it's done correctly? Go to a Chick-fil-A and observe the Gemba firsthand.

This is why Lean is so powerful! Leadership sets the expectations and then behaves in the communicated manner themselves. Otherwise, employees exposed to hypocritical managers saying one thing and doing the contrary will see through the empty rhetoric. It's a vicious cycle for the traditionally managed workers. But when the leader is shown how to treat his/her employees with respect (as it applies to the work they are asked to do), and then expects it to be translated to every customer in kind, the culture shifts. Anomalies will, of course, make their way into these workforces, but they can't survive. The respectful culture combined with peer pressure to conform will be too much to resist or hide from. I promise to spend a fair amount talking about the respect for people element. Without it in place, results from Lean will never be dramatic or widespread. Your transformation will do endless burnouts (drag race term) and go nowhere. Process improvement tools alone will not foster sustained, transformational change.

If your company is trying to instill Lean with the sole ingredient of certified Green and Black Belts, or worse, an external consultant to solve your problems for you, you will never achieve sustained improvement. You *have* to have respect for people infused into your culture. This respect must be applied to every participant in your value stream. The Lean recipe demands copious quantities of it.

Side Story – In my rural Norman, Oklahoma neighborhood, I noticed workers boring pathways and digging trenches for installation of a heavy-duty conduit. The boss over the workers informed me it was for high-speed internet service coming soon. Now, I can't even tell you the joy this news brought me! We had been enduring painfully slow internet speeds equivalent to a pair of elderly sloths chatting with two cans and a 100-foot length of string. Not even a good string. Watching the spinning circle on our computer monitor often generated colorful language knowing only eight miles down the road, people had warp speed internet service.

But alas, the joy was about to be diminished with a broken process from a company notorious for lousy customer service resulting from not positioning employees for success. I called the internet provider and listened to the useless menu options. When the first worker finally answered the phone, I told her the conduit was going in, and I wanted to know when we might expect service. She responded, "Sir, are you calling about existing service?" VOC began breaking down at this point. Feel free to sigh along with me.

"No, ma'am, as I said, they are installing conduit in our neighborhood now, and I'm wondering when actual service will be available," Seemed like a straightforward question. She then wanted all my information – name, address, zip code, cross streets, shoe size, favorite color, dog's name, carpet color in the spare bedroom, etc., then said, "I'm sorry sir, I have no idea. If you call this other number I'm about to give you, they can provide the information." Obviously, she was following some script they instructed her to spew on the path to not answering the one simple question this customer had.

Cue the wasteful handoff.

Turns out she was not empowered with the information. I know, you're shocked. I was too. I asked if there was any chance she could just transfer me, but this was a negative. Translation – This is our process, Mr. Customer. We designed it, and you will comply with its structure the way I do every day of my frustrated life.

So, I grabbed a pen and jotted down the number she gave me, called the number, endured the menu torture again, and got worker number two on the line. "Yes ma'am, I'm calling about. . .." And I told my story all over again. This ever happen to you?

"I'm sorry, sir, but you'll need to talk to the sales department."

"But, but… the gal I just spoke with said <u>this</u> would be the right number."

"Well it sorta is, sir. The sales department does not have a number you can call, so my job is to transfer you to them."

Another wasteful handoff. It's rare, I know, but it happens. A Lean mind might be thinking, *process improvement opportunity here!* Hang with me, readers. The best is still to come. Worker number three answers, I tell my story for the third time, and he says, "Sir, I have no idea. That information is not shared with our department."

"So, is there ANYONE in leadership who can answer my question today?"

"No, sir. I will have to submit a ticket, and someone will respond to me in a few days, then I will call you back." Obviously, Lean-minded employees were not involved in designing this current state process. Incredible as it might seem, no one ever called me back. Put your hand up if you are surprised.

Go ahead, speculate on what I was thinking while I heard this broken process unfold. How can a company posture an employee to fail like this? Do they not recognize the impact it has on them, let alone the customer enduring the lunacy? The person in sales literally said, "That information is not shared with our department." They are in *sales*! Don't the people in sales **need** to know what is going on with new neighborhood installations? There is no doubt in my mind a person existed at the locations where my calls were handled who knew the answer to my question. C-level leaders probably sat around an expensive conference room table for many a meeting making the decision to branch out into my neighborhood, and then sat on the information. Intentional or otherwise, did they not recognize employees would begin to get questions they could not answer? Was there no rebel in the room to pose the question for consideration?

Imagine if a competitor was installing the service at the same time, and they positioned everyone in the process for success. Imagine they informed workers and potential customers what was coming, and when to expect it. Can you imagine the impact this would have on the other, less empowering provider? Imagine if your company stopped long enough to recognize the dysfunction of their broken processes, and then actually did something to close the gaps. Imagine they sought out broken processes and were continuously striving to increase the frequency of positive customer experiences. Imagine if every time they experience an issue like this, a team is built to prevent it from ever occurring again. Imagine if a worker bee sat in on staff meetings to alert the bosses of the repetitive hurdles they face when interacting with external customers. Imagine (now I know this one is completely crazy) if these supervisors took the time to observe processes first-hand then assisted employees in removing the insanity (Gemba walking). I imagine these things every day of my life interacting with businesses making it exceedingly difficult to give them my money.

Supplying your employees with all the tools, information, VOC, training, feedback, equipment, systems, support, positive reinforcement, autonomy, (all elements of empowerment) to fully meet customer requirements in the most simplistic manner possible is a fundamental element of the Lean-minded leader. Unfortunately, it is sorely lacking in most companies. UC grads reproduce like mosquitoes in ambivalent corporate jungles and are perpetuating frustration and pain for everyone once they are promoted into management. Swatting at them is useless. Fortunately, a much better approach exists.

3. Undue Waiting

Customers experience waiting for nearly everything. We wait for an available table at a restaurant, in lines for you name it, for resolution when something wasn't correct the first time, for answers or information on the phone, for managers when the clerk is not empowered to make a simple decision, for a website to load, for the tow truck driver to arrive, for road construction to finally complete a marathon project started a generation before you were born, for the car repairmen to start working on your car despite you showing up an hour ago in alignment with the set appointment, for chocolate milk to be retrieved because the shelves don't get restocked unless a customer asks, for another register to be opened and manned when customers are backing up like new arrivals at Ellis Island, for ANYONE to be genuinely interested in what you need as a customer, and on and on. We wait, and we wait some more. Sometimes we even wait for the opportunity to wait again! Doctor office visits, for example. You wait in the "waiting room" (I find it amusing it actually has this name to clearly identify the wasteful intent of the room), then they move you to an exam room – where you start a new period of nothingness in waiting room number two. How about we put a sign on the wall and clearly label it "**The non-value-added room.**" A description under the sign might read, *Dear customers. We don't consider your time nearly as important as ours and are unwilling to increase flow, so please sit down and be patient while we busy ourselves with the broken process we have been habituating to since we opened our doors. Have a nice day.*

Might as well be honest about it. How many times were you actually seen by a doctor at the precise time of your appointment? You may consider it accommodating to have piles of magazines in the waiting room, but if you think about it critically, the reading material is just to distract you while you endure this pathetically non-value-added portion of their process. As a society, we've become so acclimated to waiting for physicians beyond our scheduled appointment time we don't even question it. It's the norm. If your doctor made an appointment to discuss something at your office, and he/she had to sit in the waiting room for an hour beyond the agreed meeting time, would they find it acceptable? Would their objection be justified? Why is their time considered more important than the patients'? Who is the customer here? What if doctors had to deduct 10% of their fee for every minute a patient waited beyond the scheduled appointment? After ten minutes, the service would be free. After eleven minutes, they would begin to pay you. Do you think this policy would become a burning platform to improve their broken process? I'm guessing they would immediately find ways to reduce/eliminate the waiting, but of course, there's currently no negative impact on them (or so they think), so the status quo ambivalence prevails. But, customers will keep coming back, *won't* they? They will until your competitor embraces Lean.

<u>Side Story</u> – Who doesn't like taking a cruise? Endless food selections, a change of atmosphere, ocean sounds emanating from your open balcony door, fresh air, lots of time to relax and think about your last dozen Gemba walks, cold brewskies at your beck and call – all in all, a welcomed diversion from the daily grind of listening to your traditional manager yammer away about how you screwed up some assignment. Ah, yes, but this delightful escape does not come without waste in the form of copious waiting. After dropping our main luggage off at pier-side in Cocoa Beach, Florida, we assembled in the back of the cattle parade with no clue how long it would take to reach the end of the winding, yellow-brick road. It was a mass of humanity playing follow-the-leader while schlepping their carry-on bags. The flow chart steps look like this - Pick bags up,

walk a few steps, stop, put them down, and repeat. Hordes of people paying their dues to have some fun. My dad used to say, "Having fun can be a lot of damn work." In this case, he was absolutely correct. The line muddled along with frequent dead stops, seemingly forever, but this was not the most broken process element. After finally reaching the point where actual service was taking place to check people in, I counted 38 staffed stations. Each worker had a light they could illuminate when they were ready for the next disrespected customer. However, only a small fraction of them was using this visual management tool. Most of them had a variety of amusing techniques from standing there motionless like contented mannequins (perhaps giving them a chance to wonder if a better job in the ship's laundry was available), to frantically waving both hands above their head. This was comical because the next person in line couldn't necessarily see the worker alerting them to the open position, and even if they did, the passenger wasn't sure if they should take the initiative to fill it or wait for the spotter's direction. The spotter was an employee trying to monitor open spots and alert the next customer to head that way. Both situations were playing out and adding to the insanity. This disrespected spotter was continually walking back and forth between the newly found open spot and the customer who would be next to fill it. This employee was repeatedly telling the workers to use the lights, but compliance was minimal and short-lived. I overheard one counter worker comment to her neighbor sitting only a couple of feet away, "I'd like to tell her (the spotter) what to do with this light." At least the waiting ordeal came with entertainment.

My inquisitive mind was in overdrive at this point, so I started collecting some data with the stopwatch on my phone. Go ahead and laugh, I can take it. I labeled the metric "Open Spot Time." It was consistently more than 20 seconds and soared to as much as 38 seconds until the empty counter spot was filled by another weary passenger-to-be in the line from hell. With hundreds of people to be attended to, this lull was obviously adding up and extending the overall wait period for everyone. Let's not forget the people at the end of the line. They were outside in the blazing sun waiting for their turn to be disrespected.

A no-brainer process improvement to me would have been to create a Kanban system. Designate space (with visual management floor markings) for 2 customer parties at each worker's station – one at the counter being serviced, and the next party positioned directly behind them. Call it an on-deck circle if you will. As soon as party #1 is finished at the counter, party #2 immediately fills the empty spot. Then, the on-deck position could be back-filled by the various methods. This would nearly eliminate the wasteful lull (Open Spot Time) for arm waving, spotter recognition, and customer travel to the idle counter. Time lost at the counter is time unrecoverable. I debated if I was going to share this with Ms. Counterperson.

Finally, it was our long-awaited turn to stand at the counter and get our precious boarding cards. My opening comment to the worker was about the long lines, and she defensively responded (using a tone appropriate for a child about to get an inoculation) with, "Oh, it's not too bad."

My pent-up frustration kicked in immediately. "Excuse me ma'am, but you didn't just stand in that one-hour line." This totally fell on deaf ears. Obviously, I was not at the combination Get-Your-Silly-Card/Customer-Complaint window. So, I went for broke and shared my Kanban idea without using the label. Didn't want to consume more time explaining what the name Kanban meant. Ms. Counterperson agreed this would help but proclaimed, "Well, I'm not in charge." To which I said, "You are the worker in this process, just *take* charge!"

Her next response cracked me up. With demonstrative gusto, she bellowed, "*If I was in charge, heads would roll around here!*" Maximum emphasis on the word "I."

Perfect! We've identified the root cause of this broken process. It's the lousy workers. All they need is someone to lay down the law, and that'll fix this jacked up mess once and for all. Whew! Got that solved. Someone promote this supervisor in-queue. Her managerial preparation has reached its zenith.

It was all I could do not to give her my *blame-the-process-not-the-worker* elevator speech, but I resisted. She clearly wasn't interested in a lesson on Lean leadership and making customers behind me wait longer would not have been fair to them. Perhaps the most salient lesson for me with this experience is a condition where a supplier – the cruise line in this case – repeats a process hundreds of times each year and isn't improving conditions for the employees or the customers. One has to wonder why this is the case. Are they asking the counter workers for ideas, or is good enough the mentality? Does recording this nightmare on the post-cruise survey have any effect? Now, of course, if you wish to pay a premium at the time you book your cruise, you can enjoy a much shorter line. Translation – pay extra or be treated with disrespect. Real leadership is needed here.

Side Story - My wife was referred to a medical specialist, but first, naturally, she had to wait a few weeks to even get an appointment. New patients are not exactly treated with the highest priority for some reason. Perhaps they are just an annoyance to these already busy professionals.

So, the appointment date was given along with instructions to fill out papers. Now, this would be wasteful enough, but the physician's office was going to mail hard-copies to our home. She was to complete same, then arrive twenty minutes before the appointment with this paperwork for who knows what reason. Ah yes, the non-value-added drudgery of filling out papers redundant to the ones you filled out for the last ten doctors you might have seen for some ailment they were unable to diagnose, but of course charged you for just the same. *Defect!* Sorry, I digress with minimal stimulus. Doctor language. No charge.

The appointment was only a couple of days away, and the mailed paperwork had not yet arrived. It was bound to be someone's fault here – no chance the doctor's office had a broken process. Not wanting to show up without the silly documents, she went online and found the doctor's web site. Please note – living with a Lean zealot for many years will infuse the mentality of challenging stupid processes with high consistency. My wife fell victim to the Lean Kool-Aid® (at least a sip or two, not a big gulp mind you) long ago.

Lo and behold, the website had a place to download the paperwork for new patients. She then called to question if the electronic papers were the same ones being sent via pony express. The receptionist was clueless, and it took a physical description of the information on the documents by my wife (by phone, after the menu options) before the person realized it was the same mess of papers they were trying to mail out. Non-Value-Added activity just keeps coming. Keep the tab running here.

"Oh yes, I suppose those are the same forms," she proclaimed without prior knowledge the forms even existed electronically. Alert the broken process police—we have another opportunity. One can only wonder if this poorly empowered employee (a type of disrespect to her and her customers) would repeat her more familiar process of mailing the stuff out after this incident because of habit. If historical patterns are dependable, she will inquire about the electronic forms to another uninformed employee, and then nothing will change. Status quo will prevail.

Let's take a step back and imagine the scenario if this was a Lean-minded office. The receptionist would have a checklist to follow for setting up new patients. It would walk him/her through the most updated procedure to inform a patient about the online documents, and they could be completed and submitted electronically. No hard-copies, wasted toner, envelopes, postage, transportation waste trotting it to a post office, sorting of mail at the doctor's office by already overburdened workers when they arrived, etc. The patient would have been given a prompt appointment with no need to come earlier than the scheduled time, and would be seen at the precise, agreed upon time. This would occur because the provider realizes processes should accommodate customers (who keep the doors of the practice open in the first place), not the other way around. And, all of these improvements would have been conceived and implemented by the workers in the process (based on customer input and continued measurement of process performance), not by management throwing fixes over the wall. Novel concept, isn't it?

Customers should not be forced to adapt to your broken process, and even more atrocious, have to pay for the completely wasteful steps you inflict on them. But, we all endure this standard treatment as though it simply cannot be avoided. Really good processes shock us. Why aren't they the norm?

It's not just physicians, although their processes are notoriously laden with confusion and void of engaged employees challenging the madness. I won't even delve into the insurance processing nightmares. Status quo prevails globally across the health care and service industry in general. Take your car in for a repair or go to the social security office—be ready to get really comfortable. It will NOT be similar to an Indy car pulling into the pit for service. Do we all just habituate to this lousy service? Be honest. Aren't you shocked when you get outstanding service? Aren't you inclined to share the experience with someone because you are just amazed it happened? Unfortunately, it is the exception. Service is usually dismal, and we've stopped noticing because waiting and lack of improvement is now as common as five o'clock traffic jams in Houston. Customers deserve better, and when they begin to get it with regularity because it has become part of the culture, the previous supplier of the goods or service will become the last resort. Please keep in mind – someone is in charge of these wasteful processes. What are they doing about it? Yelling at employees to work harder, to stop making mistakes, and to go faster? Demanding more overtime? Hiring more people to accommodate the waste, only to lay them off when company income diminishes?

Stop the madness, America. Wake up and get some Lean-mindedness in your world to improve the customer experience. Everyone is waiting for it.

Side Story – I took my Honda in for a recall to replace the airbags. After calling the dealership, I was informed I needed to make an appointment so the parts would be available when I arrived (First wait event). Most people would consider this reasonable, right? Except, the person telling me this was a hand-off from the person who initially answered the phone because her job did not include making appointments (Second wait event). She just answers the phone and inserts electronic motion waste as per the process design. Finally, someone in the service department picked up the call and set the appointment. I scheduled time off from work and arrived a few minutes earlier than my 8:00 AM appointment on the assigned day.

The service person promptly took my keys and told me it was a ten-minute task according to the Honda standard work cycle time – because I asked. This was not unsolicited information. Ten minutes, not bad, huh? I'm already thinking I will waste less than an hour of charged vacation time for this chore.

Two hours later, I inquired as to the status of my car (third wait event) and was told it hadn't even been started yet because they were "very busy." The employee then walked away from me without the slightest awareness his process was failing or motivation to further explain why or how much longer it might take. This is probably because it is not an unexpected process condition; thus, he doesn't get alarmed. Just business as usual. No bells or whistles going off here just because a customer asked about an undue delay. Perhaps the language on their documented value stream map says *Inform customer in waiting area their appointment didn't really mean anyone would begin work on their car at the prescribed time.* Let's go ahead and put a red dot on this post-it task and call it non-value added. ***Waste***!

"Excuse me Mr. Service Manager, but I was here on time for a ten-minute task, and now I'm told two hours later it hasn't even been started yet. Exactly how long do you think I will have to wait?"

He went on (politely I will add) to list excuses about tasks taking longer than anticipated, chasing needed parts for customers' cars, mechanics not showing up to work, blah, blah, blah. Charlie Brown adult talk. No projection of completion time offered. I have no proof, but I suspect the lack of first-in-first-out (FIFO) courtesy was because other repair jobs were far more lucrative than my lousy ten-minute airbag replacement. Honda pays the dealership for the labor, but they don't make squat on the parts since customers aren't paying for anything. Regardless, I was being disrespected as a customer and was expected to just wait some more. This was costing me personal time off from work, but of course, this was no concern of theirs, nor a negative impact on them. I was being forced to accommodate their broken process. Finally, I reached my threshold of tolerance and gave the service manager my elevator speech on Lean and customer service. Sometimes I can't stop myself. He admitted he had never heard of Lean. Incredible irony here when you realize the manufacturer of the car sold/serviced at this dealership lives and breathes Lean. In retrospect, I wonder how long their cycle time on my car would have been had I sat patiently in the waiting area and not complained.

By the way, their waiting room was awesome! About a dozen big comfy chairs, colorful brochures available to entice new car sales, a snack bar to purchase fancy coffee, freshly made sandwiches, and a huge flat screen TV to keep your mind occupied on something besides waiting. It was state-of-the-art when you compare it to other non-value-added rooms. Intentional distractions to offset a broken process, because, this is what customers want. Right? Might as well just add a charge on the bill for the use of your premier waiting room. Customers not willing to pay for the premium option will have to sit on the curb outside the dealership. Cushions could be made available for a nominal rental fee.

As if all this painful waiting was not enough, the service manager finally came out to the waiting room to tell me the air bags were replaced, and my car was next in line to get washed. (Fourth wait event). They wash every car after any service activity without asking if you want it or not. Nice touch, you might think, but my car was clean when I got there. Now I was waiting for a push-process task I didn't need or want. *Excess Processing Waste* – doing more than the customer wants or is willing to wait for in this case. The service manager never asked if I wanted to wait another fifteen minutes for a free wash (as though the overhead costs are not passed onto the customer), which is how it should be presented. Customers declining the offer would be giving the dealer time back in their day to do something value-added (insert sarcastic laughter here) for other customers. But instead, it's a 100% push activity. You get it (and wait for it) regardless of your input. I'd call this a VOC improvement opportunity.

I can only imagine how horrified Toyota and Honda must be when they hear how customers are treated at dealerships in this country. The service manager assured me he would do some research on Lean, and no doubt he is a total Lean zealot and a Gemba-walking fool by now.

In a book called *Transforming Health Care* by Charles Kenney, there is a story about a Japanese sensei digesting a schematic showing waiting rooms in a large medical building. The company was Virginia Mason – a health care provider based

29

in Seattle, Washington. His comment to leadership was, "You have one hundred waiting areas where patients wait for an average of 45 minutes for a doctor. Aren't you ashamed?" Powerful stuff, and if I stopped the story there, you might assume Virginia Mason is not such a great provider of health care, but you would be mistaken. They began their Lean journey around the same time I did (2000) and are now a stellar example of how to treat customers with respect. It's a great book – highly recommended for a service-provider example of what can be accomplished with Lean. Dr. Gary Kaplan was the influential force behind the fantastic improvements at Virginia Mason, improvements adapted directly from the Toyota Production System. He fully understood the potential and was the courageous champion to make it happen in his world. I challenge other CEOs to make the bold decisions Doctor Kaplan did, or at the very least, explore them. Unfortunately, traditional managers aren't typically known for seeking out ways to improve their leadership skills.

The list of companies making us all wait could be pages long, but the fact remains, processes are filled with wait time. Why is this? Is any of it just a fact of life, or is some reducible? Who is at fault here? The retailer, the retailer's supplier, the store clerk, the owner, the supervisor of the clerks, the guys stocking chocolate milk on the shelves, the woman ordering plumbing fixtures, the doctor, the receptionist, the car dealership owner, the service manager, the president at the University of Cavemen, someone else? Ponder who you would suggest we poke in the eye, and then realize you are probably incorrect. **None** of these people are at fault. The broken processes they utilize are at fault. I only blame the person-in-charge when they know their process is broken and make a conscious, deliberate decision to leave it this way. Disgraceful managers in my eyes, and they most assuredly are negatively impacting the workforce. I have zero respect for the way they treat people. These are the folks you should encourage to go to work for your competitors. Everyone wins.

Side Story – I went into one of the large chain home stores for a few bags of wood pellets for a stove we have. Pellet stoves are very efficient sources of heat by the way. The bags of pellets are 40 pounds each and usually sitting on ground level out in the garden area of the store. On this occasion, none were on the floor, but I saw full pallets of them high up on a shelf. No salespersons were in the garden area, so I went back inside to seek help. Waiting my turn at the service desk behind customers returning things for various reasons (more waste), I eventually inquired if someone could lower a fresh pallet onto the floor so I could get a half dozen bags. The employee told me they would have to use the forklift. No new information there, given the unlikelihood of a 20-foot human being capable of lifting a few thousand pounds, but then he added, "We probably have someone with a forklift license today, but I will have to find out who it is."

When I asked how long it might take, he didn't really know but assured me it shouldn't be more than twenty minutes.

I tried not to show my immediate displeasure in this broken process, so I waited there for a few minutes more. The employee got involved checking in unwanted merchandise from another customer, and it seemed evident to me I was about to wait until the Cubs won their next world series before the forklift certified person was found and the pallet lowered.

Plan B. I corralled another employee walking by and repeated my request. Sharing your story only one time, to one employee and getting a resolution is just an unreasonable expectation. This employee then got on his walkie-talkie to call the forklift driver report to the garden area. Now we were getting somewhere.

Trotting back to the garden area, I waited (yes, more waiting) for the driver to arrive, fence off the aisle at both ends, maneuver the forklift in an incredibly tight space between the towering shelves, lower the pallet onto the ground, shut down the forklift, and remove the portable fences. Then, after hunting for a box knife to remove the shrink wrap (it was in the temporary booth to pay for Christmas trees during the holiday period instead of on the forklift), the employee exposed the precious bags of wood pellets. I loaded six of the 40-pound bags onto a dolly and headed back inside the store to, yes, you guessed it, wait in line to pay. Only one register was open. Another option would have been to lift the 40-pound bags up to the scanner in the self-check aisle. I ruled this out. Total process cycle time was about sixty minutes. Had the pellets been available at ground level and a register in the area open for business, I estimate the cycle time would have been under ten minutes.

Let's recap the fault points in this section of their less-than-stellar value stream.

1) An employee at the service desk (gotta love the label "service" desk) took no ownership in helping me with my request.

2) The employee with a forklift license was unknown to him. Perhaps the visual management board was out being refurbished. Just imagine the makeshift process he might have used to find out who, or if, a driver was even working this day.

3) The forklift driver, busy doing something else, had to stop and traverse across the store to the garden area. Makes you wonder why only one person can operate the machine.

4) After getting the pallet onto the ground, she didn't have a tool handy to unwrap the product. She had to hunt for it.

5) The forklift employee walked away without asking the customer if they needed assistance with the 40-pound bags after pallet was on the floor. Culture driven not-my-job syndrome.

6) The customer (me) had to load the bags then navigate 240 pounds of pellets back inside the store because the temporary booth in the garden area was not staffed with a cashier. Good thing I'm not elderly.

7) Wait in line after pushing dolly of bags back into the store to pay at the only available register, because…who knows why.

All in all, a fairly jacked up process, but let's take a deeper dive into this example of lousy customer service. The plentiful waiting is just the tip of the iceberg here. Consider these questions. Why isn't there a visual trigger to lower a fresh pallet of the bags when the one on the floor gets to a certain point of depletion, thus preventing a customer from ever having to ask for a forklift and its associated delays? This is not unlike the chocolate milk example. Should your customer be tasked to tell you when inventory needs to be replenished? Why, when a fault point like this unfolds during a customer experience, doesn't the employee document or communicate it in some manner to someone so analysis and preventative measures can be considered for the next time? Are the managers of these employees encouraging reporting of these broken process conditions, or waiting for them to be spontaneously brought up? And most important of all, why does their culture not promote this as standard employee behavior in the interest of continuous improvement? Chances are 100% it will happen again, but the employees were collectively oblivious anything was even the remotest bit out of standard. Maybe this is the problem—this firefighting condition *is* the standard! I wonder if the mission statement is to get faster at fighting fires.

The fact is, all of these processes are in a larger value stream, but the players in the sub-processes just don't see it. The bigger picture eludes them, and it's probably safe to say management has never taken the time to communicate it to them. This assumes they (management) even know what the larger value stream looks like. Bottom line: the players are not focusing on how all the pieces are negatively impacting each other. At best, they worry about their own piece and typically blame other people when something affects them or the external customer. You wait for me, the person upstream makes me wait, and so on to our collective left and right. We all play in the overall value stream, but we don't have a clue what it looks like or how the pieces collaborate to maintain flow. When something becomes burdensome, we blame someone. As an employee in this traditional environment, why would I care in the first place? It's just a job. Take your damn wood pellets, Mr. Customer, and go away.

Ultimately, the external customer is burdened with waiting while we all perform our disconnected and dysfunctional pieces in series. To compensate, we hire more people as though it will fix the mess. Well, it might reduce the wait time by sheer force, but the Lean mind knows it is a costly and incorrect approach. At some point, you will end up laying people off. The process is loaded with wasteful activity, and more people are just a bandage to accommodate it. *WHY* customers are waiting is not analyzed. We just throw more bodies at it, or worse, do nothing and hope the customers will tolerate it. The sad thing is, in the absence of alternative providers with better service, they typically will. And should an employee rebel and complain to their traditional manager about the lousy service they are providing, well, now, this simply is unacceptable. They get labeled a troublemaker, a rebel, and soon the challenging stops or the employee simply quits. Not to worry, more warm bodies are eager to backfill the slots. Oil up the bearings on the revolving door. Then hire more people in accounting to track the turnover rate so it can be reported quarterly and ignored too.

Ask yourself, *what do I wait for that really ticks me off?* I bet you can come up with a list in no time; I won't even have to wait for it. Now, I challenge you to make another list, but be painfully honest here. This time make a note of what you make *your* customers wait for and begin to question **why** the wait time persists. What are employees doing while your customers wait? Are they hunting for information not readily available, or looking for the box cutter or some other dang tool? Are they printing useless hard copies to back up the electronic ones because someone unfamiliar with their tasks decided it needed to be done? Is the medical scheduling process bringing in more customers than can be serviced in the allotted time because of the wasteful activity heaped onto providers? Are the employees asked for ideas on how to reduce some of the waiting or have you conditioned them to shut-up-and-color? Are they waiting for you before a task can be accomplished, or for what to do when a crisis erupts? Are they empowered to alter anything?

If you can cut just some of the wait time – a tiny bit - on a single customer encounter, isn't this a notable achievement? Now envision doing it again, and again. Pretty soon, you'll begin to experience the difference between continuous improvement and firefighting. Ignore the waiting, and soon you'll have plenty of time to yourself – to wait for customers to come back. And please, don't order better chairs and a big screen TV to distract us. Your free coffee isn't free – it's buried somewhere in your overhead costs and passed onto me, the customer. Strive to eliminate the waiting room entirely, and you will be accomplishing something recognizable to your customers.

Side Story – I went into a large convenience store while traveling in a northeastern state. My mission was to get a few bottles of flavored drinks to keep me hydrated for a class I was going to teach that morning. This particular store was quite large, very clean, and offered sandwiches along with other fast food items. Aesthetically it got high marks. So, I grabbed my three bottles and headed to the register to pay. They had two pay stations, but only one was staffed. Four customers were in line in front of me. After a minute or two, there were now several more people behind me enduring an obvious bottleneck. A second employee stood just behind the cashier, stocking items on the shelf. Not a single chance this employee was unaware of the long line because a couple of the waiting customers were grumbling audibly about the wait. No effect. The person working the register continued with a non-urgent, emotionless pace, and the shelf-stocker showed no inclination to open the second register. Maybe they were not trained to operate the register because this store uses the specialist model. Cross training might not have entered into the manager's empowerment options to employees. Who knows? I was amused because I was not in a hurry at the time and could mentally document this process, but other customers were more vocal. Fed up with the waiting, the gentleman behind me set his selections on the counter and just walked out. He was obviously intolerant of the poor service given his exit message to the cashier. It was not "have a nice day." Still zero reaction from either employee. Flat affect from both. It was as though it hadn't even happened. Zombies. They continued as if this were completely normal and within the acceptable process parameters. I'm going out on a limb here with my speculation neither of them was an owner.

So, who do we blame here for this lousy service? Who is at fault? The person on the register working at a snail's pace? The shelf-stocker who didn't take the initiative to open the second register, or at least alert another employee of the backup? Both of them? The owner? There were several more employees in the store not serving customers at the time – maybe they are at fault for not pitching in? At one point, every customer in the store was in the line to pay, and yet nothing triggered a change in anyone's behavior. Maybe all the employees suck! Perhaps the manager should hold an impromptu meeting and chew them out collectively. Or we could fire them all and hire a new batch of drones. That ought to fix things. C'mon employees! Step up and do your dang jobs, right? What are we paying you $7/hour for? You're lucky to have a job.

It's very tempting to blame the employees and abuse them with the previous suggestions. One could argue the employees should have realized too many customers were waiting and taken steps to alleviate the situation. It seems reasonable, and I must admit I was a bit shocked the shelf-stocker showed no sense of alarm, especially when the disgruntled customer shared his displeasure and then bailed. But if we did an analysis of the culture, I bet the desired behavior is not being communicated properly, let alone modeled by management. How are employees on-boarded? Do they have the training to react when the line reaches a certain threshold? Does the culture promote placing the customer's needs above the non-urgent shelf-stocking activity? If an employee is told to stock shelves, are they autonomously permitted to cease this activity and open a register, or do they need to go ask a supervisor? I would have liked to Gemba walk this store's onboarding process to get a better sense of the preparation employees are exposed to. The point I am trying to make here is the severe lack of good customer service in many businesses and the underlying culture likely permitting its prevalence. Indifference is a learned behavior, and I look directly at management processes to see what transfers it to employees. Correcting this is not a matter of yelling at, punishing or replacing employees who behave in this matter. Traditional managers would disagree.

On the contrary. You need to go further upstream in the value stream, where the dysfunction emanated. My Lean journey has shown me it is far more effective to determine what permitted the undesirable behavior in the first place by getting the employees to determine the root causes and countermeasures. Who knows better what the current state is and the drivers of bottlenecks in their processes? This gets them directly involved and creates a sense of ownership for the process to work as intended. Their creativity is being held hostage by learned indifference.

34

Bottom line, blaming employees without understanding the culture behind the behavior is an effort in futility. Its disrespectful and will resolve nothing long-term. I have endured many a traditional manager in my life – some who were keenly aware of the dysfunction yet deemed it someone else's job to fix things. At one company I worked for, we had a motto. *You see it, you own it.* I loved this display of trust and autonomy. Eliminate the mother-may-I requirement to tweak a process and watch people spin up. I can attest the opposite generates distrust and contempt in both directions. Employees will not behave like owners, and good customer service cannot thrive in such environments. Leadership processes can be much better, but first, we need to awaken them from their status-quo slumber.

4. Businesses not listening to the customer

Have you ever tried to communicate a need/want with a business and it seems they are so fixated on their process they simply can't alter their tasks or script to accommodate your request? In fact, the provider shows annoyance at your inquiry to provide something outside their established process. Ever run into this behavior? Some of you didn't raise your hands yet. I'll wait.

Side Story - I called our home internet provider because the service stopped unexpectedly. After enduring the automated menu which challenged my patience with advice to go online to attempt resolving my issue – an interesting recommendation given I just reported I cannot **get** on-line – a very nice gentleman walked me through his process to test this and that. Finally, he declared the problem was not in my equipment, but instead was something outside my home. He said they would need to send a service representative out to troubleshoot and resolve the problem. Good deal, right? Oh no. We had just gotten to the process flow task labeled "fault point".

He explained I would not need to be at home when the service technician came out, given the problem was with their equipment outside the residence. Next, he offered me a couple of choices for scheduling this visit. I asked him why he could not just schedule a technician at their earliest opportunity since they would not need to enter the home. I just didn't understand my role in the process at this point.

No doubt conforming to some scripted process he was trained to follow from his computer screen, he then repeated, "Sir, which of these dates will work best for you?"

Now mind you, we'd already been through the litany of questions related to property accessibility. *No, we don't live in a gated community, no there isn't a hungry dog named Cujo guarding the home, no there isn't a 20-foot electrified fence, no we won't have the Klingon cloaking device on during the day to hide the house* – and on and on. Exterior access to the property was clearly available and permitted by this homeowner, but the insistence of me picking a date continued. Finally, realizing I was not going to get him to exercise flexibility outside of his established process, I relented and chose a date from his offered options that would *"work best for me."* Immediately was not among them. I could literally hear the relief in his sigh when he recognized I was beaten into submission. How unfortunate to burden an employee with such rigidity and lack of autonomy to make a decision outside of the standard process. It is a form of disrespect, and most assuredly does not make for a good customer experience, but hey, that's how we've always done it. Shut-up-and-color.

Which begs the question – why are some companies so out of touch with their customers' needs and how the process needs to flex (or be permanently altered) when it should? Anytime a negative experience materializes for a customer, it should raise red flags. I completely understand setting up the employee for success with a standard script so they don't have to wing it every time, but can you not empower said employee to use their own discretion when it's obviously applicable? If something in the standard script does not apply, is the employee not permitted to adjust accordingly? And if not, **why** not? Does the company recognize the negative impact on the customer, and how it just motivates them to seek alternative providers? And what about the negative impact on the employee? Is anyone in management paying attention to **this**? Do they even recognize it is disrespectful to employees? Do they care how a lousy day at work can subsequently impact a person's home life, and in turn, make them more miserable (disengaged) at work? It can be a vicious cycle, and the traditional manager has but one arrow in their quiver – work harder.

Oh, <u>wait</u>! (Sorry, couldn't resist typing the word) I almost forgot the best part of the whole story. When the technician arrived and found no one at home, he left a message informing us to make an appointment to be home to let him in the house! Fed up with the whole mess, my wife reset the modem again herself as a trial countermeasure and the system was miraculously back in action. It turned out the problem was with our equipment, contrary to the assessment the provider made over the phone. Then she had to endure the online menu and laborious process to cancel the service appointment we no longer needed. We were so hoping for a customer service survey, but it was not forthcoming. I guess they don't want to hear what people think of their "service."

As a consumer of products and services, ask yourself what percentage of the time customer service meets your needs reasonably and respectfully. When you buy an appliance, car, or something from the big-ticket list, do you feel like you were treated as you should have been? Did the salespeople listen carefully to your questions and provide the answers necessary for you to make an informed decision? Did they represent the product or service exactly as it turned out to perform? If wasteful warranty work was required, was it expedited to meet your needs, or were you tortured with their lengthy process and excuses? Chances are you know precisely what I'm talking about and could share a horror story of your own. Recognize it doesn't have to be this way. The provider with Lean running through their veins knows the impact of lousy service and treats customers in a manner conducive with repeat business. These kinds of companies do exist. Be honest - do you work for a company obsessed with increasing the frequency of good customer experiences and your empowerment to make it happen? If the company across the street was paying the same as yours but had Continuous Improvement + Respect for people (CI +RFP) infused into their culture, how many employees would immediately bail to the better gig if given the opportunity? How many are staying put because these opportunities are not widely known to them? Do you listen to your customer (and employees) and alter processes accordingly? Or are your hands tied to follow a process handed to you by someone in management who doesn't perform the task or take the time to observe it firsthand? Is it any wonder employees in this situation dread going to work every day? Imagine how your external customers feel about it. The disrespect isn't limited to the employees. Imagine the financial impact this is having. It's clearly a leadership issue influencing undesirable workforce behavior but traditional managers are not ready to admit it. Arrogance is chosen over humility.

"I have learned to imagine an invisible sign around each person's neck that says, Make me feel important!" – Mary Kay Ash

Good Processes—They Really Do Exist!

"The greatest gift you can give someone is the power to be successful." – Ray Dalio

I love the quote opening this chapter. I wish every person in a formal authority position would give serious consideration to the contributing influence they have over cultural conditions.

There are so many examples of broken processes in the world. After doing this kind of work for a while, it became impossible for me to enter a store, a restaurant, or any establishment offering a product/service and *not* instantly see the dysfunction. My friend and fellow black belt Larry Fisher and I used to do it for entertainment if we went out to lunch together. We still share stories regularly. For us, it's unavoidable. Like seeing dead people was innate to the kid in *The Sixth Sense* movie, we see waste. But the contrary is also the case – a good process cannot elude my attention, either. They do actually happen from time to time. All of them by intentional design, not the crossed fingers approach.

Side Story - My wife and I tried a new restaurant in Norman, Oklahoma – home of the Sooners if you were not aware. Can I get a ***BOOMER SOONER!?*** College football, by the way, is an excellent example of continuous improvement. Every coach has it on his radar daily. Winning becomes the more prevalent outcome if constant improvement is the strategy.

The name of this place is Tucker's Onion Burgers. When you walk in, a simple menu is on the wall in the pathway to the counter, and then another at the end of this narrow path guiding customers to the ordering counter. This allows you to decide in advance, so you are not delaying the process at the point of ordering. Nothing too unusual there but hang with me. When you get to the counter, the employee has a felt marker in-hand and a collapsed white paper bag to capture your order. A very intuitively designed bag, I might add. First, your name is written on the top of the bag. This is the end of writing any words. Food choices are facing the customer (on the bag), and the counter person just asks the logically ordered questions on options then circles your preferences on the bag. Burger? Single, Double or "Mother Tucker"? Kid size, Turkey burger, Impossible burger (vegetarian), or a Tucker Clucker (chicken)? All these are on the bag waiting to be circled or left alone. Onions? Cheese? Fries? All the same process. This replaces the typical situation of an extensive, mind-numbing menu on the wall behind the attendant.

In those cases, the customer can be overwhelmed with all the choices. It's like watching fireworks, you don't know what to focus on with so much visual stimulation. Customers will look back and forth at the various items, say *umm* a few times to fill the internal debating portion of their process, probably squint to read the small font menu, spend time interpreting the language in their head to decide if the option sounds like what they want and eventually settle on this burger, that side order, etc. Generally, there are many questions from the novice not familiar with this establishment's food choices, and the cycle time ticks on. Customers behind them are waiting, of course. For the life of me, I don't know how a customer ever learns the items on the Starbucks menu. Wow! The language alone needs an interpreter. New employees must struggle with it for a long time. Great products, but the sheer volume of items doesn't position the customer and employee for speedy success like the white bag approach at Tucker's.

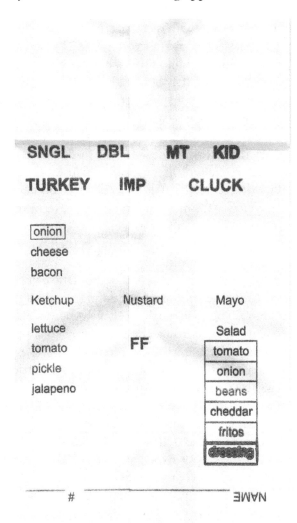

After populating it with the order, the bag (still flat, not opened) is slipped onto a cable (directly behind the counter person – minimal motion waste) at eye-level for the cooks to prepare the meals in the correct order. First in, first out.

The cook doesn't have to handle any paper (less motion waste). After the items are cooked, they are inserted into the same bag and delivered to customers sitting at the tables, or if they are very busy, the customer's name is called out for counter pick-up. Slicker than snot! What low-tech simplicity. I was immediately impressed and complimented the employee on his process. He probably doesn't get a lot of positive feedback and deserved to hear it even if he wasn't part of the design team. Properly dispensed positive reinforcement is worth its weight in gold. Servant leaders are well aware of this. They recognize they don't do any of the real work and understand their role is to position workers for success and encourage them – not beat them into submission with disrespectful decrees.

There's always a better way, even after you find it. Don't replicate what you've seen just because it's been done a billion times before in other similar businesses. Get creative! Challenge the holy hell out of things slowing down the flow and making people wait. Solicit ideas constantly from the smartest people in the dang process—your employees doing the actual work. They deal with your broken processes every day. Get their insight. Ask them what slows them down, what gets in their way, what frustrates them, what confuses them, what they have to hunt for, what is stored in the wrong location, which tools suck, what they run out of, what doesn't work correctly. Ask them what customers complain about. Also ask them if they view you, their supervisor, as a resource or a constraint. This is what brings opportunities to awareness. If you wait for them to do it spontaneously, it will only happen when they are at their wit's end and about to run out the door. Kinda like the airline employee who was so frustrated with his job he deployed the escape slide and quit with a dramatic exit. Did his supervisor even see this coming? *Culture* sets the stage for employee input. In time, you won't even have to ask anymore. They will quickly believe you want the frustrating waste identified and then, with 100% consistency, you dig in to support their ideas on making something better. *You see it, you own it* comes to life. And when they are fully empowered to resolve problems, they will do it in your absence without even asking. Supervisors will cease acting as bottlenecks. Imagine the work a supervisor could get done in this scenario. They could finish their non-value-added activity in a fraction of the time it took them before. Score!

Let's talk about return processes. Ever get the run-around when you take a product back that didn't meet your expectations? It didn't fit, stopped working, or was missing a button or a what-not? Maybe the quality was just inferior. Doesn't matter the issue, you just want a replacement or your money back. After all, you didn't get what you paid for. The supplier didn't meet their end of the bargain, but the process to reconcile it is so painful it encourages you to just live with the defective product and avoid the hassle. We've all been there, but stellar alternatives to this dysfunction do exist.

Enter Zappos. This online retailer (mostly shoes) has free four-day shipping. Want items in two days? There's a small fee for this option. Pick out a slew of footwear you want to try on because there is no maximum and have them sent to your house. Only like one of the ten pairs you ordered? No problem. Send the other nine pairs back – no shipping fees for this, either. Didn't get around to trying them on promptly after delivery? Also, no problem – you get 365 days to return them. The entire process is designed to make purchasing their product easy and as painless as possible. Almost like its design was to maximize the customer experience to generate repeat business. Got a question about something? Their customer service is available 24/7. They are obsessed with first class customer service. Now, this is a process designed around customer needs instead of forcing customers to accommodate supplier preferences.

Zappos doesn't stop there with stellar process examples. As a way to intentionally infuse exceptional customer service into their culture, they have a unique way to weed out people who are not suited for a job dealing with customer issues on the phone all day. It makes perfect sense to accept the reality not every person will understand the demands of a role before taking it. Employees receive four weeks of training at full pay, and partway through the experience, they receive "The Offer." Zappos will give you your full pay to-date plus $2000 to walk away. No questions asked. After training, the offer still stands and increases $1000 per year, capping at $5000. Essentially Zappos is paying people to quit! Culture will motivate the best suited to stay. About 14% of employees find the offer too good to refuse and exit the company. Now think about this: if the process is designed to motivate employees to leave, which ones would you expect to remain? This is an incredibly creative approach to generate cultural excellence, and as proof of the concept, Amazon adopted a similar pay-to-quit policy. If this isn't thinking outside the box, I don't know what is. I love it when one company adopts a good process they became aware of at another company and have no arrogant sense of "it wasn't thought of here, so we aren't doing it." That's humility.

What about hiring processes? Is there an opportunity to improve them? Do broken processes occasionally (and disrespectfully) select the wrong person for a job or incorrectly reject good ones? Can this selection process be improved over the traditional routine most of us have experienced? When I worked for the federal government, their structured interview process required the interviewer to introduce themselves to the applicant. Seems reasonable enough, but I once interviewed for a job posted by my current boss at the time. She was one of three people on the interview panel. She extended her hand to shake mine and proclaimed, *"Hi, I'm Sally Smith. It's nice to meet you, Brian."* I wanted to laugh out loud but refrained and played the game. This fake demeanor continued during the interview as if we had never met. It was ridiculous for both of us, but not uncommon for the government interview process to be a mindless, check-the-box routine, often with a particular job recipient having been previously selected before the moot interviews get conducted. Everyone knew it, but it persisted. Undoubtedly the policy and process can be far improved from the method Uncle Sam was using back-in-the-day. I'll give you a stellar example for comparison.

I'm not sure anyone would challenge the claim of Google being a company continuously seeking innovative ways to do things. It seems like they are always making the news with a new process to increase the customer – and employee - experience. Consider the way they approach hiring new employees. The Google policy is to "*Hire someone smarter than you, who you will be challenged by and who you will learn from.*"[ii] How's that for fresh air in a stuffy room? Imagine this being the standard at your company. Managers intentionally seeking candidates smarter than themselves, and someone who will challenge them! This screams out humility to me and is in direct alignment with the Lean leadership model. Also, the process is not narrow-mindedly limited to management. Fellow team members are involved to ensure a good fit. I experienced this approach myself when I interviewed for a job in the energy business and was pleasantly surprised to see it. It gave me a good feeling about the company right off the bat. The process improvement director, Phil Logsdon, interviewed me first then the entire process improvement team had their opportunity to ask me questions. How refreshing is this? While not void of opportunities to improve, this was hands-down the most respectful place I was ever employed. Two thumbs up for this style of interviewing people.

The direct opposite is the stale process used by a traditional manager. I know of one outstanding candidate passed over for a process improvement job because the interviewing manager said this person would be "*difficult to manage.*" Wow. I knew this applicant personally. He was a master black belt, had a Ph.D. in chemistry, and was easily one of the smartest, most creative persons you could ever want on your team. Passing him over was pure insanity from my perspective, but I also think the traditional culture he was applying in would have eventually driven him away. Sad for everyone involved. Obviously, the Google policy was not being replicated in this environment. What does the hiring process in your company look like? Is it more traditional, or does it lean towards the model of involving players on the team? Menlo also has a unique and respectful way to interview new employees. I'll leave it to you to digest their respectful process when you read the book, *Joy, Inc.*

Side Story – During a few relaxing days in Cocoa Beach, Florida, we had breakfast in a mom and pop place called Southern Charm Café. My process-seeking radar is permanently fixed to the on position, so I immediately began evaluating current state after walking through the front door. It was quite busy, so I expected to stand around waiting for someone to finally recognize us and turn on whatever chaotic seating process they used. It's amusing with poor service being so prevalent in service establishments one just expects to be ignored for at least a short time. The contrary was the case in this café, however. There wasn't a hostess specializing as is often the wasteful process condition. The first wait-person to see us immediately asked if we wanted a booth or table then walked us to our seating selection. She was most definitely exhibiting engaged employee behavior. Points began to rack up on my impression meter. The table was clean, and I also noticed despite the very busy atmosphere, no tables were waiting for someone to clean them. More points. The norm is for busy places like this to have multiple tables filled with dirty dishes sitting idle while customers at the entry point wait longer than necessary. Employees are focused on what they have to do as individuals and lose sight of the larger value stream picture (not-my-job-syndrome). Teamwork is sporadic at best because workers assume someone else will take care of things. This broken process element was missing here. Everyone pitched in to seat customers and clear tables. Ordering was prompt, and food delivery the same. Ding, ding, ding– the point totals still moving in one direction. As for the food – excellent! The owner, who previously had no restaurant experience, makes a habit of going around and speaking to nearly every table. I also saw him carrying around a pot of coffee to top off cups. While table service is obviously not his assigned role, he embraces the teamwork mission to pitch in, combining hospitality with assistance to his busy servers. Impressive. I couldn't help sharing my thoughts about his establishment and learned it had only been open for about a year. We talked about customer service in general, and he immediately picked up on my mantra about posturing employees for success and respecting their efforts. He said he is always asking for their input on things and never fails to thank them at the end of their day—every day—before they walk out the door. Serious points! At one of my places of employment, I cannot recall a single time my boss thanked me for anything, let alone a daily ritual at the conclusion of a day. He was a traditional manager to be sure, but certainly not the anomaly either. Such a simple thing to do, but many supervisors don't recognize the nearly effortless approach to develop a sense of value in employees. Why do you think this is the case? Why are the simplest motivators missing in their management process? Why do they fail to view their role as a supplier to the employees? Instead, they see themselves as the customer to the employees. I certainly have my personal data and thoughts to these questions, but I challenge you to discuss yours with peers.

The wait-staff at Southern Charm Café were all friendly and attentive. They spoke to customers beyond the minimum requirement to capture food choices and were genuinely interested in where people were from, if they were vacationing, what their plans were, etc. Customer service as it should be, coupled with an excellent product. What more could you ask for? They also inquire if someone at the table is a veteran, and if so, you get a 20% discount. How refreshing is this for a way to treat customers who have basically chosen to give your business their money? The restaurant business is highly competitive, and customers collect informal data regardless if you realize it or not.

As it turns out, this small, non-chain restaurant was rated #1 in the Cocoa Beach area by a well-known traveler website. This is after only one year in business. Proof of how a supervisor in supplier-mode (instead of command-control mode) coupled with processes directly designed and re-designed by employees can recognize organizational success. How many new restaurants can soar from startup to top status in a year? Ask me where we went for breakfast the next morning and the day after that.

We tried a popular place for dinner the same night (same town) and observed far fewer accommodating conditions. They made us wait several minutes because the table was being bussed, then after finally being escorted to this table, we realized the plates had been cleared, but the top was filthy. Inserting their broken process countermeasure, the hostess said, "I'll find someone to clean this for you." Apparently, she was untrained to perform this task. Better find a specialist. More waiting. Points, but not in a positive direction for this place. Someone finally arrived and dragged what looked like a well-used soggy rag across the table a few times. Chances are high root cause analysis was not used to prevent this undesirable outcome from repeating. Firefighting was their model. We did not have multiple meals at this establishment despite the external curb appeal it had. Looks proved deceiving, and management was influencing employee behavior, just not in a positive direction.

Rather than me citing more companies with excellent customer service, I invite you to collect your own data. Ask family and friends which companies/providers they love and loathe. I bet they will have to pause to cite the outstanding ones but can instantly fire off the lousy ones. You'll likely get standouts on both ends of the distribution, but I will also speculate it will be more on one side than the other. Some of them might surprise you. Which companies do you dread doing business with, and why is this the case? Do you see large variability with some, one time they are really good, and the next time they fail to measure up? Why do you think this happens? Are there some establishments you will go out of your way to avoid until all other options are exhausted? I'm betting it's because of the way you were treated. Sure, product quality is important, but customer service is what tips the scale for most people. If I fail you as a supplier but openly admit it to you, then turn on my process improvement machine to prevent re-occurrence of the unwanted outcome - and you as a customer recognize this - you might give me another chance. If I merely correct the defect (or make excuses for it) then subject you to it again because my preventative measures were absent or failed, you will seek another supplier. Seems like companies would pay attention to this and engage the genius of their frontline workers to close the gaps and reduce service variability. The ones with Lean coursing through their veins are doing precisely this continuously. They recognize the collective genius of their workforce and choose not to leave it untapped. The others? Well, your guess is as good as mine. For some unknown reason, they are content with mediocrity and status-quo in their caveman world of traditional management. Good enough is good enough. Process improvement activity is reserved for crisis situations when conditions reach critical mass, or a threat of legal consequence is present. Improving a process void of a just-experienced defect? That's just crazy talk to the traditional manager. Get back to work.

Please note – even the companies trying their hardest to provide excellent service will fail occasionally. Processes are built and executed by human beings. Unforeseen defects, delays, and safety issues will occur. It's how these companies **react** to undesirable outcomes making them shine above their complacent, old-school competitors. Rather than stopping after recooking the improperly prepared steak or correcting the mis-shipped order of parts, they will seek to understand the problem, determine its root causes, and insert employee-driven countermeasures to prevent the problem from ever occurring again (Fire prevention). They will also accomplish this without adding more inspections, more people, or further burdening the ones they have now. Short of a structured approach, the non-Lean company remains in what I call wish-and-hope-mode. If this is your business model, be honest, and answer the question: How's it working out for you? Do you see the same undesirable outcome occurring over and over despite the countermeasures you throw at it? Where do the majority of process changes come from? Management or employees? Do you tend to place blame on employees when defects/delays occur? And finally, to what extent does your company contain outstanding processes respecting both your employees and customers, and how do you know? My Lean journey gave me countless examples of process improvement opportunities presenting themselves only to be ignored. I once had a boss in the federal government say…" can't you just leave things alone?" Not exactly a logical question to a black belt you spent tons of money training to recognize wasteful activity. Status Quo won out in most cases, but there were the occasional bright spots. I learned from both situations.

"Chaos is the enemy of any organization that strives to be outstanding." – Karen Martin

The Puzzle Pieces

"Sometimes the hardest pieces of a puzzle to assemble, are the ones missing from the box."
- Dixie Walter

Following some of the Lean classes I taught, people often asked me what the required elements are for radical, sustained transformation in a company. What are the **HOW** pieces to make employees engaged to the point they freely challenge process dysfunction and have the fortitude to dig in and make things flow better? Explaining it is the easy part. The hard part is making it happen, especially in a culture where the CEO is not on board. He/she is the person with the switch to turn on anything by decree.

If you want to make Lean puzzle come to life, there are several sub-pieces necessary to assemble correctly. Leave pieces out, and the picture remains incomplete. Let's start with the broadly labeled pieces from the Lean puzzle box, then break those down to contributing pieces within them. Please note, I didn't come up with this. It all systematically sank into my awareness over my entire Lean journey by seeing first-hand what works, what doesn't, reading everything related to the topic I could get my hands on, and tweaking the alignment over and over (continuous improvement). It's been an endless learning opportunity for me, and I want to share it with others.

The two high level pieces are as follows:

1. **A trained, relentlessly uninhibited, enterprise-wide mentality of _Continuous Improvement_ of every process by every employee based on VOC.**
2. **_Respect for people_ as it applies to the work they are asked to do, and the culture they are asked to do it in.**

This is the Lean business system, and I take zero credit for it. I'm merely giving you my interpretation of it. Toyota has been doing this for 60+ years, and I am but a humble student of their magic. No sense trying to reinvent the wheel here. Make those elements come to life, and you will recognize no upper specification limit of success. People will look forward to coming to work every day. Employees will not get their feelings hurt when a team member challenges something they proposed because they recognize the inquiry comes from the motive of making the product/service better and not from a petty agenda to attack the person suggesting it. Improvements, along with the desire to make them regularly, become a reality. It's spontaneously happening every day without a need to nudge from leadership. Nudges came at the beginning of the journey but now are unnecessary. New, incredibly productive habits have emerged and happen proactively on a daily basis. There is no such thing as a task which cannot be done more efficiently, assuming it is needed at all. The entire enterprise marches to the fact every process task can be performed in a better way, even after the improved way is discovered.

With training, coaching, and autonomy to experiment, employees are focused on making processes simpler to accomplish with better results for the customers. Relationships between workers and supervisors are based on mutual respect for the contributions each can provide (Adult-Adult), rather than subordination (Adult-Child). This equals collaboration. Absent is the suspicion, fear, and internal competition far too common in workplaces. Leadership doesn't dispense solutions but instead supports trained teams to find root causes and countermeasures. Managers who have now evolved into leaders give clear direction based on VOC and act as suppliers to get employees what they need to meet customer requirements with far less effort and confusion. They are also coaching other leaders new to the business system. Cycle times plummet as flow continues with nary an interruption, and quality levels soar along with customer satisfaction. Single persons don't strive to be heroes because teamwork versus individualism is culturally valued and rewarded. Employee review processes are collaborative, not punitive. Organizations and individuals are setting dramatic stretch goals (based on customer requirements and levels of behavioral shifting) rather than monetary, comfortable, achievable goals because getting partial success on the former is typically larger than fully achieving the latter. Employees are not financially penalized for partial versus complete goal attainment. If bonuses and accolades are tied to goals, just watch how conservatively they are set. People are not stupid. Only processes are stupid, so Lean cultures are rewarding team behavior relentlessly driving performance gaps toward zero as they relate to what customers value (VOC). Processes are held accountable, and people are not afraid to try something new with the unyielding spirit of continuous improvement flourishing in their hearts and minds.

Let that cultural condition wash over you for a moment. What CEO would say no thanks to it? Perhaps *none* of them, if they're open-minded enough to recognize they are not omnipotent beings who have mastered the activity of efficient business processes and generating engaged employees. Just because they understand most of the mechanics of running a business does not mean they have a clue about creating employee engagement. They also need to be willing to do the heavy lifting instead of delegating a transformation to someone else.

Titles alone indicate success to some extent, but not to the levels postured by traditional managers focused on themselves to the exclusion of the employees. Perhaps you have one or two in your company. Left unchecked, they will suck the spirit right out of a workforce. They are a malignant influencer. I have experienced it firsthand many times on my Lean journey. I can remember dreading going to work to the extent I'd sigh and shake my head before going into the building because I knew it would be an instant replay of what I experienced the day before and the day before that. Sunday nights brought on feelings of sheer dread. Supervisors playing cop and taking pleasure in beating subordinates into submission as though it was their assigned mission. It was demoralizing and destroyed even the remotest chance of anyone stepping up to help make a process better. I'm not sure how I survived the madness (especially back in the mid-1990s), but it taught me many of the caveman behaviors to avoid. I've also witnessed the opposite, and it brings joy to my heart recalling the exceptions. There were some outstanding servant leaders along my journey, and they embraced the two elements of a Lean business system – often without even knowing about the labels or the concept of Lean. This desirable human behavior is not limited to those rare individuals naturally wired with it. It can be taught, nurtured, and widespread in a company, but only if it is intentionally cited as an expectation, modeled, and enforced by those highest on the leadership ladder. If the tree is to grow, it must become the basis for continued employment and promotion. Continuous Improvement and respect for people cannot be voluntary. The greatest impediment to aligning CI + RFP is the self-serving arrogance of defending the status quo.

"At Toyota, we strongly believe that it is people who make cars, not machines: if management takes care of the team members, team members will respond positively. This comes down to our belief in respect for people, which also teaches us that everyone can and should contribute to the continuous improvement of the line." – Isao Yoshino[iii]

Improvement is Relentless for the Lean-minded

"Lean is not about making your current organization more efficient but fundamentally transforming how managers think in order to grow a business designed for constant renewal and change through continuous improvement." – Michael Ballé

"Perfection is not attainable. But if we chase perfection, we can catch excellence." – Vince Lombardi

Let's break down the two larger pieces into their lower level contributing elements. Be aware they do overlap each other. As Michael Ballé puts it in his book, *Lead with Lean*, "In true lean thinking, the continuous improvement pillar is balanced by its respect for people counterpart."[iv]

The first, high-level puzzle piece is a mentality of **continuous improvement (CI)**. This is the Lean alternative to a rear-view mirror, after-the-fact firefighting model. The leader engaged in CI is encouraging small, relentless improvements to processes daily from every employee. He/She recognizes every process can be better, regardless of its current state condition. Everyone is nibbling away at the individual task activities with the objective of making things easier/quicker to accomplish. His counterpart, the traditional manager, is a long-standing member of the management-by-crisis club. He waits for something to go south then blows the bugle to rally troops towards the emergency. Employees are directed to grab the hoses and knock down the fire. Mind you, the impromptu "fix" will do nothing to prevent the unwanted outcome from occurring again, but it recategorizes the fire into the tolerable status, allowing him/her to move onto the next blaze. As managers, they absolutely see this activity as their role and mission. Perhaps they should be issued firemen helmets to clearly distinguish their purpose in the value stream.

Notice these approaches could not be more different. CI mentality accepts nothing as good enough and improves everything persistently. It doesn't wait for defects to occur or customer complaints to arrive. Every process can benefit from small changes to increase customer satisfaction and simultaneously simplify tasks for employees. Traditional management embraces a status quo condition for the process and spends time minimizing the current impact of repetitive, undesirable outcomes each time they materialize. If no crisis erupts, process changes are off the radar. This is the reactive verses proactive model of process improvement.

Of critical importance to mention, the Lean leader absolutely insists this CI journey be conducted from the perspective of voice-of-the-customer (VOC), always! Who are the customers? What do they need? When do they need it? What quality level do they deem minimally necessary? What are they willing to pay for? How do our processes negatively impact them? What are we making them wait for? Basically, are we providing an ever-increasing positive experience for them according to their definitions, instead of ours? Unless you fully understand these sub-pieces of the puzzle, you might inadvertently be improving a process the customer couldn't care less about (like phone menu systems) and be ignoring processes your customers are most interested in (like product/service quality). Make them unhappy enough, and they will seek other providers unless you are the only one on the planet. Think about it; if a restaurant mistreats you, are you inclined to go back? If you have a bad experience with an appliance manufacturer, do you discard such data the next time you are in the market for something? What about bad service at a particular hotel chain? Are they your first choice the next time? Most customers have excellent memories, and they share bad (and good) experiences with other potential customers. Social media has given customers an instantaneous global voice they never had before, and it behooves the savvy provider to remain mindful of this. Most important to consider, are providers *continuously* improving their processes based on solicited and unsolicited VOC, or do they just continue on, hoping for things to get better by chance? How would your company answer these questions?

Side Story – I bought a high-end dishwasher with a very well-known brand name. Got that sucker home, installed it, and sat back to experience the sheer delight the salesperson promised me. It was marketed as energy efficient and super quiet. Who doesn't want whisper-mode in a dishwasher?

Problem was, this marvel of engineering would leave any plastic item dripping wet. Ceramic, glass, metal—no problem. But plastic cups and bowls? Forget it. Get a towel out to dry these items yourself because this expensive machine sure wasn't going to do it for you.

Allow me to describe how this painful process played out. Many calls to the manufacturer resulted in two different repairmen coming out (on separate occasions) to diagnose the problem. Unfortunately, a resolution was unattainable. Both technicians explained to me how this unit saves energy. The stainless-steel interior walls absorb heat, and this is used to dry the dishes without the need for an electrical element in the bottom of the unit. The problem is, the physics of the heat transfer did not work on plastic in this machine. They told me they get the complaint all the time from customers, but when they report back to their management, nothing happens. They actually shared this with me because they were frustrated as well. They knew the service calls to people's houses would be a complete waste of their time. By the way, no mention of this limitation was communicated by the salesperson, or in the owner's manual. I chuckle when I recall the phone calls back to the company. Without fail, (after the compulsory menu delays and eventually connecting with a human being), when explaining my dilemma over and over to different employees on each call, they would ask me the same set of questions—no doubt prompted by their computer screen script—and they always started with asking about rinse agent.

"*Sir, do you have rinse agent in the dispenser?*"

"Yes ma'am, plenty of that blue stuff."

I always provided the information plastic was the only thing it was not capable of drying as part of my up-front story, but the rinse agent question came anyway. Then, eventually, I would be told that there was nothing "mechanically wrong" with the dishwasher and therefore no corrective action warranted on their part.

It was like a standard dance each time I called. I could project the amount of time it would take from dialing the number to the point the rinse agent question would arise. Naturally, my dance partner was new each time because assigning a point-of-contact for the complaint was beyond their tolerance for customer service issues. I made sure they documented entries about each call so at least there would be a trail of conversations. Unfortunately, this added to the cycle time because they would have to read through all the notes each time I called. Ultimately, I wanted my money back.

I repeatedly asked for a refund because of what I considered non-disclosure of the machine's inadequacy. Phone persons were not even remotely empowered to provide such financial reconciliation, and the pain continued for an entire year of emails and rejections. My wife had given up, but I was a pit bull holding onto a plastic bone. Finally, my persistence paid off. I hit the lottery with a supervisor who truly listened to my story (VOC). I asked her how she would feel after spending over a thousand dollars for a dishwasher incapable of drying plastic items and getting nothing but excuses and apathy from the manufacturer. I'm not sure why this particular employee was inclined to empathize, but fortunately, she related to my situation. A full refund was issued, and I purchased another brand—with a freakin' heating element in it! The chances of my buying anything from this manufacturer ever again is zero (they make all kinds of appliances), and I share my story with other consumers in the market for dishwashers. Imagine the negative impact this could have.

The point here is multi-fold. The process to describe the unit to customers was intentionally missing critical information. Obviously, I wasn't the first person in the value stream (this includes repairmen, engineers, assemblers, management, customers, etc.) to recognize the unit could not dry plastic items. The repair technicians who came out to my house knew all about it and were being ignored by management. Not exactly continuous improvement, is it? The first one coming to my house actually said, "Sir, I'll go ahead and do my standard diagnostic tests on this machine, but I can tell you right now what the problem is." His feedback voice was mute at corporate headquarters. This is sad given the firsthand information of customer experiences employees could be arming leadership with – if they were seeking it out or receptive to it. The next broken pieces of this process receiving no improvement was the lousy customer service on the phone and the lack of empowerment for employees triaging customer complaints. All failures in the utilization of VOC. Just a job—read your computer screen, dispense the correct answers to deflect responsibility on the manufacturer's part, and hope the customer just stops calling. Maybe if we make the menu options longer, they will hang up without us having to listen in the first place. This is not exactly the stellar example of a company embracing continuous improvement as customer feedback is collected. Perhaps someone in finance did the math and decided the few complaints did not warrant compensation without a fight. I at least hope they made engineering changes for future models.

When companies do not recognize these data points as opportunities, they just continue on their merry way in status quo land. Perhaps they determine the man-hours to deal with the complainers is unjustified in light of capitulating customers who shut-up-and-color. It's an ugly, disrespectful place to work when you can't be honest with customers and you are not authorized to correct the problem. Shortcomings will happen in engineering and design. In Lean land, humility kicks in, and customer satisfaction takes front and center. Then after the situation is resolved, structured problem solving is employed to determine ways to prevent the undesirable outcome from every happening again. Without this second step, a CI mindset is entirely lacking. In this eventuality, CI stands for Continued Ignorance. The approach is to minimize the re-work costs with a wish-and-hope model. Ignore the need to recall items, and maybe only a few customers will exit the value stream. Do you work for one of these companies? How does it make you feel when you are forced to deflect a legitimate customer complaint, and then your management team is non-receptive to you sharing your thoughts about improving the situation? Is shut-up-and-color the preferred behavior of employees in your world?

By now you realize that I cut traditional management processes virtually no slack. This is because people in positions of authority alone hold the power to influence a culture with the leadership model they practice. Only they have the authority to set the standard of behavior based on VOC. And the influence can go in either direction, positive or negative. Cutting slack to management in the face of traditional behavior is synonymous with an endorsement of it, and I will never be capable of bowing under again in my life. Lean changed all that for me. It opened my eyes to the naked emperors so prevalent in companies. Fearful employees don't point it out in public settings, and the managers in the middle of it just continue marching in step behind the command/control boss in front of them. It's a debilitating virus most people know exists, but they ignore it to protect their career. At least for a moment, try to reimagine yourself as a Lean leader who inspires employees to challenge waste in their process, and then supports them with training and autonomy to reduce it. Begin to see waste as opportunities to continuously get better, and not something to be shameful of, make excuses for, or lay at someone else's feet. The quality directors cannot undo all the madness by themselves. Nor can your Black Belts with constricted autonomy and inadequate support. *Continuous* improvement, not just improvement when a process is horribly out of control, becomes an all-hands effort for companies serious about becoming the provider of choice.

George Koenigsaecker says this in his book, *Leading the Lean Enterprise Transformation*: *"Perhaps it is good to go over this word culture. An organizational culture is defined by the behaviors or habits of its leaders; in other words, the culture is formed by what these leaders do. "What they do" is essential to the company's success, and when you add lots of these "what they dos" together, you see the fabric of a new culture."*

Think about your "dos." Are they shaping the culture in a positive direction based on VOC? Does your company view improvement as a continuous, daily activity regardless of the process condition, or do you fight fires then move on? Are your employees empowered to engage with wasteful task reduction, or do you force them to ask permission before enacting any changes to the process?

I spoke earlier how everything relates back to VOC, but I want to explain this is not limited to the external customer. Yes, they are the ones eventually consuming your finished product/service. Of course, they are ultimately the most necessary player in your value stream, but you cannot ignore the internal customers. That guy down the hall waiting on a drawing from you before they can order parts or the lady in the next pod who needs information from you before she completes step 3 of a 15-step process. Suppliers to internal customers need to know the same kind of data captured from external customers and be continually improving the internal flow of information/material to them. Negative impacts occurring to internal customers will find their way to the external customers in some way – even if only the cost of operating in slow motion. How long do things sit in people's inboxes with no activity? Is this by design or resultant from the mounds of waste the person is dealing with while other tasks collect dust in their to-do basket?

And by the way, just because you captured VOC information once does not mean you are done. You need to be asking again and again. If your downstream customer's requirements change and you are not aware, you'll be guaranteed to miss the mark with them and begin firefighting again. Are you willing to take this chance?

The following are some of the excuses I've encountered when suggesting a shift from the status quo, crisis management to continuous improvement.

"We have enough on our plate now. There is no room/time for this approach."

"We can't afford to continuously improve our process."

"The job of workers is to work. My job as the manager is to improve the process when necessary."

Notice how each of these are short-sighted and limited to reactive cultures. Plates are full and time is seen as unavailable because it is currently spent on dealing with the same defects/delays over and over to heroically get a product out the door. Cost is an invalid argument because the closed mind doesn't realize continuous improvement will actually free people up to perform more activity—more *valued added* activity. And limiting improvement activity to just managerial employees? Well, this is just plain nuts. You have a whole workforce of creativity waiting to be unleashed, and choosing to not solicit or to ignore their ideas makes no sense at all. Thinking should never be limited to the person with the corner office and fancy window views because those folks are not in the trenches doing the actual work. Affixing a formal management title after someone's name does not automatically increase their capacity for insightful ideas by a factor of 100. Management's perspective is often limited to reports, meetings, and emails. They don't see the pastry worker chasing all over the place for raw materials or listen to the phone employee struggle to deflect customer complaints – the same customer complaints over and over.

I fully grasp this is a dramatically different way of behaving, thus the emphasis on Lean being a business system and not a tool. Moving from an entrenched way of doing anything can be at a minimum uncomfortable, and even paralyzing without guidance and coaching. Asking a manager to try this could be catapulting them from their comfort to alarm zone. I get it. Please understand this is a forever journey and not a sprint. The activity of continuous improvement is not going to wholly materialize overnight. This would be unreasonable to expect regardless of the executive level support. First comes rolling over, then crawling, followed by standing up, careful walking and eventually running. Running would be defined as every employee is autonomously experimenting with small changes continually as they conduct their daily activity (based on internal and external customer VOC) because they have been trained, empowered, and provided positive reinforcement for behaving in this manner. It becomes the norm of everyone in the value stream and not the anomaly. Nothing this dramatic can happen quickly in a large company. But without the want, it will never happen.

Many are the managers I've encountered who haven't even strayed into the Gemba yet, let alone proclaimed an expectation to improve things continuously. In their defense, the culture they were developed in conditioned the resistance to alternative approaches. The mantra is "march like the guy in front of you, and we all get paid twice a month." At the end of the day, however, management teams need to decide if status quo is good enough for themselves, their employees, and their customers. If yes, I suppose transforming to an environment of continuous improvement is not right for you. But if you want to reach the cutting edge of excellence and become the provider of choice to more customers, something beyond a New Year's Eve wish and a spirited email has to be employed to make it happen.

If management would at least try to improve their processes on a continuous basis, they would see the powerful effects it can have—beyond just making the customer experience better. Employees begin to view themselves as change agents empowered to be looking for opportunities every day. Hundreds of small, sometimes tiny tweaks to a process over time add up to enormous savings in time and frustration for everyone involved. The flow will immediately improve. The cumulative effect is what justifies this dramatically different approach, and companies embracing it will benefit in ways they never imagined.

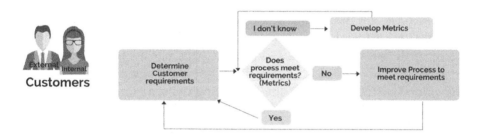

Looking at the 50-thousand-foot process map of VOC again, please note the decision block immediately downstream from determining customer requirements. *Does the process meet the requirements?* If you do not have specific performance indicators (metrics) to evaluate the extent you are meeting VOC, you are again operating in the dark. How do you know what to improve, or where to start in the process? Without VOC performance indicator feedback, how will the workers in the process know how they are doing, and what to adjust when? Should they keep doing the same thing they did yesterday or is there a metric highlighting a widening performance gap? Are VOC charts posted in their work area or do they have to rely on some boss to tell them things are going south? Does a wasteful meeting substitute for posted metrics? How do you typically answer the question, *"How are we doing at this exact moment based on VOC?"* Only a tiny fraction of the environments I've experienced along my Lean journey could quantifiably answer this question. Typically, the answer (void of posted VOC metrics) was, *"Pretty good."* Your gut is incapable of alerting you to undesirable trends, and when process performance related to VOC gets to a critical threshold, stand by for the panic reactions to ameliorate the issue. This is traditional management by crisis. Continuous improvement can be misguided if you don't know where the gaps are and how extensive they are. My analogy of foolishly scrubbing stains out of the carpet – because this issue hit the bosses' radar today - when the curtains are on fire is applicable here. No metrics means I don't recognize the more impactful curtain fire. Without metrics, you made an ill-advised decision to improve the carpet aesthetics when the impact of the burning curtains was much higher. Perhaps our customers couldn't care less about the carpet in the first place. No VOC metrics = no awareness = poor prioritization of improvements.

Downstream from the No answer on the decision block is the high-level task *Improve process to meet requirements.* When teaching Lean classes, I ask my audiences at this point, "*How long do you think this will take?*"

My favorite answer ever came from a very senior person in a company. He replied, "*About three weeks.*"

After the subtle chuckling subsided in the audience, I challenged him to consider whether he really believed three weeks was sufficient time to reach zero defects, delays, or safety issues and have all VOC requirements satisfied one hundred percent of the time. Faced with this description, he admitted that it would take far longer to reach this status.

Indeed, sir. It will take forever. No process (when analyzed from the VOC requirements) is void of defects (something not right the first time), delays (something done correctly the first time but taking too long in customer's view), or safety issues 100% of the time you turn it on. I'm describing perfection, which is the unattainable brass ring to be chased forever.

I always use this opportunity in training classes to tie in the concept of continuous improvement. CI is the polar opposite of continuous firefighting.

A mentality of continuous improvement means employees—*all* employees—are picking at the process with a relentless intent of making the outcome better for the customer and at the same time, making it easier for the worker to accomplish. ***If improvement waits for a defect to occur, you are doing it wrong.*** Even if you are meeting customer requirements, could you potentially make it easier for the employees to accomplish this? Of course, the answer is yes if eyes are wide open. What if you are not meeting the requirement? Is improvement on the radar before complete pandemonium occurs, or are some defects impacting customers tolerated?

Suppose the customer wants to have their vehicle serviced in one hour (maximum) and it currently takes three hours, the players in the process determine the waste elements blocking achievement of one hour. On their first pass, they realize the process to schedule the maintenance is not aligned with the volume of cars coming in, so adjustments are made, resulting in the cycle time dropping to two and a half hours. Great. We didn't make it to one hour, but it's better. Once they eventually get to one hour reliably, they continue picking at the process to reduce the cycle time even more, and these tweaks go on forever. Let's take another run at the various tasks in the overall process and see where more activity can be shaved or made easier to accomplish. Oh, look! The mechanic is leaving the repair stall to chase parts. Let's have the people in the parts storage area deliver the parts directly to the mechanic so he (the only person in the process doing value-added work) can continue working on the car. We just cut another thirty minutes off the overall time by reducing his motion waste. And on and on the effort goes to cut more waste in order to meet VOC requirements more efficiently. Score!

Pick any process in your value stream and imagine what it would look like after a year of employees shaving just a few seconds off it each day. Not talking about home runs here, just an endless string of base hits by the value-adders. Flow continues to speed up, employees' sense of value increases with every small accomplishment they feel proud of, customers notice the changes and share their impressions with others, and shareholders see the payoff. Now imagine conditions after two years, and then five years. There exists no upper limit of excellence.

Note: Let there be absolute clarity here—all the improvements are based on what the customer has deemed important to **them**, not to you the provider. They reported they want the process to take no more than one hour, so the process has to be pounded on until this maximum cycle time is never exceeded. Bust the one-hour threshold even once, and the process still has a performance gap. You should never be marching to an average here to determine if a gap exists—unless the objective is to hide the ugly. Averages are useless indicators of process performance. Employees are encouraged, and expected, to continually offer up opportunities to make the process better. *"Hey, boss, you know how we have to go find the keys to a customer's car before we move it to the stall. . . not sure how to fix that, but it adds time to my process. I think we should look at this."* In response, the boss engages to support the team who will figure out the cause of the delay, and the appropriate countermeasures to reduce it. Sometimes the countermeasures won't work. No big deal. Failure is part of learning. Let's take another look at the root causes and go again. The boss resists every temptation to dispense fixes. He/she knows this is the role of the people doing the real work. In a Lean environment, this behavior is the focus of every employee, every day, in every process. They relentlessly ponder how they can make the task easier, quicker, better, and more consistent. This then gives them time back in their day to do other things. There will always be activity the customer couldn't care less about or has to wait for. Scrutinize it and shave off more waste by intentional design, instead of chance.

Side Story - My post-government job in Corporate America came with quite a bit of traveling, which I thoroughly enjoyed. Getting out into the Gemba, mixing with the employees, and experiencing the real work in the company was always refreshing. Working behind a computer was part of the gig—developing training, answering customer email requests, etc.—but the most rewarding part was spreading the power of Lean to the masses and coaching their efforts to enact it properly. The company preferred we use a specific major rental car company. I won't say which one, but they were notorious about handing me two keys + two key fobs + plastic advertisement and car information all bound on a swaged steel cable. This wad of crap was ridiculously large to carry in my pocket, and I could not temporarily take the excess off because of the cable. After a couple times of dealing with this mess, I took a shot at conveying my dissatisfaction with the provider and asked the airport agent if it would be possible to get only one key and one fob for the car.

"But, Sir, what would we do with the spare key and key fob?"

I told her it would be up to them to make a process decision on what to do with the spares, but I didn't want to carry the giant wad of things around with me. The discussion wasn't making much progress, and in my frustration with the young lady's lack of interest in my complaint, I shared how I used the same rental company in Ohio and New York, and they only gave me one key and fob.

To which she replied with a less than endearing tone, "Well, this isn't Ohio or New York, now, is it?"

She realized she had just crossed a line with a customer and immediately revectored her message and tone. Eventually, she contributed the most entertaining part of this story in a friendlier manner when she offered up, "Actually, sir, we get this complaint all the time."

Allow me to resort to redundancy to give you the full effect. "***Actually sir, we get this complaint all the time.**" Almost sounds like VOC, doesn't it?

I can only imagine what became of this data, but obviously, I was not a recipient of improvements from a kaizen event targeting a method to maintain custody of the spare key and key fob to not burden the customer with them. And why did they have policy variability from one city to another? Didn't this city receive learning opportunities from the Ohio or New York office? Do they strive to behave as independent entities or one team? I asked all these questions in the formal survey the company emailed after each rental event. Without fail, they would respond back with standard appeasement verbiage saying they were *sorry my rental experience did not meet my expectations.* No mention of addressing the issue I brought forward, just apologies for the lousy experience. It always made me chuckle. At least they had a handy standard message ready to send unhappy customers. I have to give them some credit here for making it easier on employees responding to customers with a canned, *We hear you but don't plan to do anything about it,* message. Sound like a traditional management influenced process?

This is obviously not stellar customer service, and most certainly not a culture of continuous improvement. Their attempt at capturing VOC with a post-rental survey is commendable, but how they respond is all a customer really cares about. Don't just ask me about your process, *do* something with the feedback you solicited. I wonder if they keep track of various complaints for trend analysis and train all their employees on the art of root cause analysis. One can only speculate how most companies deal with it, but experiencing continued ambivalent service is a good indicator. Obviously, their Ohio and New York offices were listening to customers. But why is there silo variability? Why do performance gaps remain in place despite obvious opportunities to improve the customer experience? Why do employees not behave like owners and get involved?

The bottom line of this first major puzzle piece: The objective to get everyone in the company involved in continuously improving processes all based on VOC, not just an office of professional problem solvers. The reality is, this is no more an integral part of most companies than leadership development training is for a fast food worker. If you have ever corrected a defective product or service then moved on hoping it would not reoccur in the future, you are guilty of contributing to the likelihood of repeat lousy customer experiences and burdensome processes for the disrespected employees. You endure and contribute to these undesirable effects because that's just the way it is at your company. Perhaps you feel powerless to change anything because your manager doesn't encourage your ideas to improve things. You fix things when they fall apart; no time to be tweaking them daily. In time, the madness becomes a normal culturally expected process condition. Continuous improvement is absent from the corporate lexicon. Those black belts you hired will take care of improvement activity. Don't get me wrong, having trained Black Belts on staff is helpful, but if you are expecting them to solve the woes of the entire company, you are in for serious disappointment and/or long delays. This model cannot succeed. It is a guaranteed bottleneck doomed to failure if the larger objective is to shift culture toward Lean behavior. Convert those people from doers into teachers, guides and coaches. If they have no background or passion for Lean, they will not move the needle for you. Your guides need to be instilling excitement for continuous improvement across the enterprise. If they don't have it, how can you expect others to be infected with the Lean bug? If they are faking it because they don't really have a background in Lean, your Lean tree will wilt. Just imagine the impact of a faker translating incorrect concepts to the eager minds of your company. I've seen it, and it's not a pretty sight. Recognize the fakers are being disrespected the same as their audiences because they were put into a job without empowerment to succeed.

There are so many elements involved with continuous improvement: leadership communication of the vision; VOC; formal training; coaching; posted metrics; soliciting customer feedback at process completion; structured problem solving with a single agreed-upon model (like the 8-step model); true root cause analysis; and positive reinforcement for employees making incremental improvements to processes, especially when it doesn't take a crisis to spark it. The CI piece basically includes all the tools, but certainly overlaps into the respect for people piece. The list is far too long to address in any single book, so please continue to seek out more knowledge and act on it. Never allow your CI label to degrade into Continued Ignorance. Read everything you can get your curious hands on and encourage your peers to do the same. Learning needs to be continuous, as well. Have discussions across your enterprise to share opportunities and wins. The educational journey is perpetual if you are serious about Lean.

"Management is about persuading people to do things they do not want to do, while leadership is about inspiring people to do things they never thought they could." – Steve Jobs

Respect for People - It's Not as Intuitive as You Might Think

"I'm not concerned with your liking or disliking me. All I ask is that you respect me as a human being." - Jackie Robinson

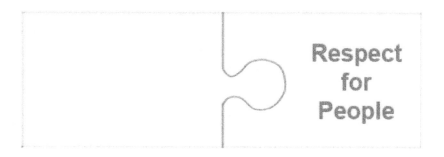

Let's touch on the second of the two large puzzle pieces, <u>Respect for People</u> <u>(RFP)</u>. Your initial response might be, *well, this isn't so difficult. We might not have continuous improvement infused into our culture, but we do respect people. Our mission statement posters even say how we consider employees our most valuable asset. We plaster them all over the place, including our website. If Sally needs off unexpectedly to accommodate an opening with her doctor or Joe wants a new monitor, we have no qualms granting these requests. We have competitive compensation and even give out employee awards quarterly and matching funds in the retirement program. Is this the RFP piece you're talking about?*

Not even close!

RFP extends far beyond the intuitive description. Saying hello to Sally and calling her by name when you speak to her is common respect you would afford anyone, even an estranged acquaintance you meet on the street. The RFP I'm referring to goes much deeper and relates to the cultural, work environment you and your management team have developed for Sally to perform her work in. Disrespect is frequently being dispensed in copious quantities and few if any of the traditional managers driving your corporate bus even recognize it. It's often unintentional. Before my journey had several years in the rear-view mirror, I was oblivious to many of the examples myself.

The posters adorning your conference rooms and common areas may express the concept (to some extent), but are your leaders modeling it—***really*** modeling it? All of them? Does their behavior reflect the language, or are your posters mere wallpaper scoffed at by the employees experiencing contradictory action from their supervisors? If you asked them, how would the employees describe the alignment between the corporate message and actual behavior? Be painfully honest when you consider these questions. Assumptions will not serve you well.

Let me explain further because this is absolutely critical to grasp. Get this RFP part wrong, and a Lean transformation will, at best, see a few brief pockets of excellence here and there, but enterprise-wide culture change will forever elude you.

When the Lean-leader speaks of respect for people, it goes *far* beyond the common decency one human being displays to another. Your grandmother passes away, and as your boss, I offer my condolences. I see you in the hallway, and I speak to you by name and inquire about how your day is going. You ask for the afternoon off to take your 4-year-old to the doctor, and I shift some workload to accommodate your request. When you are speaking, I avoid the temptation to interrupt you. You have a competitive salary and health care program. These are all examples of common decency to employees, but it is lightyears short of the respect necessary to get sustainable, cultural shifts and outrageously high employee engagement. I'm talking about respect ___as it applies to the work people are asked to perform, the extent you position and develop them to perform this work successfully, and the enterprise-wide culture they are asked to do it in___. I'm speaking about *profound empowerment* here. Leave this to chance, and you will experience wasteful re-work in your company as a rule, not the exception. This doesn't even include the negative impact of degrading the relationship between managers and employees. And if you think it doesn't warrant your attention daily or isn't important in the first place, you are indeed a traditional manager. I've worked for many of you along my Lean journey, and I came to loathe the degrading behavior you subjected people to. I'm talking about the command/control mentalities, the vindictive my-way-or-the-highway types, the do-as-I-say-and-don't-challenge-me managerial styles. It also includes the management cops who hover about waiting for mistakes to occur so punitive action can be administered instantly, the pattern of giving lousy instructions then expecting stellar results, or the unreasonable tendency to expect employees to step-up and deliver when you haven't even given them a stable platform to stand on yet. These styles of management suck the spirit right out of people and make them dread coming to work every day. Perhaps you've worked for these types before being promoted to management yourself. This is how supervisors learn the dysfunctional behavior in the first place. Culture molds behavior, be it intentionally or by chance, in both positive and negative directions. If you agree employee engagement is critical for organizational excellence, your radar needs to be in overdrive looking for opportunities to remove disrespectful conditions.

Some Examples of Disrespect:

1. **Tasking employees with something they have not been trained to do**

This is a formula to posture people for failure, frustration, and guaranteed rework. It is disrespectful, even if unintentionally done. Restaurants realizing this will have a new server shadow an experienced employee so they can get the hang of it before soloing. Any number of examples can drive this situation home, so apply the concept to your individual workplace situations. What are *you* asking people to do without sufficient training, information, or guidance? How did you feel when it was done to you in the past? By chance, did it drive wasteful re-work, unnecessary frustration, and wasted time? Did you feel like a valued employee as a result of the experience? Did you hope another job opportunity would present itself so you could run for the exit? How excited were you about getting to work each day? How was your mood on Sunday night knowing five more days of this misery were in front of you? Chances are your supervisor was oblivious to your plight, and you carefully concealed the negative impact on you to avoid their wrath increasing. I see examples of disrespect every single day.

Side Story – A young engineer came to me one day asking for assistance with an electronic survey she was tasked to develop. Her boss didn't ask if she had any experience doing this, nor did he give her definitive information on the intended audience of the survey. All she had was the basic instruction to build a survey. Perhaps he thought an engineer should be competent in all things and could easily accomplish this task. I'm not sure, but I can attest the young lady was very frustrated by the time I entered this process. Her tone was clear desperation. Somehow, she found out I had experience with survey construction and reached out for help. So, first things first, I asked who the intended audience was. She had a basic idea, but it obviously was going to need a more definitive analysis so we could narrow the language accordingly. And then I digested what she had built so far. Oh my. It was . . . well, really bad. Far too long, compound questions destined to yield no actionable data, leading questions, ambiguity all over the place, and sentence structure complicated enough to confuse any responder without an engineering degree.

Admittedly, she had never attempted survey construction before, and the undesirable outcome was predictable. Adding to the disrespect, she didn't exist in an environment where it was acceptable to say to her boss, "*I really have no experience with this task and will need some assistance from someone.*" Admissions of incompetence are avoided at all costs in a traditionally managed culture. So, she begrudgingly accepted the assignment knowing it would be beyond challenging and unnecessarily stressful. Disrespect is the label I assign to her boss' process, even though he likely intended nothing of the sort. But please understand, just because people don't recognize they are being disrespectful, it doesn't offset the impact. The outcome is the same.

Now, managers, ask yourself and be honest: Do you ever set an employee up for frustration/failure because you assumed they could do something when it turned out they could not? If yes, when the scenario was similar to the example above, did you apologize to the employee, explain how your process failed them and learn from the experience, or did you shame the employee for failing? Or worse yet, did you punish them? The most ignorant of all managerial processes will chastise an employee for poor results when they were not positioned to succeed. If your process was flawed even though you were not intentionally trying to make the employee fail, you still receive no pass. Remember, it's your process

I'm describing here, not you as a person conducting it. Unintentional disrespect is not as objectionable, but you still have the same performance gap to close. Maybe it happened because you were swamped with things to do yourself and you didn't slow down long enough to do more than toss out the assignment and run to your next meeting. Whatever the reason or excuse you claim, in the Lean world, we label this disrespectful to the employee. If you disagree and want to spin your behavior in a manner to justify your process, then you have not yet crossed the threshold of grasping what I am describing here. You haven't quite come to recognize you work for the employees. Your job is to be their supplier of everything necessary for THEIR success. Not the other way around. This is the fundamental essence of servant leadership. Please realize a hefty dose of humility and an open mind is essential to incorporate the respect for people piece of the Lean business system. Entrenched traditional management styles are incapable of being conducive with sustained engagement levels. Oil and water. Sooners and Longhorns.

Side Story – This example takes the disrespect in the opposite direction and assumes an employee is ill-equipped to do something without even consulting them to determine capability. One of the more traditional managers I worked for in my civil service job had the inclination for a new training class targeted at leadership. Ironic, I know, but bear with me. She announced one day they had hired a contractor to build this training, and I immediately pushed back with clarifying questions on her motive. I asked why we, the black belts in the transformation office, were not asked to do this in-house. Back came the response, "Well, I didn't think you guys knew how to do something like this." *Hello!* Who do you think built the Green Belt training we have been delivering to hundreds of people these past several years? This is how out of touch she was with what we did.

Not surprisingly, the product delivered from the contractor was unusable, mainly because the VOC process up-front was bypassed. Basically, the contractor took slide decks we previously developed for other classes and re-shuffled a few dozen slides into a new deck they deemed appropriate. Total waste and we threw the disc in the trash. Our boss remarked on the product by saying, *"They really hit the mark."* Well done, traditional manager! You succeeded in disrespecting the organic capability by not even asking the question, wasted thousands of dollars paying a contractor for an inferior product which never got used because there was no customer pull for it in the first place, and degraded the relationship between the employees and yourself yet further. To be fair, she was a very nice person, but when it came to respecting employees as it relates to the work they do, her process earned a consistent F. It was not her fault. The manager processes molding her were at fault. She learned from the worst. I could write an entire book on some of them. These managers didn't know any better, so we'll let them off the hook to some extent, but also understand they had no desire to learn or explore Lean leadership techniques. They were completely content with their command/control managerial style and had no motivational catalyst for improvement. Sustaining the dysfunction, their bosses did nothing to encourage continued development. Human beings will replicate status quo behavior when they don't think they **need** to improve. If you are convinced you are fantastic at something, you tend to rock on without introspection. For this caveman posture, their process gets a failing grade and is destined to be transferred onto future managers. The epidemic continues unabated as these traditional managers promote, mentor, and reinforce more like-minded grads from UC. Satellite campuses are plentiful.

Some honest questions here for existing managers. Do you ask people to perform tasks they are not trained to do? Do you take the time to confirm in advance their comfort factor, capability, comprehension of the deliverables or final state to achieve, and then continue the support dialogue accordingly? Or, do you just expect them to figure it out, and if they don't, you respond in a disrespectful manner that basically says, "*Worker bee, **you** failed?*" In reality, your process failed, not the employee. At this point in my explanation of Lean, can you at least admit there is a negative impact on the human psyche and subsequently on their potential to develop as an employee? Can you recognize your managerial process is at fault here—at least to some extent—and not the employee?

Most importantly, are you motivated to correct the situation if the pothole presents itself in the future? People want to do a job correctly the first time, but it is the task dispenser's responsibility to make sure instructions are clear and capability exists. Otherwise, the employee will experience disrespect, and your management process is directly at fault. Rework is almost guaranteed, and please don't lose sight of the costs in self-respect degradation, not to mention the financial impact to the company every time it happens.

2. Dispensing a fix in the process with no input from the person actually performing the task

This happens with alarming frequency. The people doing the work are far more in-tune with the specifics of the current state, and no amount of reports or meetings can ever get you, their supervisor, to their level of constraint awareness. Only arrogance and disinclination to permit autonomy stands in the way of recognizing the subject matter expert (SME) is a far more valuable voice in process improvement than you as the formal manager can possibly become. Just because you are the boss does not mean you must be the sole source to recognize every fix for every problem. It is both unrealistic and burdensome, but often the case when the supervisor believes this is their role. If the boss's boss is expecting this, then they are disrespecting the supervisor. Not being directly in the process doing the actual work makes it unlikely you will even be aware of the problems until they reach critical mass. The people doing the work immediately know the hurdles and should be intimately involved in the process change decisions. This generates a sense of process ownership and ultimately increased engagement levels. The misguided traditional managers will struggle with letting go of this power because dispensing decrees reinforces their sense of self-worth and self-imposed hero status in a traditional culture. But the absolute worst outcome of providing solutions is the undesirable, conditioning effect it has on the individual contributors. You will be training them to turn off their creative minds when problems arise because it is the boss' job to deal with these things. You do the working; I'll do the thinking. Employees conditioned to this disrespect won't even consider the possibility of making decisions in your absence. You become the bottleneck, and drone employees will wait for fix after fix. It's a parent-child relationship. Resentment will build, and nothing good can come from it. Insightful input from your employees is going to waste. As a formal leader, are you okay with this condition? Do you feel stressed by it? Does it seem reasonable? To what extent do you believe it exists in your process of management, and are you even willing to imagine it being an opportunity you will address?

Side Story – This story was shared from a friend of mine in a different company. A new boss took over in the process improvement office, and it seems he did some preliminary turf evaluation informing him about the pattern the black belts had of autonomously supporting facilitation and consultation requests from customers when bandwidth permitted. They saw no need to get approval because they knew what they could and couldn't handle, and it would only slow down the process to ask permission to do the job they were tasked to do in the first place. This was something he sought to abate by dispensing an immediate countermeasure of what I call, the Mother-May-I step. As this posturing manager with his metaphorical chest pumped up and shoulders thrown back put it, *"You guys had way too much autonomy, and now it is going to stop. I will approve or disapprove all requests for facilitation."* There was no recognized, let alone confirmed problem, no root cause, and no group discussion, just a process change decreed to clearly remind them who was in charge. It was posturing in the purest sense. A traditional manager sees collaboration with employees as a sign of weakness. It is their job to evaluate conditions and throw decrees over the wall for the lower paid, less capable to blindly follow. The more the alpha points and barks, the more employees will know who is in charge. Makes me nauseous even to recall the disrespectful situation my friend experienced.

Here is how the new process was to "flow." A customer would call or email the black belts asking for assistance, and they were to tell the requestor, "we will get back to you if permitted to engage with said request". Then, they sent the request (by wasteful email) to the person doing the new boss' administrative tasks. The assistant was then to forward the email to Mr. Manager and await approval or denial to provide help to the customer. If Mr. Manager wasn't available to respond, it just sat in limbo, and everyone waited. This same wait ensued if the assistant wasn't available when they emailed her. Emailing the boss directly was not permitted (more posturing to reinforce recognition of status inequality).

Eventually, Mr. Manager would respond, but sent his answer back to the assistant (with more waiting if the assistant was not available), who was to send it to the black belts, and **then** they could accommodate the customer request—assuming it was a yes from Mr. Manager. If the customer had a follow-up question/request, the process started all over again. This was taking days, sometimes weeks to play out and in the meantime, they sat around doing nothing, just waiting. Maintaining status awareness of the request was another nightmare altogether. Imagine the response from customers when told they (the BBs) were not permitted to help without the boss' approval first. It was embarrassing for them to even convey this, and downright disrespectful to be subjected to this intimidation. Eventually, when triaging all the email became such a burden on top of his other wasteful duties, he relented to allow them the discretion to make decisions as they did before he arrived. One humorous outcome was his email account always shutting down in Outlook because the quantity exceeded a max threshold limit.

It's important to point out the lack of a validated problem before Mr. Manager made the decision to vet everything customers were asking for support on. There was no documented performance gap between the current state and the organizational goal. Even more pertinent was the complete lack of any root cause this countermeasure was addressing. His arbitrary decision was solely an effort to flex his managerial muscles and display without ambiguity that he was calling all the shots. Collaborative interaction was not an option. Minions fall in line. Being new in this particular office, perhaps he felt a show of alpha dominance was necessary to start things off on the right track, in alignment with his cultural upbringing as a traditional manager. It obviously backfired and created a rift he would never be able to repair. Even after the ridiculous decree was rescinded, they at best tolerated each other for the duration of his reign. He never apologized for the misguided decision, something not unusual for a traditional manager. In their minds, admitting mistakes shows weakness. The exact opposite is the case for a Lean-minded leader. Admitting mistakes shows humility and a continued desire for collaboration. They deemed him nothing but weak. It is all so backward when you break it down with process analysis. Readers who experience this disrespect regularly know exactly what I'm talking about. These managers do not qualify as Leaders, and as such, I only afford them a label of manager. Again, I do not blame the person unless they recognize the dysfunction and make a conscious decision to remain on this arrogant path of disrespect. This is intentional malice.

To be clear, I'm not proposing decision-making trust be given entirely over without proper capability. Discussion on the thresholds when asking for manager's approval is necessary, but to withhold autonomy just to exert one's authority is pure disrespect. Conversely, to hand over full decision-making autonomy to workers without providing proper training and ensuring they are prepared to take on the responsibility is equally disrespectful. This would also posture them for failure. Ever know a person who was promoted into management and turned loose in the new role without support, coaching, and continued development? It would be equivalent to handing the keys to a forklift over to a new employee and telling them to move pallets when and where they saw fit. Full considerations should be given on both ends of the spectrum, and understanding current state capabilities is paramount before deciding anything. But when employees have proven they can perform their job correctly, get out of their way and let them do it. Stop slowing down the process just to remind people who the boss is. It is both disrespectful and wasteful.

As with many managers I've had, traditional managers were the nicest of persons when you got to know them but were utterly inept at generating engagement from employees. Adversarial conditions in the workplace flourished between supervisor and worker. Servant leadership was so far from their vision, they couldn't have detected it with Lean binoculars. The advantages completely eluded them. They were indeed a product of their culture. Accordingly, I never held a grudge against them personally, but I viewed their profound lack of leadership skills a function of the widespread broken processes preparing them for the role. I've often told my peers and leadership alike, if I were king for a day, these concepts would be mandatory training before a person could even apply for a supervisory role. In fact, it should be part of on-boarding for every single employee in order to level-set the culture on how formal leaders should treat people. It should also be mandatory for all business college students prior to graduation. This would define the behavioral expectations for everyone. The alternative is allowing a culture to morph into whatever it does by chance. It's not worth the risk, in my opinion, especially when proven methodologies exist. The wheel has been invented. Why continue dragging your cart down the road on its frame?

Do some analysis. Why are you throwing decrees over the wall without allowing employees to weigh in? Have you done it in the complete absence of a confirmed problem and/or root cause to some negative effect? What makes you think you know best what will improve a process? Think about this and be open-minded enough to realize you are disrespecting your employees as it applies to the work they are asked to do and the environment they are asked to do it in. Lack of trust sends a powerful message and diminishes loyalty to the company overall. It creates conditioned drones performing tasks without the slightest inclination to offer opportunities to improve the process. They will carry out their duties in an obviously wasteful manner just because you said to do it. My phrase, *Shut-up-and-color* describes it completely. Be advised traditional managers, blind compliance does indeed harm the human spirit in a work environment and ultimately the bottom line for the company financially. Disrespect is costing companies a fortune.

3. Giving confusing direction or instructions to an employee

This is disrespectful. If you ask someone to perform a task (assuming they are qualified to do it in the first place) and you don't spend the time getting consensus on their comprehension of the deliverables, you are disrespecting them. Think about it. You give them ambiguous tasks, expect them to fill in the blanks according to your unspoken vision, and then you want stellar results. Frustration, stress, multiple attempts, and re-work are guaranteed. If you think re-work is free or has no impact on flow, your periodic checkup with the business optometrist is way overdue.

You've probably been put in this precise position yourself with traditional managers. How did you deal with it? Did you feel comfortable asking continued questions until you fully understood the task, or did you just stop because you recognized impatience from the task provider and decided more probing would only annoy them further? Did it lead to a relationship of mutual respect, or did you just try to do your best in the face of confusion and hope for a good outcome? The Lean-minded leader takes the time to be clear with instructions, making sure the employee has what they need to be successful on the first pass, not the second or sixth. This is empowerment. Until we have the capability of reading each other's minds, we need to patiently make sure we are all on the same page of music before the band begins to play. And, if the culture is one where employees are disinclined to ask questions, the misguided assumptions will be plentiful from both parties. If you ever respond to an employee with, "*No, that is not at all what I wanted/expected/needed,*" recognize chances are high the instruction process was flawed, and **this** is an example of disrespect. The worst of the traditional managers will then vent their frustration by blaming the employee. They might also berate them for not asking clarifying questions without realizing they have created an atmosphere of fear. Employees don't want to ask more questions if they're afraid you will respond negatively. Incredibly, these managers see no part of the broken process attributed to their behavior. It's disrespectful, and your process needs to shift if you intend to set employees up for success. Arrogance and impatience have no useful part in the process of giving instructions.

Side Story – First day on the job with the aircraft maintenance planning gig. Mind you, I had not worked in an office environment before, and neither had the other two mechanics who scored this opportunity. We were the folks performing the value-added work and were now shifting to a support position. Taking airplanes apart and putting them back together, no problem. Operating computers and such—clueless. Where is the on-button? Planning material for jobs in the electronic systems we had no exposure to – which way is up? We had intimate knowledge of the job being accomplished on the production floor, but this was a mission to Mars for us. It was the exact opposite situation for the current planners. They had spent their careers in offices and wouldn't consider straying out into production areas where the noise, danger, and filth was plentiful.

That was a foreign world to them and avoided by design. What did it matter their only reason for existence was to make the maintenance activity flow smoothly and that the mechanics were their direct internal customer? This was the world they had been indoctrinated into. It wasn't their fault; culture takes the rap here. Fortunately, someone in leadership recognized the distinct gap between the current planners and their customers, the mechanics doing the actual work. Technical language alone was something they had never been exposed to. We had it in spades. Eventually, we were able to help each other interact more successfully, but not for quite some time.

Now you might be imagining a transitional mentorship program, or formal training existed for this industrial engineering technician (IET) job, and it would be reasonable to expect, especially for a mechanic who had never worked in an office before. I certainly expected it. Basically, the onboarding instructions were, *"Here is your desk, get to work. If you have any questions, ask the other planners."*

Are you kidding me? I might as well have been placed into the pilot's seat of the space shuttle moments before launch and been told, *"The buttons and switches are here, here, and here. If you need help after launch, ask your fellow crewmembers. Do the best you can. See you at the crash site."*

The job involved the use of a completely foreign computer system (to us). I eventually became quite familiar with it, but initially, it was like learning French from a Chinese speaking person, over the phone, with a scratchy connection.

I'd ask my fellow planners for help, but they would quickly become impatient with my lack of understanding. What seemed entirely intuitive to them was nebulous to me. In frustration, I finally asked someone in the leadership chain when the training for this system would commence. His rather curt answer was, "Training? It began when you got here, now get back to work!" This is just how it was. The process, be it ever so broken and unstructured, was to ask peers how to do something (when they had time for our questions), try it, then do it over again multiple times until it was eventually correct, or at least marginally acceptable. This assumed we would even *recognize* when it was ultimately correct. If it negatively impacted our customers (the mechanics), not to worry; more re-work would take care of it. If it seems to you that we were not positioned for success, you are correct. This was a stressful transition, and in retrospect, a perfect example of disrespect in the form of confusing instructions to employees. When thrown into a situation of ambiguity, unnecessary stress for everyone is guaranteed, not to mention poor results, rework, frustration, and delays. How often does it occur in your world? How many times have you been thrust into a task with little or no awareness of how to do it, or what the deliverables were supposed to look like? Opportunities abound here, and the Lean leader knows there is a far better way to avoid most of this insanity just by giving more precise instructions. In supplier-mode (Lean leadership), you are continuously striving to fill the gaps and clear the hurdles in the way of employees satisfying customer requirements. This is your primary mission as a leader. Skip this, and you will remain an ineffective manager at best – never achieving the status of leader.

Side Story – Here is the complete opposite side of the coin. Many years ago, I was to teach a class in a conference room I had never been to before (a rather fancy conference room, I might add). I entered the room, and approximately 25 participants were already there eagerly anticipating the magical message of Lean. Anyway, the electronic equipment (I call it gadgetry) looked to be state of the art stuff and was plentiful in quantity. Dealing with a 4-foot rack of boxes with knobs, switches, dials, and wires was the hurdle I needed to overcome if this class was going to happen. So, I queried the audience, "Does anyone know how to work this stuff?" Cue the blank stares from students. "Anyone at all? Bueller?"

Someone finally responded. "We normally get the IT guy to work all that stuff for us."

"Great! Where is the IT guy right now?" Rework on the blank stares. Cue my growing panic.

By now, I noticed a laminated booklet attached to the side of the rack with a string. Turns out no one in the audience was even aware of it. What the heck, it was worth a shot. Students (my customers) were waiting. Can't have that. Plan A wasn't working, and plan B hadn't been developed yet. So, I picked it up, and all became right with the world. It had a picture of the rack with a giant red arrow pointing to a particular button on one of the electronic boxes. The arrow didn't identify the name of the box or the button's purpose—who cares, right? It just said, *Push this button first*. So, I pushed it!

Things started to come to life. The screen came on. The second picture in the folder said, *when this screen comes up, push this button*. Another arrow pointed to the button. Magic! Within sixty seconds, I had my slides up, and I was ready to rock-n-roll. It was awesome. My heart rate was returning to normal.

Point of the story: Someone—an insightful human being who understood the power of posturing people for success—built these intuitive standard work instructions so any goofball (including this goofball) could get the equipment going with minimal effort. I was incredibly thankful for an unknown person's efforts creating this simplistic, completely understandable document. Imagine the delay if we had to track down the IT person, interrupt whatever he/she was doing (assuming we found them in the first place), drag them to the room, and wait for the equipment to become functioning. Imagine further how many more times this insanity might play out in the future. Also, imagine if the instructions had been built with nothing but lots of confusing words and no pictures to make it easy for a technically challenged person. Now imagine if **every** process with likely negative outcomes was designed to make sure everyone in the process – from the super SME (subject matter expert) down to the novice—could easily be successful.

Are you imagining this? Looks good, right? I bet all your conference rooms have this blatantly intuitive standard work instructions for the gadgetry, so this opportunity probably doesn't apply to you. It's just for those *other* folks who haven't recognized the disrespect and negative impacts of delays yet.

In a similar situation when I had conference room equipment not working correctly (different room), I called the help desk (gotta love the label) for immediate assistance prior to the start of a training class because that's what the little sticker on the equipment said to do. Points awarded for visual management. The person who answered told me to fill out a trouble ticket online. Ha! Now there is a useful process step for someone needing assistance within the next ten minutes. Customer service at its best. When challenged with the urgency of my issue, the employee responded with, *"I'm sorry sir, but this is what our process dictates I tell you to do."* Translation: *My traditional manager couldn't care less about your requirements or empowering me to be flexible, so please conform to the process we are mandating you follow. Thank you, and have a nice day.* At least I didn't have to listen to menu items when I called. I'll give them some points for that, but the outcome was a delayed class start time. Thirty students and I waited for someone to show up and fix the gadgetry. **Waste!**

Positioning employees and customers for success in **_any_** process increases dramatically with the right motivation and respect for the people in the process. Helping people succeed isn't an annoyance, it's a frame of mind for the Lean/Servant leader because they see their role as a supplier, not a customer. They work for the employees, not the other way around. Before you just agree and move on, decide what your contribution to the confusion is. Do you dispense vague instructions and then blame the employee for inadequate results? Do you receive lousy instructions then hesitate to push back for enough clarification to be successful on one pass – perhaps because you fear your supervisor? Both situations contribute to the performance gap.

"Understanding your employee's perspective can go a long way towards increasing productivity and happiness." - Kathryn Minshew[vi]

4. Being quick to chastise but slow to praise

This is disrespectful. Are you the finder of flaws in your employees? The defect cop? The manager with laser-focused radar to detect mistakes because you consider this your mission? Well, perhaps it is to some extent, but what you do *after* you find flaws is the critical part. I've had bosses throughout my decades in the workforce who wouldn't hesitate to trash an employee—even in public settings—for every mistake detected. My wife had a boss who berated workers for errors they were not even involved with, and it only exacerbated the situation if the disrespected employee brought this unwarranted blame to his attention. They just took the verbal beating to minimize its duration.

On the flip side, these same traditional managers are typically very stingy with a compliment when something goes according to plan. Not even a thank you comes from them. I had many a boss who told me, "Getting it right is what I pay you to do. Why should I have to thank you?" At some level, it might be a valid argument, but consider this: What is the cost of saying *thank you* or *good job* to an employee? How long does it take to say these words? And then consider the impact it can have on a human being, especially when dispensed in the presence of their peers. The Lean leader understands this completely. By contrast, the traditional manager is in cop-mode and is forever on the lookout for mistakes so they can pounce on someone. Blaming people instead of the broken process handed to them is easier. They tend to use language targeting the individual; "*You made another mistake,*" as opposed to realizing the employee probably had no intentional malice. More respectfully, the boss might say, "*Sally, can you help me understand why the process is resulting in mistakes?*" The difference is profound and reinforces the fact employees are often set up for failure with broken processes. Unfortunately, the misguided manager doesn't have the process filter attached to his or her glasses. A defect has occurred, some*ONE* must be held accountable. Critiquing the broken process allowing the defect to occur in the first place is not in their behavioral repertoire. A person must pay. Indeed, they all pay.

Are you the manager stingy with a compliment and do you seek out a person to chastise when an undesirable outcome occurs? Do people fear you? Is accountability more important to you than understanding the root cause of the defect, delay, or safety issue? If you do hand out praise, is it immediately and in front of their peers, or do you save it for some batched meeting with the employee? Why are you waiting? The positive effect diminishes significantly over time between the action and the praise. It won't produce the preferred behavioral effect you could be achieving. Do you dispense a thank you via email when you could just as easily take the time to pick up the phone or do it in-person? Are you too busy? How much research have you done on the effect of positive reinforcement done correctly? The technique is not as intuitive as you might imagine. Is it part of your leadership development training? If not, why?

One of the significant contributors to my Lean journey has been the insightful words of authors. I read—a lot. Anything related to process improvement, especially the leadership aspect, remains front-and-center on my radar. Reading a book two or three times is the norm because I will invariably digest an intriguing new morsel of value missed on the first pass. Why continue to learn the hard way (trial and error) when you can learn from the pioneers who have stepped in potholes before you? If you are not continually seeking new insight on your particular niche in the world, then you risk stagnation. You will *never* have everything in your behavioral repertoire or reach a stage where more insight is not useful to improve your technique. Imagine a respected physician who stopped exploring new practices and procedures because he/she decided their medical proficiency was sufficient, complete, and good enough. At some point, their customers would have begun objecting to leaches being applied to their rashes or bloodletting to relieve migraine headaches. I continue to be amazed how in the year 2019 I still encounter people in senior levels of management who have never even heard of Lean, let alone taken the time to explore its incredible potential for their company. My message here is simple. Seek new input and incorporate the useful elements to improve your leadership style, your process improvement approaches, your techniques for performing root cause analysis, your patterns of selecting countermeasures, and most importantly, your process of interacting with, empowering and *respecting* human beings. If you think you have everything you need to be the most effective leader you could be, you are sorely mistaken. No one does. Your development as a leader is perpetual if humility is part of your makeup. Arrogance is your enemy.

One book in particular I recommend to everyone, formal and informal leaders, is *Carrots and Sticks Don't Work*[vii], by Paul L. Marciano. Great book! You won't find the Lean language in this book, but it is loaded with insight on how to interact with human beings to get them engaged. Below I share a few quotes which tie directly into the Lean leadership model I have been describing. I encourage you to read them multiple times, then contemplate the applicability to your personal leadership style. Gloss over them with the belief that they don't pertain to you, and you will have explored/learned nothing. To learn, one must open his/her mind to new and sometimes uncomfortable input.

"Today's leaders who wish to maximize the productivity of their employees must fully understand and embrace the notion that employees work for more than just money; they work to feel good about themselves."

"My education, research, and experience have led me to conclude that powerful leaders who created highly engaged employees do so by fostering a culture of respect in their organizations."

"…when people feel respected, they exhibit greater discretionary effort in order to benefit the group and organization."

"Unfortunately, most supervisors don't bother helping employees to understand the importance of their work and its connection to the big picture. To remain fully engaged, employees must leave work every day feeling that they have contributed in a meaningful way to the organization and its goals. Do your employees feel this way?"

"Those who empower employees encourage them to take educated risks, seek novel solutions, and treat mistakes as learning opportunities."

Notice how these thoughts directly conflict with the behavioral patterns of a command/control traditional manager. If you see yourself as the defect cop and are quick to chastise people, you are missing enormous opportunities and systematically (even if unintentionally) degrading the employees' self-worth. This, in turn, reduces their motivation to challenge broken process elements, and eventually, you get frustrated with them and vice versa. The outcome is undesirable for everyone involved.

When is the last time you praised an employee for a desirable outcome, or for anything? Did you do it immediately after the positive result occurred? Did you do it in public? Was it sincere, or obviously dispensed for the sake of sounding authoritative? Do you ever just thank someone for being an employee? To what extent do employees feel appreciated and valued? Do they leave at the end of the day feeling like they accomplished something of importance and inspired to come back tomorrow because their supervisor took the time to recognize their effort? Recognize your actions, positive or negative, directly influence the actions of others.

"Appreciate everything your associates do for the business. Nothing else can quite substitute for a few well-chosen, well-timed, sincere words of praise. They're absolutely free and worth a fortune." - Sam Walton

5. Attacking people versus the process

People rarely come to work with the intent of messing up some process or creating defects with purposeful intent. On the contrary. They generally enter their Gemba trying to do their best, but you have inserted them (most likely unintentionally) into a broken process laden with opportunities to generate mistakes, delays or safety mishaps. Vague or unreasonable instructions, undocumented processes, lousy tools/equipment, burdensome software, missing informational elements, inadequate training, etc. Then, when something goes south, you want names to start assigning blame. We all know the next step in this traditional process of demanding accountability, as though it will somehow prevent the mistake from ever happening again. Maybe you don't directly punish the employees, but you might insert one of the lamest countermeasures on the planet, re-training. The initial training we provided worked so well the first time, let's just do it again. Maybe the outcome will be better this time.

Ineffective responses of this nature attack the person just as surely as if you had admonished them or generated a useless, degrading performance improvement plan. How often do those silly things produce an engaged employee? My experience says they are paper trails used to set the legal stage for future termination. Nothing generates loyalty and respect for a company like the threat of getting fired. Perhaps, in some situations, PIPs become the last resort effort, but if it is your first choice, your process of developing employees has failed miserably. If you insist on using them at your company, provide them to the supervisor of the employee instead. Their process failed. Attacking the person in any form is misguided and doomed to cause a repeat of the defect by other people in the process. Not to mention the relationship degradation between the parties and the non-collaborative element growing inside the company. Distrust and fear become entrenched quickly. Here comes the boss. Shields up!

Recognizing intentional malice was probably not in play, the Lean leader asks a different question. *"What went wrong with the process to create the undesirable outcome here, and how can we alter it to prevent reoccurrence?"* The demeanor going into the discussion is a solid understanding of processes being flawed, not people conducting them. Try this and watch the magic. People begin to abandon the fear they will get in trouble when process errors occur and will soon enthusiastically embrace them. Mistakes become opportunities to improve a process, not to abuse a person. Leadership now understands if the process is redesigned (with full participation from the people doing the work) to prevent the defects in the future, everything, including the culture, improves. A sense of co-ownership develops in the employees, and they want to participate even more. The aim is positioning people for success with a good process, always. Never to berate them in the absence of intentional malice on their part. If you insist on focusing on employees when defects occur, then give them the right to do the same to you, Mr./Mrs. Supervisor. Wouldn't this be a fairer situation? *"Boss, do you realize you made yet another mistake? Try to do better, so I don't have to recommend a demerit on your batched performance review, will ya?"* Disrespectful you say? I agree completely. The right to disrespect a human being should not be granted to anyone, regardless of their title or lack thereof. But make no mistake about it, the first move of respect has to be from the leader if you expect the employees to replicate it. Conversely, if the leader has behaved disrespectfully, don't be alarmed if the employees give it right back.

Side Story — After teaching one of my short classes on Lean to a group of first- and second-line supervisors, this woman from the class called me the next day. Always an encouraging sign because it means they are processing what they heard and not just discarding it the moment they leave the room. She said she really liked the class but wanted to take issue with something I said. Great! I love it when people challenge my message. It means they are critical thinkers at heart, precisely what I'm encouraging they promote in the entire workforce.

So, what struck a chord with her was my mantra of processes being broken, not employees. She wanted to give me an example of when the opposite was the case. I instantly knew this was going to be interesting because I've heard similar stories start off the same way hers did. The conversation went something like this:

"So, I have this one employee, and she simply cannot conduct the job she is tasked with to an acceptable level. All her peers seem to get it, but no matter what I do with her, she continues to make mistakes. It's just so frustrating for me." *(Notice she didn't convey any sense of frustration on the employee's part, just her own. Also, note her language of "no matter what I do with her." She didn't even realize she was attacking the person.)* "I've tried talking to her, re-training her, counseling her, mentoring her, even doing the task in front of her so she can see how to do it properly. Still, she fails. This is **clearly** a case of the person being at fault, and not the process; don't you agree?"

I carefully asked her a series of questions intended to help her think this through a bit more. My goal was to have her arrive at the correct analysis process instead of me just handing it to her.

"So, ma'am, help me understand what the selection process is like for employees performing this task."

She immediately came back with, "Well, you need to understand I didn't hire her! It was my predecessor. I inherited this employee."

Ah! Now we're getting somewhere. If only we could get the hiring person on the phone, we could beat her up with "What the hell were **you** thinking?" questions. Surely this would lead to a better fix, right?

I asked her the criteria for hiring. She said there wasn't anything documented in particular, but it needed to be someone who could process a lot of information quickly before acting. She then immediately shifted back to bouncing solutions off me, as if I would know just the right thing to do. After all, I taught the class. Obviously, I must have a vending machine filled with solutions at my disposal for all maladies.

One of the resolutions she was considering in desperation was dismissing this employee. Wow. How sad is this? Considering a last-resort action without even examining the situation that put this employee in a position she potentially wasn't suited for.

So, let's assume for just one minute this employee was indeed ill-suited for the job. We'll say for discussion sake she will never be good at it. Plenty of people are bad at some tasks. Put me into an internet technology task, and I will fail despite whatever training you subject me to. It's just not my forte and never will be. Coach me, mentor me, berate me, re-train me, threaten me, hit me with a stick, spend countless wasteful hours generating a performance improvement plan and the results will forever be less than desired. Would this mean I am the source of the problem?

When presented with this hypothetical question, my student's answer was an immediate YES, and you might be inclined to think the same. The employee is flawed.

But suppose we take a look at the selection process putting me in the position. I fill out some application form, and someone asks me a few questions, like, "*Have you used a computer? Do you have experience with Excel, PowerPoint, Word, etc.?*" I can honestly respond to all these questions in the affirmative, but that doesn't make me equipped for a job in IT. Then, I'm hired and expected to perform at a high level.

When I fail to measure up, you counsel me, retrain me, mentor me, etcetera, and I still fail to measure up. Is it reasonable to say I am the problem here?

With a reluctant tone after hearing this alternative perspective, she said, "Well, no, in that case, the process failed to filter for the correct competence level to perform the job."

She then paused and said, "Now I see where you are going with this. I suppose the process of selecting this person could have been flawed."

Score!

In many cases, this person has a skill the company can benefit from. The best scenario plays out with transferring the individual into a job suited to their skills and abilities. This is a win for everyone involved. If this is just not possible, it may ultimately be necessary to dismiss the employee, but the Lean leader should subsequently attack the hiring process, so this disrespectful situation never occurs again with another employee.

I must say I've run into variations of this story many times on my Lean journey. People are conditioned to attack other people as though it will prevent the problem from ever happening again. It's easy and quick, but more times than not, it skipped the critical root cause analysis step. If an employee gets into a job they are not suited for—regardless of the reason—can they be held accountable for the mismatch? Shouldn't the job selection process get the bulk of scrutiny here? I would claim yes. The selection process is to blame, and to skip straight to adjusting the person in some manner (re-training, performance improvement plans, etc.) could lead to undesirable outcomes repeating for other employees and relationships degrading across the board. Another round peg employee will end up in a square hole job and we will keep pounding with increasingly bigger hammers to make them fit. A futile effort and incredibly disrespectful.

Respect (as it applies to the work people are asked to do) builds employee engagement without fear of ridicule or punishment. The mantra to remember here is **ATTACK THE FLAWED PROCESS, NOT THE EMPLOYEES IN IT**. Traditional managers will need to consciously catch themselves when the old behaviors become tempting in situations where previously they reacted quickly to blame a person for unwanted process outcomes. As with all of these alternative behaviors, the transition doesn't happen overnight. The more experienced Lean leaders need to coach others until the desired behaviors become muscle memory. Be patient with each other because the payoff is well worth the effort. This isn't a competition among the leadership group for one person to shine above their peers. Everyone needs to pull the rope in the same direction with a single value stream mentality. This is why I emphasize the enormous advantage of having the CEO, or person at the top of the organizational chart, fully on-board—someone like Chris Hammes (COO & Executive Vice President at Integris Health care), Art Byrne (author and former CEO of Wiremold company), or Dr. Gary Kaplan (Chairman & CEO of Virginia Mason health system). These people are shining examples of what executive support for a Lean transformation can look like in a company. They didn't sit back and wait for a change to occur at its own pace, or worse, delegate it to someone else. They embraced the role of a passionate champion who intentionally initiated a culture shift by communicating traditional methodologies (like attacking employees first) would no longer be an acceptable approach. Behavioral expectations from the top of the food chain are not likely to be ignored.

During my journey, I've seen pockets of excellence briefly emerge in sections of large companies (including the federal government job I held for over three decades), but the Lean magic wasn't spreading across the entire enterprise. Something was limiting the cultural shift from overtaking the previously entrenched good-ole'-boy system developed shortly after the earth cooled. Certain organizations latched onto the power of Lean and set off with a motivated spirit to infuse it. But without the executive support at the top, it predictably sputtered. The energy was unsustainable long-term. Perhaps you have seen this in companies you worked in, researched, or heard about. It's a sad thing to witness because you recognize the incredible potential remains just out of reach. Until the C-suite inhabitants put their hands on the wheel and intentionally steer the bus onto Lean Boulevard, the isolated cheerleaders will continue to struggle convincing everyone to stay the course. Imagine a middle-level leader touting Lean success stories in their department during a meeting only to have their passion be dismissed by senior management. The lack of positive reinforcement is essentially a message to discontinue. Culture wins every time. Why not use this fact to your strategic advantage?

Side Story - In 2017, I had a powerful experience after a two-hour Leading with Lean class I taught. The audience of mostly informal leaders numbered about 35, and they were intrigued when I described what a culture of Lean leadership looked like. It is typically the case for people to stay around after a class to ask questions and bounce ideas off me, which I enjoy because it affirms to me they are actively processing and genuinely interested to learn more. In this instance, one particular young lady obviously had a question but hung back away from the rest. She waited for everyone to leave to share her thoughts in private. When the room was completely empty, she explained the concepts of Lean leadership and its techniques were new to her. She had never heard of Lean before, let alone the leadership style I had been describing. He words will forever remain etched in my memory because they were both encouraging and depressing at the same time.

This young engineer told me my description of respect for employees was like a fantasy, and it would be a breath of fresh air to go to work every day in such an environment. So far, so good, right? But then came the more salient message element. I give her high marks for being courageous enough to share because she had never met me before thus didn't know what I would or wouldn't take back to management. Frustration can be the catalyst for bold behavior.

"I've worked here for about a year now and don't know how long I can continue. The relationship between my boss and me is toxic. He couldn't care less about my ideas or challenges to process fault points, and the more I bring things up, the more he considers me a troublemaker. I would kill to work in the respectful environment you just described to us. What can I do to change things?"

Wow!

I was trying to process her thoughts and at the same time formulate a response to give her hope things could change. She obviously didn't want her fellow classmates to hear this frustration—a clear indication of her cultural predicament. I explained to her how Lean transformations take time and are expedited only when senior leadership is fully on board as a knowledgeable champion of the efforts. This obviously gave her no comfort because she knew the critical ingredient was unlikely to manifest in her department. I often wonder if she decided to bail from the company or hang around in hopes things would change. She clearly was an employee who was begging to make a difference and be valued, but her glow was systematically being extinguished with the broken management process her boss utilized. How unfortunate for everyone. It seems UC grads often win this battle, but consider this: do they really win? How about the company—are they winning with managers behaving like this? Are external customers of the company winning?

I have processed this conversation dozens of times since it occurred and have used it in subsequent training classes as an example of what traditional management can do to the human spirit. Unfortunately, the debilitating conditions she was exposed to are not uncommon in corporate America. I could absolutely relate to her story because I have worked in those toxic environments myself over the years. If you are tossing this situation into the anomaly bucket, I can only encourage you to look more closely. It's happening everywhere, and companies will not, cannot, reach their full potential if it persists. Still not buying it? Collect some data in your company and reevaluate your assumptions. Engagement levels are probably much lower than your gut-data indicates. Incredibly creative employees are being conditioned to shut-up-and-color. Many of them will simply move on in frustration or sit idle at their desks, wondering if they will ever have a supervisor who fully appreciates their spirt to contribute.

Side Story – In 1999, I was at rock bottom with my job conditions. Going to work had evolved into a sickening chore. I would rather have been cleaning gas station restrooms in the dark, using my own toothbrush. We had been subjected to mandatory 12-hour shifts because production had gotten so far behind. Things were ugly. Traditional managers reached into their inept box of fixes and latched onto their go-to countermeasure of overtime. Unfortunately, it wasn't impacting the delay, so it seemed logical to hire more people and work those drones twelve hours a day also. All this aside, the management team (and I use the label very loosely) was nowhere close to inspiring a culture of continuous improvement + respect for people.

With nearly twenty years of federal service under my belt, I was seriously considering resignation as my only outlet. I did not have enough time to retire, and equal paying jobs were non-existent in the local area, so this was not a trivial decision. Conditions were to the point I literally got sick to my stomach before going into the building some days. The dread I felt driving to work would build as I got closer. It was an awful situation and when I announced to my wife I was seriously considering quitting she didn't challenge it one bit. My plan was just to escape and find something, anything, to pay the bills. Leaving a federal government job before retirement is something very few people do, but my physical health needed priority over the financial security aspect. I was miserable, and the negativity consumed me. When employees are subjected to relentless disrespect—which comes in many forms (intentional and unintentional)—everything begins to degrade – at home and work. Fortuitously and without active intent on my part, I was presented an escape route to the planning office. Had it not been for this, I'm certain I would have resigned. Instead, I was able to take the first step on a path that would ultimately change my life—and my perspective of leadership—forever. It was the genesis of my Lean journey.

If you haven't done so already, I encourage you to digest Dr. Deming's 14 points for management. Number eight says, *"Drive out fear, so that everyone may work effectively for the company."*[viii] I implore you not gloss over his words. Think about it to the extent you as a leader utilize it within your daily approach, or as a frontline worker as you may or may not be subjected to the fear of speaking up.

Once you grasp the respect for people piece of the Lean business system, you begin to shift your focus of leadership from cop mode (command/control) to supplier. Your mission becomes supplier of **everything** missing in the employees' world keeping them from accommodating customer requirements in the easiest, most efficient manner possible. As Deming insightfully said, *"The aim of Leadership is to help people do a better job with less effort."*[ix] I don't think the concept could be conveyed more plainly. The problem is, it doesn't reach a front burner for traditional managers. They are typically focused on their own world, making the monthly numbers, how they can advance to the next rung on the ladder, and spending time knocking down hurdles for employees doesn't make the to-do list. Other priorities prevail. If not ignorance of the adverse outcomes, perhaps egos and inflated senses of importance are getting in their way. It's very unfortunate, but far too common and acceptable in companies today.

If you are not familiar with Dr. Deming, I invite you to become so. The man was a genius when it came to explaining how to be successful in business and how to position employees for success using the principles of Lean, despite the absence of the label during most of his lifetime. He should be required reading for all managers and business owners. If you have an MBA or even an undergraduate degree in business and have never heard of Dr. W. Edwards Deming, you should contact your degree provider and demand a partial rebate. Their educational process failed you. For the life of me, I cannot understand why a Lean leadership class with an introduction of Deming is not required in all business colleges.

In servant/supplier mode, the leader is continually looking for employee hurdles or gaps. If they need training - supply it. Workers have confusing (or missing) instructions - get the A+ worker to build standard work to eliminate the confusion for the less experienced and then continue to polish it to a brilliant finish with continuous improvements. Workers say the performance feedback they get is lacking? Determine precisely what they individually need and make the changes. Workforce not completely clear on how their process is performing? Use the VOC information and develop (with the employees) performance indicators so everyone can instantly see where the gaps are. The sole purpose of your existence as a leader (if you are embracing Lean leadership), is to *position your employees for success every chance you get*. This is the activity of empowerment. Then, when it's time to hand out the atta-boys, do it immediately in front of their peers. Don't wait till the end of the quarter just because you have a batch process to dispense accolades. The positive effect is diminished when you wait weeks after the act.

Another thing to incorporate into your leader's respect toolbox is the avoidance of credit-grabbing. Nothing is quite as nauseating as a boss seeking, proclaiming, or accepting credit when they should be bestowing it on their employees, especially in public settings. Instead, heap praise on the teams so they are motivated to challenge more opportunities in their processes. When employees do the grunt work only to witness the boss taking credit for it, they are disinclined to go the extra mile next time. Discretionary work will vanish. Their respect for you will plummet, assuming it existed at all. It costs nothing to deliver praise properly, and the impact on people will pay dividends. You appreciate it from your superiors, why would you not correctly provide it to your direct reports? *This* is the respect for people I'm describing here. As you can see, respect goes far beyond politeness or a robust compensation package.

If you wish to evaluate yourself as a leader, consider measuring the extent to which you posture people for success or failure. I provide a method at the end of the book to help you get started. This is the rudimentary indication of your effectiveness. You have no more important mission element. If humility prevails, you will determine the baseline, the gaps, and the path forward.

Another vital point to understand here is the connection to customer requirements, both external and internal customers. Employees need to know what the requirements are, and then, the current state condition of the extent their process is accommodating these requirements. To withhold this information, or not develop it in the first place is yet another form of disrespect. Employees not only have the right to know how their process is doing, but without it, they will struggle to recognize their own value on the job. Additionally, without this knowledge, the motivation to improve a process will be lacking or misdirected. The simplest remedy is to capture VOC, translate it into performance indicators, then post your performance conditions so every employee is keenly aware of how things are going. Please don't bury them in some shared database with nested folders where only Indiana Jones could find them.

It's impossible for me not to be passionate about this critical element of leading with Lean because I know firsthand what it can do to a culture. I've seen Lean tools make a process or two better, but it just can't have the dramatic impact possible until respect for people becomes culturally intermingled. Think about the bosses you've had who you'd walk on hot coals for if they needed something accomplished. Remember how you felt working for them? Remember the joy it brought you to show up in the morning because you felt valued in their eyes? Remember how you felt when they shared your accomplishment in a public setting, and it was absolutely genuine? Maybe you even turned down other opportunities just to stay in their organization. Now think about the ones you worked for who generated nothing but dissension among workers, looked out for themselves first, took credit for your work, and habitually withheld recognition unless it was to highlight negatives or promote their own standing. We've all worked for these self-serving bosses and tolerated the conditions. Everyone loses.

As Jeffrey Liker put it in his book, *Developing Lean Leaders At All Levels*, "*As a senior leader, they cannot make the improvements. They cannot do the work. They are dependent on the people who report to them. Understanding this leads to humbleness. My job is to serve the people who can actually do the work; help them in any way I can. This is often referred to as servant leadership.*"[ix]

So, what does research say about this? Patrick Lencioni talks about it in his book, *The Truth About Employee Engagement*. He says, "*It would be impossible to accurately measure the amount of misery in the workforce, but my experience tells me this: more people out there are miserable in their jobs than fulfilled by them. And the cost of this, in both economic and human terms, is staggering. Economically, productivity suffers greatly when employees are disengaged. The effects on a company's bottom line or a nation's economy are undeniable. But it's the social cost of misery at work that seems particularly overwhelming, because it has such a broad ripple effect.*"[xi]

In their book, *The Enthusiastic Employee*, David Sirota, Louis Mischkind, and Michael Meltzer put it this way, "*People want to be treated like responsible adults, but many workers – primarily in factories but also in many white-collar settings – are, as they see it, treated like children or criminals, subjected to strict monitoring of their work and other behavior to coerce performance and conformity to the rules.*"[xii]

I can recall several managers I've worked for who required a report be sent to them depicting everything I'd worked on the previous week. I'm not talking about just the highlights; I'm talking a detailed account of everything. It was used as a monitoring system and was beyond degrading. If these managers had learned to Gemba walk instead of demanding wasteful CYA reports, they would have known precisely what I was working on, and what I needed their assistance on. The difference should be undeniably clear.

In his book, *Lead with Lean*, Michael Ballé says, "*Toyota grounded its management on learning and, over the years, developed a continuous on-the-job learning model based on two pillars: continuous improvement – continuously challenging oneself and learning by continuous small steps – and respect – making our best efforts to understand the obstacles each person encounters, supporting their development and making the best possible use of their abilities.*"[xiii]

Ballé also says in this same book, "*Based on our long-term commitment to researching Toyota, we can at least conclude that the company is indeed serious about employee engagement. Respect for people has been a mainstay of its business model for as long as we can tell.*"

By all accounts, Toyota has mastered the element of respect for employees. They recognized long ago the causal effect it has on human beings and ultimately the bottom line of company success. The mystery here is why most companies fail to walk this talk. Why, knowing all these causal connections and how they interact to sustain the employment energy of human beings, do they ignore the opportunity to actively incorporate them into their cultures? Many companies pay lip service to the ideas in their mission statements hanging on their walls, but does the behavior match the rhetoric? Only the employees can best answer this question, but if the answer is no, then the posters are mere wallpaper mocking employees and reminding them of what could be. Every reader should do some introspective analysis on the extent their company is respecting employees as it applies to the work they are asked to perform and the culture they are asked to do it in. And if you are a formal leader with direct reports, critique yourself on the extent you are disrespecting employees. I promise you it is happening to some extent. Anything short of full empowerment is disrespectful. Managers need to broaden their understanding of what it means to behave respectfully towards employees. The alternative status quo behaviors are costing your company a fortune.

I want to spend more time discussing autonomy, and the typical lack thereof when managers refuse to trust and delegate. How many people have to ask permission for mundane or low impact things? After we hire and train people, why do we not trust them to perform their job in a relatively mother-may-I free environment? Do we have data saying they are not trustworthy, therefore we mandate our approval for tasks? Is it necessary to micromanage to prevent defects, and if so, what is done to correct the process beyond the hovering cop approach? Do you have data substantiating your premise employees will wreak havoc if permitted to make the call in your absence? If the answer to this last question is yes, what was done to prepare the person for the job? Why does this type of culture exist in the first place? Could it be a countermeasure was hastily inserted without a root cause, and the knee-jerk decision became set in stone? Whatever the case, it's adding wasteful cycle time to your processes and conveying disrespect at the same time. If you are playing compliance cop in your process, it's time you admit your process is badly broken. Do you really have time for wasteful inspections? Stop blaming these employees and attack the flawed process you inserted them into. Something is missing to ensure workers will be successful. It will give everyone -most assuredly you - more time back in their day.

Side Story – An administrative assistant shared this story with me after attending one of my Lean classes. She was tasked with acquiring office supplies for the floor when needed. Someone asked her to purchase something, but alas, this item didn't exist on the list of approved office supplies. I don't recall what the thing was specifically, and it doesn't really matter, but since it wasn't on the list, she had to get special permission to purchase it. The approver was at the general manager level and not readily available due to travel. She submitted the request, then waited. Always some waiting in processes, right? Eventually, the request made the manager's radar, the approval was granted, and she bought the item for the requestor.

Wait for it . . . the item cost $5.00

I asked her if she had ever been denied one of these requests, and her answer was negative. Not once.

Think about the message this wasteful process sends to the employee. *I don't trust you to make the call even with a $5 item so you will need to check with me first.* Really? Is this how a worker should be treated? Is it how you would prefer the process steps flow? Obviously, this list of approved items came about in an effort to standardize the purchasing of supplies—and this can be a good thing—but why is the employee not empowered to make the call on non-standard items? Imagine the cost of the process to ask permission, and the fact permission is always granted. I'm going to speculate it far exceeded five dollars, and the collateral damage was to condition an employee to remain in mother-may-I mode. Wait for the boss to say yes/no because they are in charge of the budget. Wow. This is a classic adult-child relationship. How about we let the employee make the call all the time and trust them because we've empowered them with clear guidance on how to decide without dragging an inspector into this low-impact process? And why would you have an approval process in the first place if the answer is **always** going to be yes? How wasteful can it get? When she told me the story, I asked her if she had challenged the unnecessary step. You can probably guess her answer.

Culture does this to people. The design makes no sense when you break it down into the process elements but remains in place because traditional management does not encourage people to push back. It is culturally frowned upon. Push back is incorrectly viewed as challenging the boss, not the process. The employee might be labeled a troublemaker. The waste stays in place, the disrespect goes unabated, and the worker bee is further conditioned to emulate sheep behavior until they find a suitable exit.

In an article entitled "Bad Manager Mistakes That Make Good People Quit" Dr. Travis Bradberry, states, "*More than half of people who leave their jobs do so because of the relationship with their boss.*"[xiv] Please ponder this for a moment. If a worker's boss is the significant influencer of good employees exiting more than half the time, why would companies not use this pearl of wisdom to their advantage? Why would they not be continuously developing all supervisors before and after promotions in order to achieve the more desirable outcome? What could possibly be more important? I can attest I am a data point here.

Having been in the work world since 1974, I confidently proclaim I have worked for every type of supervisor from Hitler to Mother Teresa (and everything in-between) and was able to experience and compare the impacts of their various demeanors.

I understand it's hard to halt the business machine long enough to take a fresh look at options, assuming one is so inclined. Managing the day-to-day fires can be overwhelming, and intentionally pausing to consider a new strategy struggles to find its way into a hectic schedule. It's all supervisors can do to just survive the current state, brain-draining days they exist in now without driving into the ditch on the way home. Honestly, I get it, I just don't accept it as unalterable. There is a plethora of evidence showing much better results can be achieved in your business, but status quo behaviors will never get you there. Regardless of the determination, continuing on the wrong path will not lead to the desired location.

So how does a company, a university, or the sandwich shop on the corner ever expect to transform their culture into one embracing Lean? Note I said embracing, not notionally dabbling in it or faking it. What could possibly exist to shift minds and behaviors from the traditional habits of the masses? Quite simply, you need the person at the top of the food chain to believe wholeheartedly in the journey, and this person, acting as the champion, provides the bus for everyone else to ride on. It becomes the only transportation device permitted, and he/she must have their hands firmly on the steering wheel. The traditional behavior bus and its unyielding occupants have to be permanently removed from service. I advise donating both to your competitors. Additional cavemen in their culture dispensing impromptu countermeasures and disrespecting employees can only be good for your bottom line as a competitor.

This Lean-behavior bus must include training, mentoring, and positive reinforcement for the desired behavior. If some choose to disembark, so be it. Those reluctant to get on board will have a short period of time to decide, but under no circumstances can it be a voluntary situation. If you allow Lean behavior to be optional, human beings will continue with the bad habits responsible for getting them where they are today. The transformation will be prolonged for a painful amount of time if it happens at all.

In 2014, I attended a tour of Integris, a major health care provider in Oklahoma. This was a local company on their own Lean journey (inspired by Virginia Mason Health Care), and we (folks in the process improvement office) wanted our leaders to see what Lean looked like firsthand. About fifteen people from the energy company I was working for attended.

The first part of the tour was a presentation by the executive vice president and chief operating officer of Integris, Chris Hammes. This man stood at the front of the conference room and said something I will never forget. After a brief historical account of their Lean journey, he said, "I demand my leaders lead with Lean. Should they choose not to, I completely understand, but I very politely escort them off my bus."

Score!

Chills went up my spine. I literally felt the goose bumps forming on my arms. It was all I could do to resist standing up and applauding like some groupie. Having fully embraced the power and sanity of Lean many years before this speech, I could not have been more impressed with how eloquently this gentleman phrased it. This information wasn't the least bit new to me, but I hadn't heard it boldly spoken in a public setting by a senior leader. He was describing the recipe for successful transformation, and he was the metaphorical root system of the lean tree—passionate, executive support in champion-mode. Lean leadership was the chosen behavioral methodology. It was the expectation of senior leadership, not some flavor-of-the-day program. Traditional managers need not apply.

I recall frantically writing down the quote, but it was excess processing. Shake me to consciousness after a month-long coma, and I will be able to repeat his words. They are forever etched in my memory, and I've cited them many times in classes I've taught since. Leading with Lean was not voluntary in this company. It was the expected behavior and clearly communicated by the leader. I cannot attest if the vision is still present today, but I sincerely hope it is. Just as a traditional leader might have observed and assimilated sycophantic behavior because it successfully led to promotions in their world, Lean leadership behavior is the one to replicate from mentors and other leaders. When servant leadership is *the* way to gain favor and promotions, it naturally becomes the habit of choice across a company. Board the bus or seek alternative transportation with another company.

Please recognize I have greatly simplified the ingredients to Lean cultural transformation. A company absolutely needs to have executive support if they expect process improvement to be successful, but I would do the reader an injustice if I did not delve deeper into the topic. So, allow me the privilege of continuing to share my Lean journey with you, and the immense learnings it presented this student along the way.

"You must never be fearful about what you are doing when it is right." – Rosa Parks

Transplanting the Lean Tree

"There is no elevator to success, you have to take the stairs" - Zig Ziglar

Ponder my tree metaphor.

Imagine you found a tree you believe would make the perfect anchor plant in your landscaping environment. It has all the esthetic characteristics you want, looks very robust and healthy, has obviously grown very well where it is currently located and has captured your full interest to transplant. It is a beautiful tree, and the current owner assures you it can bear significant amounts of fruit in your yard. The excitement is high as you plunge your shovel into the ground near the base of this tree. You can do this! The earth seems relatively hard, so you put your full body weight on it. Embedded rocks and roots from other trees are all slowing down this part of the process. Already the fun begins to dissipate. No one likes things hard to accomplish. Digging is delaying the instant gratification you seek, but you trudge forward. You wanted to get this tree into your yard immediately, so you can reap the benefits and show everyone what you have accomplished. Seems like the root system is very deep and spread much further than anticipated. Probably don't need all of the dang roots anyway. Don't want to get too carried away here. The objective is to get this done quickly so we can expedite harvesting the fruit and taking credit. You decide to get what you can and just cut the wandering roots short. Surely, they will grow back. No problem. I got this, you remind yourself.

Having deemed the digging portion complete enough, you grab onto the trunk at the base. After a couple of mighty tugs, the tree finally releases its hold from the ground below. Thank goodness you continued on that gym regiment you started last January. Brut force has prevailed.

Now that you have this sucker out of the ground, you begin digging the hole to transplant it in your yard. Part of you wonders if you should have prepared the new location first, but you dismiss this fleeting thought. More hassles. The ground is much harder where you want to locate it, so the absolute minimum hole size is going to have to suffice. You didn't solicit input from experts or give a lot of consideration to planning. Besides, you don't have all day to dig a giant hole. You can soften it up later with plenty of water. That should do the trick. You shove the fragile tree into its new location, backfill with dirt from the hole, and there you have it. One transplanted tree! Job well done. Take a moment to step back and admire your handy work. The local arborist would be proud of what you accomplished, right?

Well, maybe not so much.

Unfortunately, in a short time, the leaves begin to wilt. This was unexpected, so you pour copious amounts of water on it. As director of landscaping and a subject-matter-expert in organic matter, you decree manure is needed, so you have your employees spread it generously about the base of this pathetic looking tree (because supervisors don't handle the manure directly). After a week of wishing and hoping, the tree is showing no signs of sustaining life. "Stupid tree," you say. "Probably wasn't suited for our yard anyway." It might remain on life-support for a while with heroic efforts, but everyone with normal vision clearly sees this tree is not going to rebound and flourish. No amount of fertilizer or water will save it. The arborist informs you the inadequate root system was just not able to sustain life. You discard this assessment with arrogance repackaged with positive spin about how these things take time. After all, you're a Director and have led new initiatives before. "We just need to be patient and it will thrive", you tell the skeptical onlookers.

Keep this in mind: when you initially view a mature Lean culture in a company, you mostly see elements of the tree above the ground. You see the fruit and the lush new growth resultant from years of careful nurturing. It is unlikely you will experience or grasp the deeply established root system sustaining continued growth. Indulge me while I make the connections to properly infusing Lean into a company's culture.

Perhaps the leadership team heard about Lean from a convention speaker, a book, a consultant, articles online, a tour of a Lean company, or from their competitors. *Hey! This sounds like a cool thing to do. Our company needs this stuff. Let's transplant it into our world. Have an underling fetch our golden shovel and a photographer!*

Unfortunately, what seems like a straightforward initiative fails to yield the desired fruit because the architects of the effort were focused on the above-ground elements of this tree, the tools of Lean - an attractive total productive maintenance (TPM) program, process mapping, statistics training, certifying green/black belts, etc. - without realizing the critical behavioral elements to make it work and survive. The "tools only" approach is relatively easy to transplant, but it simply will not produce the long-term results you heard about. Preparation with the techniques of change management was not considered before you dug the hole. No time was allotted for that. Your Lean tree is doomed without the essential root system of Lean leadership to give it solid support, make it grow, flourish, and experience sustainment. It cannot be faked or done without the behavioral, support elements below the surface. Respect for people doesn't materialize from infusing the tools. It comes from humble, open-minded servant leaders recognizing they are the suppliers to the employees. Their #1 objective is relentless empowerment. **<u>Nothing</u>** can substitute for this. The "tools only" approach cannot produce employee engagement (the fruit from the tree), and this is the fatal flaw many well intentioned traditional managers are unwilling to admit.

In one of the highly recommended books I share with my students, Tracy and Ernie Richardson have this to say in *The Toyota Engagement Equation*. "...the key is understanding the difference between the people side of Lean and the tool side. The people side will always be the most difficult aspect – here, you need the discipline to create this thing called culture. For the tools to be successful, people must understand their involvement or the purpose behind the tools."[xv]

Allow me to describe how the dysfunction manifests in a traditional environment. Cue the empire building in a dedicated transformation office and misguided behavior of command/control managers across the company. They saw some shiny tools above ground (one-piece flow, Kanbans, visual management boards, Quick Changeover, 5S, etc.) and completely bypassed the behavior elements of what it takes to make all this work throughout an enterprise. The root system they carelessly overlooked is the Lean-minded leadership necessary to sustain the transplant. Insufficient roots mean nutrients cannot properly flow throughout the tree. It is critically essential to support the energy and help people recognize the value of their efforts. These are the folks in supervisory positions striving to be servant leaders positioning their employees for success as their primary objective. Their mission includes encouraging the relentless identification of broken process elements from every employee, Gemba-walking to find burdensome hurdles frustrating employees doing the real work and supporting the process improvements continuously based on voice-of-the-customer requirements. They are the root system feeding the tree, and without their behavior firmly established, only pockets of excellence will glimmer short term. You may get some fruit initially, but it will not be plentiful. Effort must be allotted to build the enterprise-wide root system. Without their carefully coached behavior, no amount of tool infusion will achieve greatness. It will be viewed as a "program" for some to play around with and not a widespread cultural shift. Economic storms will topple the weakly planted tree because the culture is not equipped to keep it alive. Changes in the way employees behave will fade, even if modest signs of growth were initially encouraging. They will see the dysfunction and hypocrisy of their boss encouraging identification of broken process elements (lip service) only to be met with indifference or disdain when such issues are actually brought to light. The fragile new behavior will ultimately be conditioned to extinction. Traditional managers who were tasked to make the tree grow (because someone in the C-suite thought Lean could be delegated) are ill-equipped to carry out this difficult change management mission. However, they are exceedingly adept at spreading fertilizer in the form of exaggerating a process win here and there, which might temporarily keep a few leaves appearing green. They learned the manure dispensing technique well from other traditional managers, but the inevitable outcome will not be altered. It will only be prolonged. Your newly transplanted Lean tree will die like the past flavors-of-the-day decreed from the uninformed. You might as well have just cut the tree off at the base of the ground with a saw and jammed it into its new hole. Perhaps you can sustain it for a while with an army of external consultants and creatively crafted PowerPoint slides touting success, but the facade is destined to be discovered. The culture is not shifting to a system of continuous improvement coupled with respect for all players in the value stream.

Growth is unlikely without a widespread culture of internal Lean leaders who champion the behaviors of Lean. They need to understand the concepts of Lean leadership, practice them daily with dedicated coaching, and truly embody what it means to lead people as opposed to making the monthly numbers. If they behave as cops over the process and chastise employees for mistakes instead of recognizing the process itself is flawed, the tree will die. Go ahead and spray an herbicide on the tree and get it over with. The outcome will be the same, but it will minimize the period employees are cruelly teased with promised changes to their culture. Maybe you could purchase an artificial Lean tree which equals empty rhetoric, motivational posters on the walls, etc. It won't grow, but it will look impressive from a distance and might fool customers and shareholders for a while. Perhaps some employees might even believe they are operating in a Lean environment because they have not seen or touched a real Lean tree.

"Lean" (more accurately "Fake Lean") gets transplanted into companies impatient or unaware of the necessary planning work. Maybe it's spontaneous implementation by an email decree (the traditional manager's go-to method of change management), or perhaps it's casually discussed in relentless meetings with plenty of head nodding and well-intentioned plans emanating from executive conference rooms. Chances are good a VP got tagged with the responsibility, and they take this burden onto their shoulders like any number of challenges they have embraced over the years. Regardless of the method, they set off to transplant the tree. Maybe it's a last-ditch effort to drive costs down and shareholder smiles up. Seems perfectly logical. If we can operate with lower expenses, it only stands to reason we will be a more viable company and create more massive piles of money. Off we go, let's transplant the tree! We'll hire an army of Green Belts, some Black Belts, maybe even a Master Black belt or two so we can tout credentials, house them in our corporate office far away from the Gemba, put some process maps on the walls, give inspirational speeches proclaiming our newfound initiative/program, teach the tools, and set goals of dollars to be saved. Things will spontaneously get better because we have all these new weapons to fight waste. If Toyota can do it, surely, we can. Our tree is planted! Keep the water and manure coming.

All too often, somewhere along the path of this endeavor, credibility fails to manifest. Well-intentioned leaders truly want the bottom line to be more favorable, and they work very hard to make it happen. It's the objective set forth, but they are far too busy in the day-to-day activities of attending meetings and dispensing process changes they deem applicable. Unfortunately, the transplant process they have turned to is lacking executive support setting the expectation for Lean leader (servant) behavior to replace command-control management. I'm talking about enterprise-wide support for behavioral shifts in how people are treated, not just teaching a box of tools. The required root system to transform process improvement into reality (a continually growing, flourishing tree) has been substituted with an unsustainable model laced with layoffs, office closures, smoke-and-mirror reports, exaggerated improvement project results projected well into the future, and cuts destined to make overhead numbers look good in the short-term. Company instability and shaky employee loyalty remain unaltered. Not to mention managers faking Lean leadership behavior because they were told to "be Lean." It can't be delegated, and it can't be done with a speech or an email. It has to be a long-term, strategic effort with the patience to have failures along the way. One thing I have learned about failures: viewed in the correct light they are raw material (opportunities) to improve a process. If your Lean transformation is wilting, it's not too late to begin again with a better approach. Staying on the status quo path will not get you there. Once a wrong turn has been taken, no amount of determination or motivational speeches to trudge forward will get you to the right destination. At some point, you have to admit the error, turn around, and go back to basics. A new tree must be planted. Humility trumps arrogance every single time. Google how the spray lubricant WD40 got its name for a real-world example. Failures are the interim steps toward success and are never the final outcome if improvement persistence is embraced. But, they need to be followed by structured root cause analysis, not more knee-jerk solutions coming out of thin air (traditional manager dispensed manure). It has to engage the untapped genius in subject-matter-experts doing the real work daily, and it has to strive for a noticeable culture change where people are excited to come to work because they are highly empowered and intimately involved with the process improvements, not just the recipients of it. When well-intentioned managers throw process changes over the wall to the worker bees, they probably think they are helping. Same comment if the changes are inserted by external consultants. Both are, in effect, conditioning the workforce to wait for more of the same as opposed to becoming critical thinkers themselves. It's all backward and disrespectful. More manure and water will not yield desirable results. The transplantation **must** begin with a developed root system.

So, given this proven path to success with Lean, why do companies not research the potholes others have stepped in and learn how to avoid them? Why do they fail to give real Lean a try and do the grunt work in the first place? These critical questions are debated by many authors sharing the message of Lean. I can say first hand I've bellowed the madness of trying to change a culture without the root system of Lean leaders firmly in place and have become more and more frustrated with what Art Byrne (former CEO of Wiremold company) calls the "Concrete Heads" – individuals stuck in their ways and resistant to the power of Lean. In his book, *The Lean Turnaround* he states, ". . . *there are so few Lean leaders, and, as a result, why only 5 to 7 percent of companies are successful with a Lean transformation.*"[xvi]

Lean, Smean.
I've been a boss
for many years.
I've got this.

Allow me to share my own impressions of why companies will set out on well-intentioned Lean journeys (or whatever label/methodology they use) then realize non-existent, mediocre, or unsustainable results. Traditional management processes are at the heart of these failures. This is my anecdotal interpretation of how traditional managers are born, developed, and proliferate to hold companies back from becoming the premier suppliers of choice.

Let's say your goal is to climb the corporate ladder to the highest level you can and pile up lots of money and favor along the way. You monitor the surrounding culture carefully, digest the patterns of those achieving similar goals, and try to replicate the successful model. You are also absorbing the behaviors not working for your peers. A colleague challenges a proposal in a meeting, and the result is a tone and implication from the boss saying to the rebellious boat-rocker, *perhaps you have forgotten your place in the food chain here, young man.* You add this experience to your mental logbook (probably on a sub-conscious level) and continue to tweak your own behaviors to match those of the successful players around you. Say the right things to the right people regardless if they align with positive customer experiences. Avoid saying things you know leadership is not receptive to (even if it is what they need to hear to make better decisions), and always behave in alignment with the favored employees. Regardless of the idea your boss comes up with, you applaud and march in-step. This is politics in its worst manifestation. You continue collecting data on what works. Employees trend towards replication of rewarded cultural norms. We all do it to some extent. To rebel is to draw unfavorable attention in your direction, and you can't be doing this in a traditional environment.

Lo and behold, this plan gets you to the lofty levels you dreamed of. You are now a director, a vice president, a full bird Colonel, or a GS-15 civil servant with a window office and a designated parking spot. You have arrived. The last thought on your radar is, *Well, now I think I'll abandon the approach getting me here in favor of Lean leadership.* Of course not. You continue on this path and hone the behavior even further. Your proficiency for being politically correct and saying the right things to the right people at the right time becomes your forte. You do this even when it conflicts with your ethical beliefs. It is playing the game with the unwritten rules to succeed personally, despite the undesirable outcomes these behaviors cause for the company as a whole. Not to worry, company success is not your objective. Moving up the ladder is the focus. You probably don't intend to say here forever anyway. This is someone else's ship for life, not yours.

In time, others are replicating your approach (because you are unintentionally mentoring them) so they too can climb the ladder to status. The cultural norms become more solidified in the company, and you relentlessly chase senior leadership recognition like a drug. I've heard it labeled "managing up." More power, more money, fancier offices, and other self-serving perks are your brass rings. Continuously developing your direct reports to become the most efficient and successful (success defined as satisfying customer requirements in the most efficient manner possible) versions of themselves is, most assuredly, not your primary mission. No time for them. Your advancement is the focus.

Now along comes this company "plan" to implement something called Lean leadership, and your long-practiced, reliable behaviors are in jeopardy. Warning sirens begin sounding. Regardless of the negative consequences of non-compliance, what has served you so well for many years will not easily be discarded just because someone is citing employee engagement potentials and the wild improvements possible. You listen to the lunatic Lean dude spouting insanity such as *"Encourage every employee to freely/openly challenge your processes when they see undesirable outcomes and support direct involvement from the people doing the actual work. Most importantly, heap respect upon the employees as it relates to the work you are asking them to accomplish and do everything possible to position them for success,"* and you wonder . . . What in the name of holy hell is this drivel? Does this guy even have a clue how amazing we leaders are at running this company? Does he not understand the titles we have achieved? Has he forgotten he is talking to successful vice presidents, general managers, regional directors, four-star generals, CEO's, Senators? Look at us. Obviously, we know what the recipe for success is because of the stature bestowed on us. We worked hard to get to these levels.

Recognize this is entitlement talking.

With all due respect to your accomplishments, ladies and gentlemen, employee empowerment, which leads to engagement, should be your mission priority. Unfortunately, neither the level of your title nor the longevity of its duration automatically qualifies you to successfully inspire employees and create high levels of engagement. Raises, bonuses, stock options, promises of promotions, punishment, threats and other similar operant conditioning techniques are incapable of generating long-term engagement from human beings. Profound respect is the path research confirms as effective. Despite it being desperately needed it is often scoffed at by traditional managers with commensurate results they misdiagnose. Should you abruptly discard my proclamation, I encourage you to measure the current-state engagement levels of your employees and use empirical data to evaluate your gut assumptions. What does your environment really look like? Are employees passionate about challenging broken processes or has fear conditioned them to blindly defer and remain silent to retain their employment status? Do they feel respected as it applies to the work they are asked to do and the cultural conditions they do it in? This is not the time for delusional self-talk. I challenge you to reimagine leadership using an empirical yardstick.

Are your employees waste-wolves or shut-up-and-color sheep?

For those who have followed the formula of traditional management styles to reach advanced titles, the likelihood of skepticism (and initial resistance) is incredibly high. Perhaps even guaranteed. It is also completely understandable. I totally get it. It's like asking someone to drive from the right-hand side of their car after being entirely "successful" for years from the left-hand side. It defies the intuition and threatens all which they find comfortable and natural. They are the boss. Bosses come up with fixes and hand them down to the worker-bees. Employees must view those in authority as customers and accommodate the decrees of the accomplished thinkers. This is the natural order of corporate hierarchy. Initially, the reaction might be *I'll sit back and wait. This foolishness will go away, and I can continue with my proven path of personal advancement.*

If given the option of shifting gears to Leading with Lean or continuing on the behavioral path responsible for their current stature, it becomes a non-starter for many. The catalyst for change is not significant enough. A burning platform to alter course does not exist. Habits win out if the culture permits me to remain on my previous path. I will keep driving from the left side of the car as long as I'm not forced to do it differently. Other initiatives have come and gone; hopefully, this will do the same.

Behavioral norms will naturally emerge in any company, be they positive or negative, and management is the architect in both cases—intentionally or not. Using this same argument, reimagine an environment where Lean leadership is the norm, and new employees emulate *this* behavior on their way up the ladder. The replication of acceptable norms is identical, but in the case of a mature Lean environment, the outcomes will be dramatically more attractive to every employee and customer. The culture is profoundly different by design. Who wouldn't want to work in THIS company?!

Art Byrne says, "*...most CEOs got to where they are by following the traditional management approach. Why should they change?*"[xvii]

95

Jacob Stoller says it this way: *"In light of the documented success of Lean companies, why do so few CEOs make the leap? . . . the old rules of management are deeply entrenched. Those who have made it to the top have adapted very well to an existing culture. In asking them to change, we are asking them to forsake a system that has made them and their friends very prosperous. Together, they mutually reinforce the beliefs that define the status quo."*[xxviii]

As someone who has seen the results Lean can produce, it's frustrating to be surrounded by skeptics who won't even consider trying, outright resisters, or worst of all, the fakers. At least the resistors are honest about it. Some resisters will actually try to sabotage Lean initiatives. They are so entrenched in their current traditional path, new approaches are deemed valueless even before exploring them. Do they not realize their employees are problem solvers just waiting for the chance to be heard and participate? Does the condition of highly engaged employees, deep loyalty among the workforce, and widespread passion for making processes better continuously (based on VOC) not sound intriguing in the least? Do they forget how subordinated they felt as a worker bee themselves and now view their management status as a reward for persevering and paying their dues? In my opinion, it's like saying no thank you to a pair of new running shoes while participating barefoot in a summer marathon on asphalt. *I run in my bare feet because I've always done it this way before. Hurts like hell, and the blisters last for weeks, but I manage. Besides, I'm far too busy running this race to try something new. I'll get by.* – the voice of arrogance speaks.

I recognize they feel threatened, often fearing they won't be needed as a manager if the employees become autonomous problem solvers, though this fear overlooks the critical supplier-role Lean leaders play. Regardless of the combination of variables driving the resistance, one thing is for sure: traditional management has become an entrenched habit, and there is a seemingly endless supply of these managers inducing negative impacts on employees, and ultimately customers, everywhere. Unfortunately, if this broken model is the path to personal success in a company, it will persist. As my friend Brenda Shumate says, "you get what you incent." How right she is.

Human beings are rarely excited and self-motivated to replace one habit for another, even if the projected outcome is touted as far better. They need a catalyst. Ideally, the nudge is the person at the top of the food chain saying, *"Ladies and gentlemen, I will no longer tolerate traditional management and disrespect, mostly in the form of non-empowerment to employees. From this point forward, you will learn to be Lean leaders or seek employment elsewhere."* Now, **this** is a burning platform! Unfortunately, it takes significant courage to declare something so dramatically different as the new cultural norm. Status quo, for most, will remain more appealing, especially if the shift is voluntary. I understand it and recognize the drivers, but I will never excuse it or look the other way. Nor will I cut any slack to the entrenched traditional manager when they refuse to shift. Without attempting any political correctness, I proclaim their close-minded behavior a self-serving disgrace. Many the traditional manager has told me stay in my swim lane using various levels of threats, but after Lean was transplanted into my DNA in 2000, I remained steadfast in my resistance to perpetuating or enabling their dysfunction. When something is blatantly wrong, it is worth risking one's security. You can choose to be a capitulating bystander to employee disrespect, a manager who practices and rewards it, or a necessary disruptor declaring the tree's root system is inadequate and failing to nourish the tree. I chose the last option early in my Lean journey, and it often did not serve me well – given the unreceptive environments I was in. Which camp do you fall into? How about your peers? Is it worthy of a discussion at the next staff meeting?

"One reason people resist change is because they focus on what they have to give up instead of what they have to gain." – Unknown

Process Waste. Are You Aware You Have a Mountain of It?

"The most dangerous kind of waste is the waste we do not recognize." Shigeo Shingo

Sprinkled about to this point have been numerous examples of process waste. I'd like to get more specific here for those unfamiliar with the labels. You will no doubt use/find minor variations of these names and examples thereof, but these are the set I've been working with and teaching for many years now. Feel free to challenge any of the comments or positions I take toward the topics in this book. Also, recognize these waste labels are not always exclusive buckets to identify a waste type. Overlap is common, as well as one waste being responsible for another, as in transportation waste resulting in waiting. Lean leaders need to be keenly aware of waste.

I will also assert that while there are multiple types of process "waste," there are only three types of process "problems." A problem is loosely defined as an undesirable outcome (or potential outcome) during or after a process. These include Defects, Cycle Time issues (Delays), and Safety issues.

Defects – Anything not correct the first time. This comprehensive label includes all interim defects during the process of producing the product or executing a service – not just the product/service condition at the conclusion or handoff to the external customer.

Cycle Time (Delays) – Something taking longer than expected. Note, for problems to receive the Cycle Time label, the activity was done correctly (no Defects) the first time, but it just took too long to accomplish. A customer or engineering standard of time was exceeded in the absence of defects and re-work. Because of this distinction, the labels of Defects or Delays should be carefully examined before assignment.

Safety issues – These include someone getting injured or having the potential to be injured with the current process design. Note: A process design does not have to be documented or conducted in a desirable way to be considered current state.

Given these problem labels, recognize you do not have a cycle time problem if defects are occurring. A report is submitted, mistakes are found, and it has to be corrected. The consequence is the process taking much longer than anticipated. Defects are the *problem*, and the delay is a subsequent *impact*—the unwanted result (outcome) of the problem. I say this so teams are not incorrectly focusing on cycle time as the problem, and their claim of improvement is accomplishing the rework in a timelier manner. In reality, they have a defect problem, and if the defects are reduced or eliminated, the impact of delays will be reduced/eliminated. Just because you decrease the cycle time reworking defective items, realize the actual problem (defects) still exists. Teams often confuse problems and impacts, thus my attempt to clearly differentiate them. If you believe there is a combination of problems going on, it is often the case where you have one problem and the other things are just impacts thereof. Inefficiency results if you are working on an impact instead of the fault point (problem) upstream of it. Defects are by far the most common problem in a process, but the labels of "waste" will help teams further clarify opportunities to conduct any task more efficiently. Once the waste is removed or reduced, process flow speeds up. This is precisely the intent of reducing waste in the first place. Everything is about giving the external customer what they are paying for with the least amount of non-value activity—the activity they would not pay for if given the option.

Recall the definition of Lean I provided earlier: *Lean is a business mentality of providing a product or service with minimal waste from the customer's perspective.* So, if we are to provide the product/service with minimal waste, we must be capable of recognizing the waste in the first place. It is unlikely wasteful activity will show up on your radar for reduction if you don't know how to spot it. Also, be keenly aware the label of waste is from the EXTERNAL customer's perspective, not yours as the provider of the product/service, and not from any internal customer. Most of what you deem of value (as a provider) would be met with stern objection by your external customer if you itemized it on their bill. Imagine the response they would have if you listed the man-hours expended in your staff meetings and then told your customer to pay up. Little do they realize they are already paying for all your hidden process waste. This is the motivator for companies to reduce waste and become the provider offering the product/service faster at a lower cost without negatively compromising quality. It doesn't seem to add up—faster, cheaper, and better all at the same time. To achieve this lofty outcome, you are striving to develop employees by heaping constant respect on them in many ways. This is empowerment! To the mature Lean company, it all makes perfect sense. It's not just a part of the strategy, it _is_ the strategy.

The acronym to help you remember the waste labels is **DOWNTIME**.

Defects. This bucket is for anything not correct the first time

Overproduction. Making more stuff than you have customer demand for

Waiting. For anything, by anyone in the value stream, at any time

Non-Use of Talent. Ineffectively using the skills and talents of employees

Transportation. Moving your completed or partially completed product from place to place

Inventory. Storing excess quantities of stuff (raw materials & finished items)

Motion. People moving about, hunting and gathering, driving, flying, walking, reaching to get stuff, etc.

Excess Processing. All activity in excess of customer requirements

There exists no process on earth void of waste. Let this sink in for a bit, but please don't use it as an excuse to not address waste in your processes. Even when it cannot be eliminated, it can be reduced. We don't like to admit it, but sometimes the entire process is waste according to the external customer's perspective. Allow me to explain.

Waste is there, but people in the process are often unaware of it and therefore unlikely to be on a mission to seek it out for reduction. It is incredibly easy to habituate to waste because it blends in so nicely in our processes. We must make hard copies of this document just in case. The two-hour staff meeting is important. If we don't inspect every widget, some defective units might make it to the customer. Employees must walk over to this place to get their tools/equipment/instructions because this where they are kept. Everyone has to wait their turn in line at the customer service counter. Transferring you to a specialist and playing music while you wait is just how we do things here. The examples are endless once the fog is removed from your glasses. Typically, about ninety-five percent of process steps are of no value to the external customer and non-value added (NVA) steps are waste. The terms NVA and Waste are synonymous. These steps do nothing to directly alter the form, fit, or function of the product/service the external customer is asking for. I say that, and then someone will claim re-work changes form, fit, or function, therefore, is value-added. Well, technically, you are changing the product, but it wasn't correct the first time. No customer is willing to pay you twice so re-work is always NVA.

This may seem harsh, but that is precisely the point. The Lean mind is not willing to excuse, defend, or even worse, protect waste. Remember, even if it cannot be eliminated completely, the likelihood of reducing it is almost guaranteed. Once reduced, you are now able to spend precious time on things important to your customer versus throwing more people and money at process waste to get tasks accomplished. Flow speeds up as waste is reduced. This can reduce the cost of providing the product/service, and you become more attractive than your concrete-headed competitors. Lean behavior will give you an unequaled competitive advantage should you choose to implement it correctly. *Correctly* is the operative word here. I've seen more than my share of Lean tools misused along my journey. Whew! It could be a book by itself. I won't even go into the traditional manager's decision to 5S everyone's desk (designate where every item on every desk would be positioned without their input) because it seemed like the Lean thing to do. Talk about waste! I learned a valuable lesson early on in my journey - Lean is done **with** people, not **to** people. Get this wrong, and your tree will wilt and die.

Defects. As you go through the list of waste types, I challenge you to identify each of them in a process you live in daily. Defects are everywhere. Lots of things are incorrect the first time, but broaden your perspective beyond the actual product you are providing. Did you ever show up late to a meeting for whatever reason? That's a defect. Did you ever get a report with incorrect numbers on them? *Defect.* Did you ever give someone a task only to realize the information you turned them loose with was inaccurate or ambiguous? **Defect.** How about an employee ordering the wrong item? **Defect.** A traditional manager resistant to behaving as a Lean leader gets hired for the position to lead a Lean transformation. **Defect!** You sent an employee to a training event they didn't need or want? **Defect.** They are literally everywhere once you open your mind and start being critically honest about processes and things not correct the first time. The temptation is to ignore, excuse, or downplay the need to prevent re-occurrence of defects. If your response to a defect starts off with *"Well…,"* you are probably about to cite a reason the waste needs to stay put. This is NOT how a Lean mind is wired up. The Lean mind reacts to waste as yet another opportunity, not an annoyance from the malcontent pointing at it. Worse yet, in the absence of root cause analysis, you might prematurely throw a countermeasure at the issue and end up inserting even more waste rather than reducing any. "We're getting defects at station #3. Start inspecting every widget before it moves to station #4." Instead of removing the waste (Defects), you inserted another non-value-added step (inspection) just to catch the anomaly. You added waste by addressing the wrong thing. In isolation, it may be no big deal in some processes, but, add them all up over a year's time, including the associated activity and cost of re-work, and your perception might change. Your customers are paying attention, even if you are not. I hope by now you are recognizing how arrogance is the enemy of continuous improvement.

My audiences often objected to inspection being a wasteful step. They argued, "If you don't inspect it, a bad product will make it out the door." Well, this may be valid, but my counter to the objection is to argue you have addressed the wrong problem. How many inspections would you need if the defects stopped occurring? Please understand I am not advocating you abolish all your checks. Until your process becomes far more reliable with continuous improvement to prevent defects (confirmed by data), and standard deviations approaching zero on producing to specifications, inspection will be the appropriate short-term approach. But, if it remains for eternity and is the only way to prevent defects from getting to customers, I challenge you to recognize you have fixed nothing. What if your data (after countermeasure insertion) shows the defect rate has plummeted? Maybe you can cut back from 100% inspection to spot inspection. Score! You just reduced some waste in the process and increased flow.

Still not buying my explanation? Consider this. Supplier A provides a product at cost $X. Supplier B supplies the identical quality item but at cost $X + Y. Supplier A can provide it for less money than you because they found a way to mistake-proof the step where defects had been occurring and can now rely on the process without costly inspection. Maybe they spot inspect to make sure the countermeasures are still working, but 100% inspection is gone. Now then. Equal quality, lower price, shorter lead time. Which supplier are you going to purchase the item from?

Bottom Line. Your value stream is loaded with defects. The challenge lies in admitting it without getting embarrassed or defending them as inevitable. Remember, in a Lean environment, you will be holding processes accountable. People will not be punished unless intentional malice is at play. The difference is significant. Status quo will never propel you to the premier provider of anything.

Overproduction. Producers often make more stuff than customers are ready to purchase. If we have demand for 10, why not make 15 and put 5 on the shelf? It seems logical because when Mr. Customer does want one, you have one ready to ship. Makes sense, right? But, what if Mr. Customer doesn't want one? Now, what happens to the inventory you piled on shelves just in case? Do you mark it down and try to get rid of it? Car dealers do this notoriously. Every car on their expansive lots is waiting for a buyer to appear. I hope they are not relying on their obnoxious commercials on TV and radio to make this happen. Many of us can't get to the mute button fast enough. Talk about waste! In the meantime, they are paying interest on every vehicle. Guess who ultimately pays for it. At the end of the model year, they start marking them down (leftovers) to get ready for the next influx. Production exceeded demand.

So, what are the consequences of making too much stuff? Do you just leave it there in hopes someone is going to eventually want it? Do you need more storage buildings to house the extra things you produced? In reality, you have a pile of money being held hostage in the form of inventory without customer demand. This is money unavailable for other things the company might need. Now, before you start throwing darts at me, imagine if your lead time to produce the item was slashed to the bone, and Mr. Customer could get his widget produced and shipped very quickly after asking for it? I know, this sounds like crazy talk, but Lean is not for the faint of heart or those opposed to thinking outside the box. That would be status quo land, and the population there is enormous. Continue residing in status quo land and see how your financials look over time compared to the producer with tiny lead times. I encourage you to look at a Lean-minded company and examine what their lead times look like, and how they are obsessed with continually reducing them. Anything impeding flow is subject to attack. Your finished product inventory will shrink, and monies will become available rather than imprisoned on a warehouse shelf. Make excuses for overproduction, and your traditional management membership will automatically renew. And by the way, trying to predict customer demand without capturing extensive VOC…forget it. I hope by now, you are absorbing the fundamental tenant of everything being tied back to VOC. Without it, you have a blind person navigating your bus down a crowded interstate. Hang on. It could get ugly.

Waiting. Now here is one you can absolutely identify examples of. I've previously cited several examples of it in my side stories. The problem is, waiting is an inevitable part of any process, right? Wrong. Maybe it can't be eliminated, but can you reduce it by 5%? How about 3%? Accomplish that, and you just got more competitive because flow increased. Now let's go for another 3%. The fact is, most customers (except for the Lean savvy ones) have been conditioned to wait for everything under the sun. Why is this the case? Justifications will be plentiful from traditional thinking providers, but so will opportunities to reduce it once you stop excusing it as necessary or inevitable in your processes. Providers even find ways to make the waiting process more palatable (comfy chairs, free coffee, magazines, background music, etc.) so you won't give up and go elsewhere. In reality, they added waste to the process. No mystery who pays for the distractors. Also recognize, whenever anyone internal in the value stream is waiting, the flow has stopped for them. Ultimately, the external customer will be waiting as well. Hopefully someone is paying attention, and cares about this.

If you could total the amount of time we human beings spend in lines during our lifetimes, how much would it be? A year? More? Scary thought, isn't it? We wait in traffic, in parking lots to get an open spot, in grocery stores, in restaurants for a place to sit down, on our computers watching the little spinning thing go round and round, for the doctor to see us after getting to the waiting room (I love that label) at the scheduled time, to board airplanes, to get off of airplanes, to get your baggage, to fill out forms when your baggage didn't arrive at same place you did, for a human being to finally pick up after you've been on hold for an eternity, to eventually get to the right person to answer a question about a purchased product you had a problem with, for an open toilet after the movie lets out because the capacity is exceeded by a factor of ten, for a product to be delivered, for a replacement product to be delivered because the initial one was incorrect or damaged, at the customer service counter (often an oxymoron) in a store, for our boss to make a decision on something before we can proceed, for a wasteful meeting to begin because some yahoo has not arrived yet and we for sure need the yahoo to proceed, and on and on. We wait and wait and wait some more. **Why**?! If the service/product provider cannot eliminate the waiting altogether, what are they doing about reducing it by some amount? Anything? Wait just a moment while everyone ponders this. In my experience, there is almost always a defect causing the waiting. Something didn't happen as we wanted it to, the rework machine is humming along, and humanity stands around waiting for the madness to be corrected.

Only the Lean-minded provider is continuously working on this waste reduction. He/She is asking employees how it can be reduced from their perspective because they do the real work every day. They are Gemba walking their processes to see the waiting firsthand, then doing it again after a countermeasure is inserted (one the team came up with, not the boss). It stays on his/her radar because service in the form of not wasting the customers' precious time is paramount to becoming more competitive than the other providers who embrace the good-enough model of business. Only the delusional mind ignores the causal connection of reduced flow, to reduced waiting, to increased customer satisfaction levels. So, if you're buying my argument, what are you waiting for to close the gaps?

"Time waste differs from material waste in that there can be no salvage. The easiest of all wastes and the hardest to correct is the waste of time because time does not litter the floor like wasted material." -Henry Ford

Non-Use of Talent. One of my favorites because it is notoriously overlooked. Compare the amount of time your engineers are designing something versus filling out reports or paperwork that doesn't physically move their development mission forward. Imagine the talents employees have, but you are paying contractors to do the work because you are unaware someone in-house has the skills. This occurs because supervisors don't take the time to learn the capabilities of their employees. Are you paying an external provider for training when Billy Bob used to teach incident investigation or welding in a previous life? You don't realize it because you don't really know Billy Bob that well, and of course, you didn't poll your workforce when the training need arose. You simply tasked Betty to find a contractor to do the work. Seemed logical at the time. I was once asked by a local college to build and deliver a training class on Developing Performance Indicators. Turned out the customer to the college (the federal government) was my current employer! They could have asked me to do this, and the cost would have been zero. Instead, they went to the local college and asked them to provide it, and the college, in turn, enlisted my assistance as a contractor. Non-Use of talent waste at its worst.

Are you asking Frank to do something entirely outside his skill level when Sally is an ace at it? Perhaps you didn't realize Sally is good at it because it's not Sally's current job to perform this task. You've got her doing some specialty task. Are you even looking for excess capacity—employees with spare time on their hands—when Joe is tasked to the breaking point with all the work you have disrespectfully piled up on him? If not, Joe will either quit or start failing at more tasks, and then you might be inclined to blindly tell him he isn't managing his time correctly. I had a traditional manager tell me this once. I was hooked up well beyond my capacity when other employees had significant free time. When I asked for assistance, he told me I was sucking at time management. I didn't have the patience to explain he was addressing the impact and not the cause. Thanks for the feedback and assistance, boss. Your status as a servant leader is falling below the standard. The experience served to further educate me on the effect of disrespect on an employee. Telling someone to work harder without examining the root cause helps no one improve.

A better approach would be to sit down with the employee and dig into the process causal factors leading to reasons work is not getting accomplished. The *whys*. What are they? Keeping the discussion in Process-Land (*Why is the **process** failing?*) versus People-Land (*Why are **you** failing?*) will yield far more participation from employees, thus fruit from the effort. The Lean leader knows and practices this daily. The traditional manager has no time for such nonsense. The mantra they rely on is *Go Faster!* But regardless of the reasons, non-use of talent waste occurs when you are not thoroughly or efficiently utilizing the skills employees have.

Opportunities are limitless when you intentionally seek them out. In-house talent is being overlooked, ignored, under-burdened, over-burdened, and misused all the time. The waste is there if you only take the time to see it, then act on what you see. Allow people to contribute to the fullest extent they desire. One might argue a job description doesn't include what an employee wants to assist with. So what?! Give some positive reinforcement when Mike wants to do something he is capable of. Everyone wins. Discouraging discretionary contributions from employees is just nuts, but it happens in traditionally managed cultures. Waste!

Transportation. This is a waste folks are quick to defend and excuse because they deem it necessary. "We have to move our stuff from point A to B." Recall you must look at low-level tasks in isolation to determine if they are value-added. Do not combine multiple steps into one bucket. Any time you are moving your completed or partially completed product (including the raw materials you use to produce it), you are incurring transportation waste. Yes, every single morsel of movement is waste because it does nothing to change the form, fit, or function of the product when viewed as an isolated task in the process. When you move it, it is not physically changing/getting closer to the finished condition as a mere fact of relocating it. That makes it non-value added (waste), and if your customers got itemized bills for all of this, they would be calling your service department immediately with complaints. Now, you might argue if you don't move it from point A to B, you can't do task X to it, so the transportation is necessary and thus value added. Nice try, but your argument is combining steps—the movement and the subsequent step(s) after it is moved. If you ONLY consider the movement itself, you will have to agree that the form, fit, or function of the item did not change. That is unless you managed to damage or loose it during transportation. Transportation is pure waste and should be on your radar for reduction, even if you cannot eliminate it completely. Less transportation leads to shorter cycle times (increasing flow) and less production cost overall. You will instantly become more attractive to your external customers when you pass these savings onto them.

Consider this: UPS is in the transportation business. One hundred percent of what they do is waste to the external customer buying the item! The product has experienced all the value-added work it's ever going to get before UPS takes possession of it to transport it to your front door. Once completed by the manufacturer, shipping will not continue to alter its condition. Customers tolerate this fee, but given the option of a provider across the street with the same product (same cost, same quality, etc.), they would not pay UPS to transport it. Recognizing this transportation activity is always going to be non-value-added activity in the process (as viewed from the external customer), they took the Lean approach of trying to reduce it. The countermeasure was to redesign driver routes to minimize left-hand turns. Turning left requires idling time waiting for the traffic to clear or the arrow to turn green at intersections. The result of this innovative idea is saving them about 300 million dollars annually. Delivery routes are accomplished quicker, and less fuel is consumed.[xix]

Please note, the activity is still waste, but now there is less of it. Score! Just because it cannot be eliminated does not mean you capitulate. Taking an all-or-nothing approach to process improvement—specifically, waste elimination—will limit improvements just *waiting* to be realized. Maybe you are positioning machines, material, or people incorrectly, and this is causing more transportation waste than necessary. Perhaps you could select external suppliers closer to delivery destinations. Any chance they would move their operation to your neck of the woods? Just a thought. If you can't find any ways to reduce your transportation waste, I'd argue you aren't looking hard enough. Some would call this low hanging fruit, but my experience has shown much of the initial fruit is laying on the ground. Just bend over and pick it up instead of stepping over it.

Inventory. How much on-hand stuff is enough? Let's get one thing straight immediately: not all inventory is waste. If you have idle employees waiting on delivery of raw material before they can begin work, your inventory level is too low. There is nothing Lean about that, and I have seen misguided applications of Lean declaring all inventory must go. I'm talking about *excess* inventory here. Things you produced with unreliable speculation of customer demand (push process) or raw materials you ordered in quantities well beyond what you need within the lead time from your supplier. These are the types of inventory wastes falling into this bucket. Storing cabinets full of toner cartridges because you got a great deal on a volume purchase won't make much sense when they dry out and become useless before you use them. The more inventory you have, the more buildings/space you need to store it, the more man-hours you will expend to keep track of it, move it about because it's in the way, and hunt for it because you have so much you can't see it all at a glance. Have you ever purchased an item because you can't find the one you have? So, to fix this, you install expensive inventory control software, provide training to use it, hire more IT people to maintain it, and the madness just expands to support the original waste. Achieving the right levels of everything is a continuous adjustment, but if you avoid the analysis, you will most assuredly be holding budgeted money hostage. I was at a large car dealer recently and to locate cars on their massive lot, they push the panic button on the key fob, then assuming they are in-range, they try to follow the honking noise. This particular lot was so massive we were randomly wandering in various directions to get the device to work. The entertainment begins when multiple salesmen are hunting cars at the same time and become confused about which car is honking. I'd say they might have too much inventory if they can't even locate what they have on-hand. Maybe they should buy some shuttles and hire drivers to carry people around to find cars. Of course, we'd need some parts and supplies on-hand to maintain the shuttles, more mechanics and a building to house everything. Surely customers would be willing to pay for those extra things. With the shuttles, we could justify even larger lots to increase our inventory levels.

I advise managers to capture at least two basic things when deciding on the right amount of anything to have on hand: lead time (time from item request to item in-hand) and consumption rates. Let's say you need industrial filters in stock. If you use ten in a day, and it takes two days to replenish your inventory (supplier lead time), perhaps you start out with twenty (max) on the shelf. On Monday you use ten and order twenty more. On Tuesday, you use the remaining ten on the shelf, and on Wednesday, you receive twenty more to keep the process moving without delay. Of course, the ideal situation would include ultra-reliable suppliers bringing you ten each morning, and you retain zero in inventory. Before this perfect state becomes a reality in your supply chain, you will need some on the shelf to prevent work stoppages. Perhaps twenty, but not 500 just because they were on sale and you currently have room to store them. You continue to adjust the on-hand levels to seek the sweet spot. The sweet spot is a condition where the employee never reaches for something and there is none available, but not a mountain of them either.

I once consulted for a small aircraft manufacturer who bought electronic equipment (in bulk) on sale only to find upgraded equipment was now available, and their customers had no desire for the old stuff. Material in excess of $1,000,000 remained in its original boxes for years with the inevitable fate of a dumpster. Even storing it was problematic because their space was limited, but they didn't have the heart to discard it.

The more inventory you have, the less money you will have available for other things. Think about this the next time you purchase that pallet of toilet paper from the warehouse store. How much food (especially canned goods) do we throw out because it expired? Is it really saving you money to buy in bulk? Most of us are guilty of excess inventory waste to some extent, but the Lean mind will challenge it relentlessly and continue to adjust in search of the sweet spot. The greater the cost impact, the greater the attention the excess material should receive. The impact should always be a priority consideration when making decisions on where to engage with process improvement. As I tell my students, don't spend time scrubbing stains out of the carpet when the curtains are on fire. Prioritize the excess inventory costing the most to maintain and start there. The extra box of paper clips can wait for now.

Motion Waste. This one is different from transportation waste. Motion waste is *people* moving about, not your product. They might be unnecessarily bending, reaching, stretching, or hunting and gathering because they don't have what they need precisely where the task is accomplished, going floor to floor for wasteful meetings, chasing parts, tools, information, all adding unnecessary cycle time to a task. I knew a project manager who officed in Oklahoma even though the entirety of his work was in New York. He flew back and forth constantly. Makes perfect sense, right? This is another waste left unabated because improvement processes are not looking for it. It's hiding in plain sight. What sense does it make for an employee to go to space A, gather stuff, then go to space B to do the work? And please don't say, "Well, that's the way we have always done it," or I will be forced to use your excuse in a training class. Employees don't have to be bolted in place like a machine, but is there really obvious motion waste you could easily help reduce in their day? The answer is yes, but only if you devote time to look for it. Take a Gemba walk and get ready to be amazed at what you find. I once observed an employee crawling on his hand and knees under large natural gas pipes (on gravel, by the way) to plug his air hose into the poorly located air outlet before removing some hardware with an impact gun. The outlet was at least 50 feet away from where the repetitive work was accomplished twice a day.

Obviously, the design process missed this eventuality, but the motion waste remained in place. Neither the worker nor the supervisor ever challenged it prior to the Gemba walk I coached. It's-just-how-we-do-it mentalities will overlook motion waste. Add to this a culture unreceptive to employees challenging the status quo, and you have a perfect formula to ensure waste stays put for eternity, or until a safety incident occurs. Injuries are, unfortunately, the only catalyst for some traditional managers to make processes better. Proactive analysis is a luxury their wasteful days of endless meetings all over the building (or country) cannot accommodate. This is yet another form of disrespect to employees.

What blatant motion waste opportunities exist in your process? Are your processes forcing employees to go to one location to retrieve tools, information, or materials and then moving to another to use them? I recently observed an employee at the parts department of a car dealership go back into the warehouse to search parts availability on his computer when another computer was right at the counter where he spoke with the customer. Back and forth with he went with every additional piece of information he captured from the customer. It was painful to watch. I wondered if anyone in his management chain was paying attention to the burdensome activity. Take a guess what customers were doing while this was occurring? When is the last time you intentionally went looking for motion waste opportunities or asked employees to point them out? Sure, you might observe some by chance, but is this the best approach? Be honest.

If this paragraph has induced even a twinge of motivation to go hunt down and kill some motion waste, I consider it a start towards simplifying a process for some disrespected employee in your environment.

Excessive Processing. Doing anything in excess of what the customer has specifically requested in their requirements will fall into this category. Every process has this particular waste, and it tends to increase like bacteria over time. Examples are everywhere. The story about the car dealership washing every car after performing the maintenance on it is an example. It is beyond the customer requirement, but you do it anyway. It seemed like a good idea at the time, but you failed to ask each customer if they wanted to wait for it or not. Some probably would, others would decline. Again, the power of VOC is being ignored.

You have twenty cells on some form, and the downstream internal customer only uses information from twelve of them. The remaining eight cells are ignored, but Mister-form-filler-outer populates them just the same. Make the white space go away. Perhaps because the cells are there in the first place or because they have never captured VOC from the downstream customer. I call it Assumptionland. Have you ever visited there? Perhaps someone decreed and the conditioned employees executed without challenge. Maybe this level of quality made sense ten years ago, but it is now moot. You won't know until you dig into the whys.

Meetings are another good example. How many do you attend because they have a reoccurring status on your calendar? Folks convene for a staff meeting or something equally life-altering, and one or two hours evaporate without anything of substance occurring to improve a process. I've been told this happens occasionally. Send your external customer a bill for meetings to review your process metrics and see how they respond. Would a visual management board substitute for the conference? What about useless hard-copy material or training you dispense to your workforce? Don't forget the 30 minutes you spent authoring an awesome email to the masses and the 15 minutes they each spend reading/digesting it when they have the time to stop their value-added activities. I feel certain your external customer would not find this acceptable and object accordingly if their bill were itemized to include all these costs.

Do you have reoccurring, required training which yields nothing useful for employees to better satisfy customer requirements or make their jobs easier to accomplish? Sometimes this gets inserted in the interest of safety or legal requirements, but are there alternative options you haven't explored? Are you using materials far exceeding engineering standards because someone believes it is worth it – without examining the impacts? Adding a little of this and a little of that doesn't seem like much, but it adds up. Maybe you need them, maybe you don't. Again, these are tasks the customer didn't include in their VOC to you; thus, you are excess processing. Some of it might be justifiable, but is ANY of it not? My journey has taught me this type of waste creeps in without notice, then remains the acceptable norm without objection. It becomes how you do things going forward – forever. More excess processing equals more people needed to conduct it, equals exploding costs over time.

Does any of this happen in your world? Why? Is anyone determining its utility value and alignment with VOC? How are objections to these wastes received by leadership? Are they interested in reducing them?

Do you print hard copies of things available electronically because that is what you have always done? **Waste**. What CYA forms do you have employees filling out which produce nothing of value to your external customers? If you do not recognize the time you are extracting from a worker's day, then you are missing an opportunity. It's not just the silly form and costs to print it—people are wasting precious time. If the information is essential, can you find another way to produce it besides tasking the value-adding worker? Could a support person do it?

How about approvals for things – the mother-may-I tasks? The employee is not empowered to move forward with producing customer requirements until someone says go. Perhaps some of them are cautionary checkpoints with high impacts if things go south, but do you have any that fall into the ridiculous category? **Waste.** Car salesmen are rarely empowered to negotiate with the customer. They go back to their manager with the last offer and ask for a green or red light. Why is this the case? Why are they not provided a minimum price to get and then allowed (after proper training) to make the decision? Why does a cashier need a supervisor's approval for the condition of a personal check presented for payment? Can they not be trusted to inspect for the same information the supervisor is going to look for? Your external customer didn't ask for these hand-offs or the ensuing delay, but you force them to pay for it just the same. On top of this, it conveys disrespect to the unempowered employee. If you can't trust them to perform their task according to your standards, then you have ill-prepared them for the job. Why did you hire them in the first place? This is your broken process at fault here, not the employee's assumed incompetence.

We used to get our government performance appraisal electronically (a virtually useless process of dispensing subjective grades batched once a year because this is how it had always been done in UncleSamland), and then the supervisor would print a hard copy before you left their office. I told a particular supervisor to please not print one because I had no use for it, but she insisted she was required to give me one. I often wondered if this was actually documented somewhere in a giant, dusty binder of government regulations in the Pentagon basement.

When I asked why she just looked at me in disbelief. I tried to explain to her I had no need for it and would not keep it. It was an ineffective argument. After the obligatory printing took place (while I waited and wasted more time, of course), I promptly inserted the copy into her recycle bin in front of her. We continued this mutually disrespectful dance yearly because she felt compelled to give me that hard copy. The less rebellious employee would have discarded it outside of her observation, but I was trying to make a point. It became a battle of wills, and objective analysis says we both lost. Neither of us was going to shift from our posture. I've since learned the futility of some battles and try to take a stand only when the negative impact of the waste is worthy. A Lean journey will do this to a person. Initially, you will want to highlight all waste like a town crier, but then you'll recognize it's better to leave some of it alone until the culture becomes more receptive to attack it. The *impact* of waste rather than the waste itself becomes the engage/ignore threshold until all the traditional managers have exited the bus. In the government, they occupied a significant number of seats up front. Hopefully, some of this has changed since I retired.

Another example of excessive processing is gold-plating. Metaphorically speaking, a process is gold-plated when it exceeds quality levels well beyond what the customer requested, needs, or would be willing to pay for if given the option.

Causal factors vary significantly, but this is an opportunity to examine the process. Is this level of quality justifiable, or are we doing it from an undocumented assumption the customer will be impressed with our efforts? Should we switch from a wooden fence to a decorative concrete wall? Does the company vehicle need to have self-driving capability? Do we really need one-ton trucks, or will half-ton vehicles suffice? Should we increase the wall thickness of the natural gas pipe by 50% so it will last an additional 100 years? Maybe it's worth it, maybe not, but until the analysis takes place (including VOC discussions), you might be wasting time and money with no return on efforts. Please recognize I am not advocating increasing *or* reducing quality levels unless your customer is going to benefit from it and accepts the consequences. The VOC process has to be utilized before decisions are made in either direction. To skip this step is to risk excess processing waste creeping into your value stream. Your competitor with less of it is more attractive to customers.

To summarize, I've listed the various types of waste labels, and I hope you are now pondering some of the opportunities in your world to increase flow as well as improve employee/customer experiences. If you struggle to assign the exact label with the particular waste, you're excess processing. It doesn't matter if the correct bucket name is selected because they bleed over into each other all the time. You have recognized an activity as waste (something not physically changing the form, fit, or function of the product or service, and something your external customer would not be willing to pay for if given the option), and this is the critical catalyst to reducing or eliminating it. **Score!** Take the rest of the day off with pay for your efforts. You probably have a wasteful meeting you want to avoid this afternoon anyway.

"We're here to put a dent in the universe. Otherwise, why else even be here?" – Steve Jobs

How is Your Process Doing? Pretty Good, You Say?

"If you need a new process and don't install it, you pay for it without getting it." – Ken Stork

Let's go back to those VOC elements (both internal and external) you wisely decided to capture. To use them to their fullest, they must be turned into performance indicators so you can measure/monitor the extent to which your process is meeting the requirements from customers. If you cannot evaluate this, you will guess where/when to improve any process. Seems logical enough, but how many companies are in the dark? And even if they do have VOC metrics, are the measures made readily available to the entire workforce? Do you have updated intuitive charts on the wall in a common area, or are mind-numbing data and confusing charts buried in SharePoint for only the most ambitious (or bored) employee to find? Maybe you hold quarterly meetings to brief this stuff. Sounds like a good alternative, but this batched process will not serve you well. Things can be going south between briefings, and improvement is delayed. If your charts are not continuously updated, they are incapable of driving timely process improvement as gaps begin to widen. Batch your metric updates and your process improvement efforts will become firefighting activities when outcomes have degraded to an intolerable level. Ask any college football coach if he is content with the scoreboard information being updated every 30 minutes during a game and see how they respond. Stale data tells me it has no real importance to leadership, so how can you expect your employees to care? It seems the activity of leadership fighting the fires of the day takes precedence over having useful metrics posted for employees. Whack-a-mole, as I like to call it, consumes their schedule, wears them out, and leaves no time to actually improve a process or develop employees.

Side Story - One of the best examples of monitoring VOC metrics I observed was in a Chicago based company called Sloan Valve. They make plumbing fixtures for restrooms. Phil Logsdon – the most decent human being I ever had the distinct honor to work for - and I toured through their facility and were shown their customer call center where a handful of employees take incoming calls from customers throughout the day. Mounted on the wall for all to see was a monitor with LIVE data! If a customer called in, didn't get through in a timely manner, and hung up in desperation, the monitor would record their number and the order in which they called. Employees could then call these people back to address the issue as opposed to making the customer call back again. Live data drove improved customer service, and the immediate recognition to improve call handle time, so customers didn't have to hang up in the first place. Now imagine this data (quantity and phone numbers of customers hanging up because queue times were excessive) being collected someplace remotely (out-of-sight for employees) and sent to the supervisor weekly, probably in an email to be read when the he/she has some free time. In this case, the process step might be to return a customer call seven days later to offer assistance. *"Excuse me, Mr. Customer. I see you called a week ago and didn't get through to our customer service department. How can I help you?"* Good luck with that process. I hope it wasn't a toilet leaking onto their floor. So, the process in place at Sloan Valve is one I would give high marks to, but unfortunately is the anomaly when you look at companies in general. Even if data exists, it rarely is posted visually for employees to monitor their process and react autonomously. I suspect this is because management does not consider the workers to be decision makers, therefore posted metrics are none of their concern. Yet another form of disrespect.

Please note, I'm not advocating all metrics need to be updated with live information. On the contrary. To do so would be a misuse of the Lean tools, and you would fall prey to the all-or-nothing mentality. People tend to latch onto a new tool and try to blindly apply it to everything. I show you how to use a hammer, and suddenly everything looks like a nail to you. Negative. When deciding on how often to update the charts, you need to consider this single question: *What is the **impact** of this gap getting wider without immediate visibility to the people in the process?* If it's negligible, then perhaps you can live with a small batch time between updates. Every process is different, and you need to consider the unique situations. If I learned nothing else about process improvement, I learned one size does not fit all when it comes to applying the tools of Lean and Six Sigma. Feel free to insert the voice of sanity, and using the impact question will help significantly. But, generally speaking, quarterly—or worse yet, yearly— updates are just too far apart. And if the impact is so small as to justify these long batch review periods, do you even need to measure the element it in the first place? Continuing to do so could be a complete waste of precious time. Does it help anyone recognize a useful performance gap? If a metric is not a catalyst for improving a process, I claim it might be useless to collect.

Metrics need to intuitively indicate if a performance gap exists (and how much) between customer requirements and the current state of the process. To what extent are we delivering on what customers deem important to them? To be useful, a chart needs to show two critical levels: Where we are <u>right now</u> (current state), and where we <u>need to be</u> (the organizational goal, or customer tolerance level). Having both elements on your charts will instantly convey the existence of a performance gap to the reader, and the extent thereof. Otherwise, save the paper, ink, and man-hours. Bare walls will convey a message with the equivalent value.

<u>Side Story</u> – By chance, I came across about a dozen charts posted on the wall in a production area I usually didn't frequent. I'm drawn to charts like a moth to a porch light, so I went over to discern how this organization was performing. None of them had listed thresholds on them (so discerning performance gaps was impossible), but they were very sophisticated looking. Lots of colored bars, lines, and arrows going every which way. It looked quite impressive to the novice eye. One could instantly jump to the conclusion this organization was embracing visual management. But, I could not see a threshold line where the process *should* be performing to compare where they actually *were* performing. A few minutes later, a supervisor came over to inquire what I was doing, and I asked him what a particular chart was telling the audience who might look at it because I sure couldn't figure it out.

"Ah, that one . . . hmmm, I'm not really familiar with **that** one."

"How about **this** one?" I inquired

"Um, yeah, that one . . . um, well, I'm not really sure what that one is all about either."

So, I followed with, "Can you tell me what **any** of them are saying related to your processes?"

At this point, I became aware the supervisor was obviously concerned someone of authority was testing him. He was visibly displaying anxiety in his speech and body language. I assured this manager my inquiry was strictly from the perspective of a curious Black Belt who liked visual management and charts, and no punitive action was remotely possible here. He then relaxed and became forthcoming with the straight scoop.

"Honestly, he said, *"I don't know what any of these dang charts are saying about our processes. We just put them up for the tours that come by periodically. But in defense of the people who post them, the information is ALWAYS up-to-date."*

Great! Ambiguous charts conveying no useful information to the workers in the process, but always up to date. Can't beat that. Imagine the man-hours expended producing them, printing them, and replacing them daily on the board. Let's all say it together please . . . ***WASTE!***

Ladies and gentlemen, this is wallpaper in its purest form. Charts devoid of useful information to the audience. Zero chance it will alert workers to widening performance gaps and subsequent improvement activity to close said gaps. Sorry, but no points are given for the up-to-date status.

This experience was intensely entertaining at the time, and I learned a valuable lesson from it. If the charts are not intuitively obvious to the workers in the process, driving simplistic awareness of a gap and subsequent action, then they why produce them? Also, if it takes a briefer to explain a chart to the workforce, again, it has failed from a Lean perspective. I challenge you to peruse the charts on the walls of your company, assuming there are any. Can you ***immediately*** discern a performance gap when you look at them without asking someone to clarify it? A difference between where the process <u>should</u> be performing and its <u>current state</u>? If not, ask what their purpose is. Ask who the intended audience is. Perhaps you can enlighten the supervisor in the area how visual management is intended to be used. Perhaps you are the supervisor. If so, you have an opportunity. Stop disrespecting your employees by keeping them in the dark on how their process is performing based on VOC. As you find these confusing charts on your walls, I recommend placing them back into your printer trays and at least getting some recycle use out of the paper.

While I'm on the topic of targets, or customer tolerance levels, let me say this. If **you**, the provider of the service or product, are setting these levels, you are likely doing it wrong. If you want to understand a threshold of how long your customer should wait on a product/service, or what the quality limits should be, ask them. It's that simple. Don't assume or guess, talk to them. Find out from the actual customer. This is what VOC is all about.

Side Story – I was only on the job about two weeks at a company when someone came into my office for assistance. He wanted to improve a report he compiled each week but didn't know how to go about it, so he came to the new "Lean guy."

I assured him I could help, but I first needed to know who his customer for the report was and what requirements they had for it.

"That's not important," he said. "I just need your help making it better."

I'm not sure how long it took me to get his attention, or how many times he repeated the same request with complete disregard for the audience the report was intended for, but it was telling. This poor lad was a victim of his culture and was clueless about how to begin any process improvement activity. I explained it as gently as I could, both to slow him down and to make it a coaching moment he might benefit from.

The main takeaway here is to understand VOC is the **absolute starting point** of any improvement activity, or even just to evaluate if alterations are necessary in the first place. He was about to make changes to a report without a clue if those changes would be palatable to the recipients. If you don't know what the customer needs/wants, how can you be sure your changes will be in alignment? How will you know what to measure? Stop the madness if you do this yourself. Ask the questions, get the customer's input, build metrics, and then move forward to close performance gaps. Assumptions will bring results akin to what Coke got when they changed the beloved original formula back in 1985. Apparently, "New Coke" wasn't exactly what the customer had in mind.

If you are too young to remember this gem of a decision, allow me to recap for you. After 99 years of success with their famous soft drink formula, "New Coke" was launched on April 23, 1985. The original taste people knew and loved was gone—vanished from the shelves—replaced with a different taste. Customers went crazy—dogs and cats rioting in the streets—and just 79 days later the decision to completely replace original with New Coke was scrapped. I'm assuming the company took a hard look at whatever market research was available at the time, but it doesn't take a statistical savant to realize VOC failed here. They brought back the original formula, and "Classic" Coke sold next to the new stuff. In 2002, "New Coke" was finally abandoned.[xx] Even without confidence in whatever research they utilized, a better approach might have been to introduce the new product in parallel and measure receptivity. But my point here is to highlight the criticality of VOC.

If I randomly polled 50% of the people in your company, how many could tell me—quantifiably—the extent to which their process is meeting specific customer requirements? Could the CEO even tell me the answer to this question without tasking an assistant to look it up? As I travel about teaching, I often just ask employees straight up, *"How is your process doing related to customer requirements?"* I'm fishing to see if they have metrics at their immediate disposal.

The number one answer I get is *"pretty good."* Assumed translation: *"I have no clue what my customers quantifiably need, or to what extent my process is currently accommodating it. Basically, I just come to work, do what I always have done, get paid every two weeks, and try to stay out of trouble with my boss."* Just to be fair, it's possible my cynicism of traditional management is responsible for my assumption of the translation mentioned above. No empirical data beyond my plentiful anecdotal experience was collected to substantiate it. But, when I pressed for instantly accessible, quantifiable VOC metrics, they were absent in nearly every instance. Real data there. VOC can't be all that important, can it? Let's have a Coke and discuss it.

How many of you remember the Dunkin' Donuts commercial from the 1980s? Google it, and I'm sure you can find the video. The donut-making guy is leaving his house in the morning saying, *"Time to make the donuts."* The same guy walking back in the door at the end of a long hard day says, in a tired, non-enthusiastic tone, *"I made the donuts."* This cycle repeats multiple times in the commercial, signifying (in my opinion) the soul-sucking job redundancy the employee is enduring.

Now extend the metaphor to your own company culture and explore some questions. Do employees have a clue if they made the donuts customers wanted, the right amount of each kind, or if they met the quality requirements? Has anyone in management communicated any of this to them? Probably not. So, the poor chaps just make the donuts, day, after day. If a bunch of one flavor is always left over at the end of the day, that's just how it is. If Bubba runs out of cream-filled donuts, he tries to make extra the next day and hopes it's the right amount. Seems logical. No chart or visual management exists telling him how he's doing. Can we possibly expect him to be engaged in process improvement? How would he know it even needs to take place, or what precisely to improve or by how much? Not going to happen. Make more donuts, Bubba. Do whatever you did yesterday. Keep your head down and stay gainfully employed. It's what he does in his culture void of documented VOC requirements, let alone awareness of current state performance measured against VOC. Employees in this environment are unlikely to care about anything after a while. They merely exist and look forward to Friday afternoons like a weekly lottery win. Please recognize this apathy is a consequence of the culture, not the employees. Don't blame them.

Have you ever been in a job like that? You weren't sure who your customers were, specifically/quantifiably what they required, or how well your process was providing it? No performance indicators were shared with you, let alone posted on the wall for your continuous awareness. You just kept making the donuts day after day because someone told you to. Deciders behind the magic curtain at corporate were doing all the thinking. You were just the doer. Are you in a job like this now? I believe these jobs are far more common than the alternative, where employees know how their processes are performing—quantifiably and always—based on VOC. Communicating financial results to employees is fine, but it gives them no insight into how their individual efforts are doing. Consequently, process improvement opportunities are overlooked until something is completely out of control.

After many years in the work world, not a single instance occurred where leadership told me specifically, quantifiably what our external customers wanted. Zip. Zilch. Nada. I often asked and got generic answers. When I pushed for specificity, I got the traditional blank stare from my victim. Obviously, a boss didn't want to admit to me they really didn't know. It wasn't long before I decided to build a training class to help folks understand the power of metrics—what good ones look like and how to develop them. Most of my training classes came about from broken process catalysts like this. And, for the most part, I was given full autonomy to trudge forward with the lessons I developed. No wonder I loved the work, despite some of the traditional managers inadvertently steering the bus into denser fog.

When I teach my class on developing performance indicators, I start with an exercise. Three or four random students are asked to cite the following elements about their process, and I record their answers on flip chart paper or a whiteboard.

1. Tell me the <u>name</u> of some metric you measure in your process (its metric name)
2. Tell me what the <u>organizational goal</u> is (goodness level as seen from a customer)
3. Tell me quantifiably what the current <u>gap</u> is (assuming there is a gap)

Most are able to give me something resembling a metric name—not specific, but in the ballpark. Very few can tell me what the organizational goal is (they often take a guess at it, but when pressed, admitted they really didn't know). And no one has *ever* given me a quantified current state gap value as of that moment in time. Some have guessed at the gap, but they couldn't definitively tell me as of that day what it was. No charts existed on walls outside their offices to tell them the current state, and as many would say, "*I'd have to pull a report from system XYZ to know what the gap is.*" I have taught several thousand students on this topic and gotten the same results from the exercise every time. If you are a leader in your company, how would your employees fare with those three questions? Could you answer them yourself without tasking an administrative assistant to hunt-and-gather the information? Be honest. If you can provide all three responses instantly, congratulations! If a random employee can likewise answer them, take the rest of the day off with pay. You are probably a Lean-minded leader.

Little did the audience know, but I was collecting data myself. Each time I ran the exercise, it further described the extent of unawareness. Of course, people in my audiences typically don't even understand the scope of how unaware they are. They honestly don't know how their processes are performing in accordance with customer requirements and don't engage in impact-based process improvement because they have no clue what needs to be improved, or in what order. They just come to work, make the donuts, and do what they're told. With no one complaining, they assume all is right with the world. Why would they think otherwise? If pushed for an answer to how their process was doing, they resort to the easy answer, *pretty good*. It's not their fault. They are merely the product of a culture led by traditional managers hoarding information, assuming it even exists. Most of these managers are not intentionally disrespecting their employees but are also unaware of the cause/effect relationship in place.

Now comes my favorite example of this uninformed cultural tendency. A particular metric was near and dear to this one company, and they measured it quite accurately: the number of vehicle accidents. Employees did extensive traveling in pickup trucks daily because facilities and offices were separated geographically. Avoiding these accidents (mostly fender-benders with no injuries) was high on their list. For a long time, the data was available only in a central network location, and only locatable by the determined few who went hunting for it. Every time I taught my classes on Lean, I'd ask the audience how many accidents the company had to date. Rarely did anyone know, because it wasn't overtly posted on any wall, just buried somewhere in shared electronic files.

I have no clue if I was an influence in amending this condition, but eventually, they started sending a periodic company-wide email with the information. It was still not posted on walls and updated with every single new data point, but definitely an improvement from the Grand Canyon-sized SharePoint location. Score!

Back to my favorite example. I'm teaching a class to an audience of senior individuals. The room was filled with vice presidents from around the country, and when I got to the metric portion of my message, I asked the canned question. "Can anyone in this room tell me how many vehicle accidents the company has had so far this year?"

I paused to let them ponder it. Scanning the room revealed some of the students frantically searching for the email on cell phones and laptops so they could provide the precise number. This brought me amusement because the people with the most influence on the culture were unable to answer my question—a question, mind you, about a metric on the front burner across the enterprise.

Finally, someone in the room found the correct number of accidents when they got done hunting/gathering in their stash of emails and presented it to the class. I then asked a follow-up question.

"Can anyone tell me *why* employees, including leadership at your level in the company, are unable to immediately give me the precise number of accidents when I ask?"

They had no idea what answer I was fishing for, and I didn't want to prolong their agony, so I spelled it out for them. If there exists a metric so crucial to leadership you want every employee to be aware of it constantly, why must a person go looking for it in their email stash? Why would you not post it on walls all over the place, so it becomes easy for people to know what the status is?

I got blank stares and zero comments in response. As I've said, my pattern of teaching is to hold leadership processes accountable, not to just to excuse these foundational opportunities. Sure, they were smart folks with a lot of business savvy, but they were not using the formula for successfully transplanting a tree. I did this with the intent of waking some of them up, and perhaps altering future behavior among the more humble in the audience. *They* model behavior being replicated by the masses around them. I wanted them—and you—to realize there are better ways than emails and shared file storage to convey important metrics. Of course, this was the precursor argument to capturing and measuring internal/external VOC. They weren't exiting my class without at least hearing this critical message. The hope was for behavioral alterations in alignment with the concepts. Sometimes, it actually happened, and nothing is more encouraging to the Lean town crier. I admit this approach was incredibly risky from a career perspective, but to filter it or not challenge their current state methodologies was to do my audience a disservice. It might not have been the message they wanted to hear, but I firmly believe it was the message they needed to hear. A Lean transformation doesn't happen with passivity, and I was positively willing to risk carrying the torch through the middle of town.

In retrospect, I believe it was the right approach. On my last day with this company, a mid-level manager I rarely interacted with, shook my hand, and said to me, "Thank you for showing me what all-in looks like." I will never forget his comment. People willing to declare the emperor naked take significant risks. Another senior VP labeled me a "necessary disruptor." I took this as highly complementary, because it was precisely my approach—rocking the boat to generate introspective analysis, but always striving to do it respectfully by attacking the process used by management, not the person. At least that was my intent. Some didn't interpret it as respectful pushback—perhaps because they didn't want pushback of any kind—and their interpretation of my effort was highly negative. I can live with that. Transforming a company requires radical truth and transparency. You can't preach radical change—and this is what a Lean transformation is—and at the same time excuse status quo behavior. Those are incongruent actions. A major transformation effort is obviously not for the faint of heart or people in fear of losing their job by dissenting from acceptable norms. If an uncomfortable but necessary to hear message is met with negative repercussions for the sender, then there is little hope of behavioral shifting. People will cease to speak up and powerful opportunities get extinguished. I refuse to believe any CEO wants this.

Speaking of Lean transformation and metrics, I've seen madness ensue when companies try to measure the impact of the effort. *How do we know if it is working? Is the needle moving?* Reasonable questions, given the time and money being spent to train and coach people on the Lean business system. Unfortunately, and with far too much frequency, it seems commonplace to look at dollars saved. After all, this is ultimately what will occur when all the elements are working properly, right? Seems logical to build a spreadsheet and tally the financial consequences of process improvement activity for the year, then set goals to save specific amounts next year. Isn't that what the C-Suite is ultimately interested in, the bottom line? Isn't this what shareholders want to know?

Danger Will Robinson!!

Those born after 1968 will likely have to Google the old TV show *Lost in Space* to understand that line frequently dispensed by the robot, but I share it to make a point here. Start evaluating your Lean transformation according to dollars saved, and you will doom the effort to fail. Yes, you will save on operating costs eventually, but this is **not** the leading indicator a Lean transformation is taking hold. Give me any dollar amount, and I can cut it from your current operating budget in a matter of days. 50 million? No problem! We can whack through your spending elements with chainsaws and an industrial wood chipper, but after the dust settles, I'd like to evaluate what processes became more efficient as a consequence. And ultimately, will the frequency of positive customer experiences increase, or will the status quo service be deployed but at a cheaper cost to the provider? This is not what Lean is all about, and I encourage companies serious about infusing lean to not let a misguided temptation of measuring dollars become the gauge to monitor.

Alternatively, let's evaluate if *behaviors* are shifting. Tell me the extent employees are aware of their customer requirements and the performance gaps of same. Explain to me how many managers are moving to empowerment behaviors according to surveys from their employees. Show me the trend of cited root causes listed on your incident reports so we can determine if pointing at processes is overtaking the previous tendency to point at people. Let's measure the perspective of your external customers, and if they feel like you are paying more attention to their VOC requirements, the extent to which you are now listening and adjusting processes accordingly. What do employee engagement levels look like now compared to a year ago? What does the hiring process look like now that Lean is a valued cultural element? Does the on-boarding process now include indoctrination to Lean awareness? How many Gemba walks are your leaders engaging in, and what are the opportunities they are finding? What hurdles have they helped knock down for employees? What is the comfort level of employees to highlight process fault points compared to pre-deployment of Lean? What are the receptivity levels of managers when employees are doing this? To what extent are you using structured problem solving and rapid improvement events with teams of SMEs to close VOC performance gaps as opposed to the guessing model utilized by traditional managers before the transformation began?

What does *this* dashboard of metrics look like? Basically, measure and evaluate how much your culture is shifting toward the foundational tenants of Continuous Improvement + Respect for People. *These* are the indications you need to focus on rather than dollars saved. The savings will come, I promise, but the cultural shift is what takes you from a short-term survival vision of whacking bodies and spending cuts to a completely different, long-term way of behaving across the enterprise. CI + RFP.

Traditional managers won't have the stomach for this approach because they want instant financial indications the Lean needle is moving. Please recognize you could save a bazillion dollars and still have lousy customer experiences, a culture of people afraid to challenge frustrating process elements, my-way-or-the-highway managers, and an atmosphere stifling creativity and engagement. In this case, I'll predict your turnover rate is not something to be proud of. Behavioral culture change is your objective, and this is what you need to be setting goals against and measuring. Lean entrenchment will not happen overnight under the best of circumstances, which might compel the impatient to retreat back to the cave and scratch on walls again. This is the outcome if the Lean champion is not keeping the bus within the lines on the road, assuming you even have a champion behind the wheel.

Someone once wrote to Dr. Deming asking for the formula to expedited quality improvement and was willing to pay whatever he wanted. His insightful response: *"There is no instant pudding."* The man was a genius. How unfortunate the United States automobile industry didn't listen to him sooner. One could easily argue they are still not listening. I believe the longevity of the Lean journey is what keeps many from taking the first steps.

Side Story - In my government job, we had just endured a wasteful meeting with our entire department, including the big boss. He concluded the session with encouragement to bring ideas to our supervisor's attention if we had ways to make things better. This was like candy to a Lean-minded black belt, so I seized the moment immediately afterward in the hallway to corral my supervisor, while the message was still fresh on his mind. I let him know our organization didn't have a single metric to depict our performance, and I personally had no idea if we were meeting VOC requirements, or even what they were. I suggested we sit down together as a team, capture VOC information, and develop performance indicators to guide our improvement prioritization.

Keep in mind, this man was a GS14, responsible for several employees. After listening to my proposal, seemingly with concerned interest, nodding his head up and down as I spoke, he looked me right in the eye and said, "Do you know what the main ingredient in vanilla extract is?"

I'm sorry, what was that again?

I just passionately suggested we build metrics to understand how our processes were accommodating customer requirements, and my boss responds with, "Do you know what the main ingredient in vanilla extract is?" Thank goodness my friend Larry Fisher was a witness, or no one would have ever believed this story.

Imagine your boss responded with such a detached comment. He went on to describe the ingredient to me and the animal it is extracted from then simply walked away. I was beyond shocked. Was this guy suffering a stroke, an aneurysm, or some kind of a mental break? Should I dial 911 and find out if they can save him? You can't make this stuff up. This guy was probably the most disinterested boss I was plagued with during my 35 years working for the government. He was mentally checked out long before we were subjected to his presence as a boss. He basically just wanted to exist until he could retire and was doing a fine job of exactly that. No performance gap. Some would call it "retired in place." Mission accomplished. Nice enough guy, but had zero interest in VOC, metrics, or anything at all related to process improvement. Seems like the perfect choice to be in charge of black belts in a transformation office, right? Being a nice person is undoubtedly a plus for a boss, but it takes far, far more to be labeled a Leader. If they are not listening to their employees—who should be considered customers of the boss—then they have not grasped the Lean leadership concept. This kind of behavior also trains employees not to care, and apathy can spread like a virus.

Have I beat this dead horse sufficiently, or should I slug it a few more times to make sure? Capturing some VOC here. You readers are my customers.

Whatever it takes to get leadership to realize the critical importance of VOC and visibility of associated performance gaps needs to be done. Don't let the concrete heads out there squash your motivation. The bold change agents can eventually get the attention of habituated managers consumed with personal agendas contrary to the company moving forward. Granted, it takes courage, but the alternative is capitulation and stagnation.

Another aspect of metrics became a glaring opportunity for me on my journey—the use of averages. I'm not sure a more misleading value could be selected to describe the condition of any process. Before going any further, I'll tell you straight up I hate averages. They hide ugly like nothing else and should be avoided (as organization goals/targets/process indicators) at all costs. Allow me to explain why.

A metric has one function: to help you recognize when a performance gap is occurring between a customer requirement and the current state of a process. If you accept this, then you must also acknowledge that an average is not capable of doing it. It is quite possible you can achieve/maintain a target average at the same time your variability (data spread) is increasing. All it takes to offset the higher data points is a few low ones. Knowing only the average tells you nothing about the actual performance of the process, and ugly processes can appear to be okay. If you shoot at a duck twice with the first shot being a meter too long, and the second shot a meter too short, on average you shot the duck. A simplistic example, but hopefully you get the idea.

A much better approach is to establish a line in the sand, a maximum value. The maximum value is a threshold you never want a process data point to exceed. An example would be a cycle time the customer is willing to tolerate, say 130 days to finish an overhaul of an aircraft. This value is also referred to as an upper specification limit. Hopefully, it is customer rather than supplier driven. Some processes will simultaneously have a lower specification limit, a lower end value data points should never dip below. Speed limits on a highway are a good example. Drivers should not go slower than 45, or faster than 70. Anything below the minimum, or above the max is a defect. With both a lower and upper spec limit, your acceptable data points must stay within this window of tolerance. Average driver speeds are irrelevant.

Consider this example.

When a patient lays in a hospital bed hooked up to a computer monitoring vital signs, numeric values are clearly noted with flashing numbers, colors, and audible alerts. The alarms are an immediate indicator the patient's body has crossed a minimum or maximum threshold, *Hey! Mr. Caretaker, you need to do something right now to prevent an undesirable outcome.* Imagine if your hospital monitors only displayed average blood pressure and heart rate over the past few hours. It might give the staff more time to do some non-value-added paperwork, but this isn't going to position the patient or the caretaker for success.

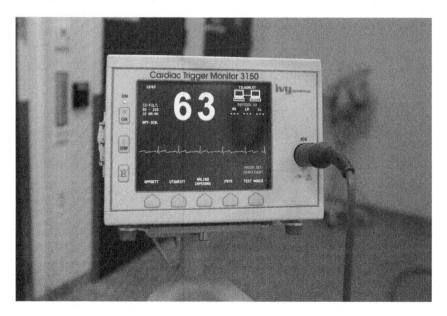

On the contrary. You absolutely want to know when something is going south in order to address the right issue with haste. You could have died five minutes ago, but on average, your heart rate is just fine during the last hour.

Metrics in your process are exactly the same if you think of them in these terms; you (and the employees performing in the process) need to know immediately when a line in the sand has been crossed so you can dig in and determine how to prevent it from happening again. The alternative will demand a much greater level of reaction when you finally realize the process has gone way beyond acceptable limits. In summary, averages have their purpose in statistics, but should *never* be used as goals for a process or reported to describe how a process is performing. Count the number of times thresholds are exceeded and use root cause analysis each time. This is far more laborious but aligns with a management team striving to employ continuous improvement based on VOC. Embrace the ugly!

Since I'm fond of metaphors, indulge me in another one. I use this when I teach my class on developing performance indicators. Imagine you are driving an unfamiliar car someone gave you for an upcoming trip. You trust all is well and climb aboard, heading down the highway on a 400-mile journey on a blazing hot summer day. As it turns out, the gauges on this vehicle are missing. You hear the engine running, but you are clueless about even the essential indicators like fuel quantity and vehicle speed. Being the adventurous type, you discount this minor inconvenience and focus on the road ahead. You recall lousier cars you owned, and they nearly always got you from A to B. No problem, you think. Let's just get going down the road. I'll match my speed with the cars around me because they are probably abiding by the limit. I'll stop occasionally and fill this puppy up with gas. It'll be okay. All is right with the world. So, you turn up the radio (it amazingly works) and plow forward with blissful ignorance.

Let's speculate on how the process of this journey might possibly go astray. You could get a ticket for speeding because the yahoos around you were all going too fast, or, the engine might overheat. Or maybe, just as you're accelerating at a critical junction on the busy highway where you have to switch routes, this dang car runs out of gas. The piece of crap. It should have gone much further, but you were unaware of a slow leak in the gas tank. If you could just have made it to the next exit, you were planning on getting some gas there. Time for some serious damage control (firefighting). Phone calls (with menu options and music), waiting (there's always some waiting), towing . . . pick an unpleasant set of outcomes and be ready to live with the consequences of this driving process without gauges. Did I mention it was 104 degrees outside? Now translate the metaphor onto your business process without VOC performance indicators.

Recognize the pitfalls of working in a process void of timely, posted performance indicators, or in this particular case, no indicators? The sane person would immediately object to driving this car, even if the destination was a short trip across town. You should do the same if you are working without specific, customer-driven performance indicators for your process just chugging along.

I wonder what the prevalence is of people going to work every day, performing some task, for some known or unknown customer, and they are clueless about how the process is faring according to requirements. Not to worry. We can look over at our competitors to see how they are doing and match our speed to theirs. It'll be okay. After all, we've got more important things to do than put a team together and build silly VOC metrics, or spend precious time updating/posting the charts we do have just because we got some new data points yesterday. Or was it the day before? Who knows, just keep making the donuts. We can batch the updates like we always have. On average, I'm sure we're probably doing pretty good. I can hear the donut machine humming (or is it clanging?) so let's relax and enjoy the day. It's nearly break time anyway.

If you choose the sane path to understanding your process performance, you will spend the time getting VOC requirements, turning them into meaningful metrics with definitive thresholds, posting intuitive charts showing how your process is performing against the requirements, making sure every single employee from the lowest to highest level is aware, and then acting on gaps quickly when the impact warrants attention. Most importantly, you will be doing this ***continuously***.

"Confusion is a luxury which only the very, very young can possibly afford and you are not that young anymore." - James Baldwin

The Elusive Root Cause

"If you study the root causes of business disasters, over and over you'll find this predisposition toward endeavors that offer immediate gratification." – Clayton Christensen

While the scope of this book was to be far more behaviorally based as opposed to a box of tools, one, in particular, is necessary for the Lean leader to grasp. If the people leading the business are not adept at understanding when root cause analysis has gone far enough, then they will not be able to guide those performing the actual activity. Leadership is all about modeling the desired behavior for others to replicate. This chapter is to share what I have learned along my journey related to root cause analysis (RCA). I'd like to clearly establish that the identification of a root cause (RC) should be a mandatory precursor to the selection of countermeasures. It's a cart before the horse thing.

The activity itself sometimes can be like nailing Jell-O to the wall, with one arm tied behind your back, in the dark, with rubber nails and a nerf hammer. No matter what someone might tell you, it is often difficult. Add to this the generic training people are provided, along with the human prevalence of impatience to achieve results instantly, and you have a recipe for ineffective outcomes. This is precisely why problems re-emerge after the activity was deemed complete – the RCs were symptoms or bypassed completely. Solving problems doesn't equal installing a Band-Aid, it means preventing the outcome from ever happening again.

Make no mistake about it. The most challenging element to uncover while problem-solving is finding this fuzzy thing we call the root cause. People throw the term around quite a bit, but I am convinced few know precisely how to wrap their arms around it. When a manager is content with "employee did not follow the documented instruction," I am confident they are unaware of what an RC is. It seems straightforward enough when you peruse available literature, training material, or videos, but in practice, it is often done poorly when it's done at all. I am explicitly lumping training classes into this broken process of developing causal analysis capability. Course designs are failing to help people understand the mechanics of doing it and/or what the deliverable should look like. If Green and Black belt RCA trainings were effective at creating capability, certified individuals would be eliminating negative effects like crazy when they returned to their companies. Undesirable process outcomes would ***never*** emerge again. Have you conducted RCA only to experience the same defect occurring again and again in your company?

The causal connection says this: The RC is the required precursor to the undesirable outcome. If A occurs, then B is the potential outcome. If you can determine the root causes (The As) and then remove them from existence, the undesirable effect (The Bs) cannot occur again. If a person is allergic to cats (the

RC of sneezing) and you pitch Fluffy out the front door (not to worry, the neighbors wanted a cat to solve their rodent problem), the sneezing and runny eyes (negative effect) cannot occur again within this person's home. Easy peasy, right? Well, not so much. Pick any problem you have tried to resolve with this treasure hunt of a process and then determine if you were successful. Success means you have found process conditions to remove (maybe multiple things), and as a result, the negative effect you wanted to avoid never happened again. If you can say yes to this, then chances are you have solved the problem. This assumes, of course, other elusive RCs are not lurking in wait of their turn to cause havoc.

So, what is the big deal? We ask a few whys, and the golden nugget driving the negative effect will just appear. I'm told *five* is the magic number of times to ask why. This was sarcasm if you didn't immediately catch it. I use sarcasm to make a point from time to time. No, really, I do.

Unfortunately, RCA is far from this simple. No amount of structure—regardless of the RCA tool chosen or persons using it—will deliver the goods unless the practitioner, 1) knows what an RC looks like, and 2) knows how to guide a team of subject-matter-experts (SMEs) around the potholes to get there. I've witnessed many certified Green and Black belts struggle with RCA and then settle on something the team labels an RC when in fact the digging stopped prematurely. Or, a team goes into the RCA activity with the intent of justifying some countermeasure they have already decided on in advance, or one handed to them from management. All wasteful activity creating useless wallpaper.

The impatience I mentioned earlier can be an ugly element in problem-solving. The number one excuse I've heard from people when I question their abbreviated or non-existent RCA efforts boils down to variations of *Ain't nobody got time for that!* Watch the news on any particular evening and listen to politicians puke out countermeasures for problems when no RCA analysis has even been considered. *What we need to do is* _____. Anyone can utilize their emotional response to a problem and toss a decreed fix over the wall with passion and conviction. Traditional managers are experts at it. Unfortunately, slot machines in the Las Vegas airport pay off jackpots more often than this approach does.

Without going into a training session here on how to conduct RCA—because it can only be done effectively in person with on-hands practice and immediate feedback from an experienced, patient coach—I will limit my scope to establishing what a *stopping point* looks like and the mentality to get there. By this I mean, when a person or team has cited what they think is the causal domino, how can they confirm they have arrived? What does a valid stopping point look like? If they have gotten off-track, what does that condition look like? Another objective of this chapter is to highlight where RCA typically goes astray, and the preferred path to seek.

My journey has taught me there are three locations the RCA bus can travel to.

1. **Crazyland**—getting into causal elements you have no control over whatsoever (*the engineer who mis-designed the valve was home-schooled by an alcoholic foster parent who modeled lazy behavior*). Addressing the behavior of the deceased parent is impossible, and even if they were still alive, the likelihood of it affecting future behavior of the engineer is, well, just crazy. Short excursions to crazyland are common and fun, but you need to recognize you have left the paved highway. It might be an entertaining side excursion, but this dirt path is unlikely to yield fruit.

2. **Peopleland**—the place where we trash the worker and affix blame under the guise of accountability. This will invariably nudge management to consider useless countermeasures like counseling, firing, vengeful punishment, performance improvement plans (PIPs) or my favorite useless countermeasure, re-training. In the rare instance when the worker created the defect intentionally with malice, addressing the person is justified. Otherwise, stay off this pothole laden path as well. Not only will it fail to yield fruit in the form of preventing problem reoccurrence, but it will degrade the culture into a blame-game environment. Five WHYs will become five WHOs, and no winners emerge. Humiliating a well-intentioned employee with the intent of correcting behavior across the enterprise is misguided. Traditional cultures are riddled with guided tours through Peopleland.

3. **Processland**—the place where almost all negative effects are conceived, born, raised, and become entrenched because *that's how we've always done it.* Please don't make me give you a multiple-choice test to determine if you can identify the desired location to guide the team with RCA. Drag them back to Processland even if they occasionally leave the designated trail on their own. Document any undesirable outcome you might be experiencing (example: *expense reports are riddled with errors*), and if the RCA activity is done properly, you will find unintended design flaws in the process. In many cases, the flaws were inserted intentionally but without malice. Example: Someone high on the food chain decrees *Let's use the Alpha system for expense reports. It'll be awesome!* Three months later, *Oh double-damn, this system is awful. Look at all the defects and delays we are getting. Whose idea was it to use this piece of crap?* Oops, we just took an exit ramp into Peopleland. Someone is about to be held accountable for a decision void of intentional malice, as though this will eliminate all bonehead decisions from everyone in the future. The facilitator's responsibility is to now direct the group back to Processland as quickly as possible.

In other cases, the process flaw creeps in from variability of application. Different employees are doing it with several different methods. Ways to do things just morph over time. No one intentionally re-designed the step – it just sort of found its way into the bigger picture and is now responsible for an undesirable outcome. We could go on and on talking about the genesis of dysfunctional process elements, but the fact remains they are what is now causing the negative impact you wish to eradicate.

It boils down to this statement. **Something about the current PROCESS design permitted the undesirable outcome to occur.** And please recognize a process exists even in the absence of a documented set of instructions or detailed flow chart. If you are currently doing the task/work in any form, you have a process – regardless of its variability, inefficiency, repeatability, or confusion factors. Even if the defect occurred the very first time you conducted the activity, you still used a process (a series of steps) to do it. The flaw is contained in this process design somewhere, and this is where you aim your RCA flashlight to find it.

The main point I want to make here is maintaining a relentless objective of dragging your RCA discussion back into Processland if it unexpectedly veers into Crazyland or Peopleland. While this might seem like logical advice, in practice, it can be a daunting task to do effectively. It takes courage to chastise a team's process of conducting RCA, and a bold, experienced change agent has to be willing to do it without hesitation. Again, my intent here is not to teach the technique but to cite the paths to avoid, and the correct one to seek.

Okay, this second element I absorbed during my journey was something never taught in any formal class I ever attended, and I went to a slew of them. The stopping criteria (knowing when you have arrived at a reasonable root cause) for RCA came from my extended stretch at the school of hard knocks (HK). Re-work was my degree major, and I was captain of the Do-Over team. We even had incorrectly fitting jerseys with Ctrl + Z on them. The two instructors at HK were brutal—Dr. Trial and his sidekick Professor Error—but the outcome was eventually worth the effort, at least for me, because I was never content with the status quo other educational options were dispensing. I've been to instructor-led classes on five whys, cause mapping, fishbone construction, etc., but not a single one of them nailed the pearl of wisdom I will now share with you. Well, I consider it a pearl. Maybe it has been obvious to you for a long time.

So, here is the situation. For discussion purposes, we'll say a team is conducting RCA to determine what caused a mishap. Bubba and Bubbette were machining a widget when suddenly the machine they operate together seized up and destroyed the expensive piece of equipment in addition to the product they were producing. The team of subject-matter-experts convened and are now trying to determine what caused the mishap. They decide to use a standard 5-Why tool. (By the way, all RCA tools are just variations of the original 5-Why tool.) The structured problem-solving facilitator is asking why this happened, and someone is recording the answers to the series of questions. Here comes the challenge. At what point do they stop and proclaim they have reached a root cause? I've asked this exact question to people claiming to be skilled in RCA, and it often gives them pause. Some of the answers I've gotten include, *"Well, it's called 5-why, so you stop after five."* Thanks for playing, but no points for this response. The label is notional. It may take 3 answers, 5, or 20. The team might get off track, entertain a brief stay in Crazyland or Peopleland, and the count of questions/answers might pile up significantly. Leaders should wave the Suspicion Flag if they are presented an RCA with exactly 5 questions and 5 perfectly fitting answers.

Other responses I've gotten to my question have been, *"Well, you stop when you have reached a root cause."* Well, yes, thank you for the insight, but what does an RC look like? How do you know you are there and can proclaim it a Root Cause?

Perhaps my favorite answer of all time was from a young lady who with conviction and confidence told me, *"You keep asking Why until you can't ask it anymore. Then you are there."*

In response, I asked her if there was a point where she literally would be unable to ask WHY, like the word wouldn't even come out of her mouth. I used a contrived example of effects and causes back to her which eventually resulted in a fictitious SME saying, *"Because the earth cooled,"* to which I could then say, *"So, why did earth cool?"* My point to her then, and it remains true now, is there is literally no point where I could not continue to ask the why question again. We could do so until the SMEs pulled at their hair with both hands in desperation and ran from the room screaming colorful expletives. By the way, asking the pure "Why" question is exceedingly obnoxious after a while (also ineffective from a design perspective). There are facilitation techniques to offset this monotony, but this is a topic I'll save for another forum. Wonder why I almost strayed from my scope. Anyone want to cite the cause?

So, permit me to answer the question for you now. Please keep in mind, this came about after my own frustration at asking proclaimed experts (RCA instructors) what the stopping point is, and not getting a definitive answer for practical translation into actual RCA activity with teams. Years of experience in the Gemba brought it to my awareness sometime around 2010. I call it the **Stop or Keep Digging Flowchart**.

As the facilitator of RCA, I'm continually evaluating a pair of criteria—questions to help me assess if a valid stopping point has been achieved by the team of SMEs with the repetitive question/answer routine of 5-Whys, or whatever structured tool is being used. It is applicable in all cases.

Stop or Keep Digging Flowchart

Criteria #1: *If the last listed answer (the "because" language) to a why question <u>could</u> be eliminated with some countermeasure (regardless of what the CM might be), would the negative effect we are trying to prevent go away?*

Recall the contrived example I started with. A machine and its product under construction were destroyed. Imagine the team answered a series of 5-Why questions and came up with, *the machine seized up because Bubbette failed to conduct the oil filter change during the preventative maintenance procedure.*

Let's assume here this is a valid and confirmed statement. We have empirical evidence to support it. Now we'll apply the first criteria question: If the listed cause <u>could</u> be eliminated with some countermeasure (regardless of what the CM might be), would the negative effect go away? The answer here is **YES**. If the filter gets changed during preventive maintenance, the machine will not seize up from insufficient lubrication, but you cannot stop here! Straightforward enough, but the first criterion is far easier to satisfy than the next one. It is inadequate by itself. Getting a NO here would trigger the Keep Digging task (meaning the *why* question/answer activity goes on), but a yes answer now triggers the second criteria question. They are designed to be asked in series (see flow chart).

Criteria #2: ***Do we have enough information to insert an effective PROCESS countermeasure (regardless of what the CM might be), which will either eliminate the possibility of the outcome re-occurring or greatly reduce its likelihood?***

If we apply this criterion to *Bubbette failed to conduct the oil filter change during the preventative maintenance procedure,* we now get a NO answer, and we are back to Keep Digging. The 5-Why activity turns on again with questions (*Why?*) and answers (*Because _____*)

Let me explain the reasoning. We know Bubbette failed to replace the filter, and we know if she had replaced the filter, the machine would not have seized up. What we don't know is **why**! She could have failed to change it for any number of process reasons we are currently clueless about (ran out of parts, was distracted with another task from her boss, the tool to change the filter was broken/unavailable, she exceeded her twelve beer a day limit and couldn't read the instructions, etc.). We need to know the **why** in order to brainstorm/consider reasonable countermeasures (CMs), which will subsequently prevent the condition of a filter not getting changed during preventative maintenance. We need to alter the **PROCESS** of changing filters, and this cannot be done when the information is limited to *the employee didn't change the filter.*

Herein lies the notoriously stepped-in pothole. If we stop at *Bubbette didn't change the filter,* imagine the ignorant countermeasure we might insert. We could fire the employee, punish her, retrain her, put her on a traditional performance improvement plan destined to do nothing positive for anyone, make Bubba do it in the future, send Bubbette reminder emails (in all capitals and large font for emphasis), hang reminder signs near the machine, remind her in-person . . . well, you can contribute plenty more useless CMs to continue my point. Please recognize the key thing I am trying to share with you here. Stopping prematurely can lead to countermeasures attacking a person, and process outcomes are likely to remain the same. Defects, delays, or safety issues are poised to occur again and again. The worker is generally trying to do the best they can in broken processes, and then the traditional manager wants to hold them accountable. Intentional malice was not present, but the broken process gets ignored. It's caveman madness. Until you have confirmed evidence on why the process Bubbette is using failed, you do *not* have enough information to insert an effective process countermeasure. If you insert some lame reminder or punishment intended to ensure filter changes in the future (basically allowing the process to remain as it was) someone else will create the same defect without intentional malice precisely as the first employee did. Bubbette gets fired, and Beth takes over. She fails to change a filter, and the negative outcome happens again. Will you now repeat the useless countermeasures used in the past as though by some magical intervention they will work this time? Keep putting the wrong key in a car's ignition switch in hopes it will somehow start the engine. What would you label this activity if you witnessed it? The undesirable outcome remains a potential outcome again unless the process is appropriately adjusted, and you don't know what to change in the process until the digging has been done to fruition. Both criteria need to be answered in the affirmative before you declare you have identified an RC at a deep enough level.

A friend of mine was a forklift operator in a warehouse filled with metal drums. All day long they were moved about like an endless game of chess. The established policy was, *Pierce a drum with your forklift, and you will be fired immediately.* No exceptions were considered. He was an outstanding employee for years and took meticulous care to not pierce drums. Unfortunately, it happened one day. During the termination discussion, his boss apologized for taking this action and emphasized how he felt so bad losing such an excellent employee. No RCA was accomplished. The go-to countermeasure of firing sat patiently on the traditional manager's shelf waiting to be dispensed repeatedly as the undesirable outcome of a pierced drum happened over and over again. The exact same process was handed to the replacement driver and remains poised to produce the same result.

Insanity.

I cannot emphasize this point enough. Attack the person because your RCA activity stopped prematurely and be prepared for the defect, delay, or safety incident to happen again. Also, be content with cultural degradation, because it is a foregone conclusion. Everyone loses, and I have seen this painful scenario play out more times than I wish to recall. It's damned ugly. Think about the safety issues your company has encountered. If the undesirable outcome (ex: employee injured performing task X) ever occurs again, your previous RCA activity was obviously flawed. No amount of threats will alter the process with definitive prevention outcomes. Automobile accidents happen when drivers are distracted by their cell phones. Will the risk of fines ever prevent this? Maybe we could put bold decals on the dashboard saying, "Never look at your phone while driving." That should do it, right? Let's get those drivers aware! Recognize we are failing to prevent reoccurrence with the countermeasures selected. What is the cost of addressing an undesirable outcome over and over? It ain't free! Broken processes are at work here, not defective employees as traditional managers would like to believe. Not even the traditional manager is at fault. Their broken process of managing is, and it will be replicated by those observing them until someone declares the dysfunction is unacceptable. I wish the root cause of this problem would be analyzed.

Caution! At the time you are answering the questions of both criteria the team is not—I repeat, **NOT**—tasked to determine what the specific countermeasure is. Brainstorming countermeasures will be a separate activity once you get a YES to criterion #2. If you feel you have enough information to insert a process countermeasure, then the criteria have been met, regardless of what countermeasure the team ultimately agrees on. This is important for the facilitator to keep in mind, so SMEs don't withhold a yes until they know the precise countermeasure it is connected to. Horse then cart, not both at once, please. Combining both tasks at once, RCA + CM considerations, is multitasking, and no human being is capable of multitasking. I also highly recommend using a Pick Chart to evaluate potential countermeasures on their impact to the problem and difficulty to insert after both criteria are satisfied, but this is yet another topic outside the scope of my RCA discussion here. So much to share, so little time left on this earth to do it.

Bottom line: the next time you incorporate root cause analysis as a precursor to determining the best countermeasures for preventing re-occurrence of an undesirable outcome, please give the two criteria evaluation a shot. Recognize the first criterion is far easier to satisfy than the second, so be prepared to keep digging until you have reached pay dirt on why the process failed. This approach will serve you much better than traditional methods. Just a little something I've learned on Gemba boulevard. Awesome road. Have you been on it lately? It pays for itself because the other routes have hidden tolls your company cannot afford.

"If I had one hour to save the world, I would spend fifty-five minutes defining the problem and only five minutes finding the solution." – Albert Einstein

Have You Been to the Gemba Lately?

"When you go out into the workplace, you should be looking for things that you can do for your people there. You've got no business in the workplace if you're just there to be there. You've got to be looking for changes you can make for the benefit of the people who are working there."
- Taiichi Ohno

I've alluded to the power of Gemba walking but now wish to take a deeper dive into the topic. The word Gemba (or Genba, both spellings are used) is typically unknown to the people in my classroom settings. Most of the business people I shared conversations with in airports, on flights, and slow shuttle bus rides to airport rental car lots were clueless to it. I am continually astounded how in the year 2019, 32 years after the term was coined by John Krafcik and subsequently mentioned repeatedly in articles, books, and videos, many business people have never heard the word Lean, let alone Gemba. How is Lean leadership not a required class for any business degree, most assuredly for MBAs? In defense of some, I have met people who are doing a version of Gemba walking but haven't familiarized themselves with the label. Let's give them partial credit here. Maybe a B minus. Their grade can be bumped up to an A+ if they learn how to Gemba walk properly and increase their frequency to at least once daily.

Gemba is a Japanese word which translates into "The real place." It is where the work is accomplished. If you are a software person and you spend your day in front of a computer writing code, this environment is your Gemba. Perhaps you are a cook—the location of your food preparation tasks is your Gemba. Aircraft mechanic? The shop floor where you physically work on the planes, this is your Gemba. A Gemba *walk* is the activity of a person going to the actual place of the work and observing tasks being accomplished. You are watching, learning, and seeking opportunities to remove hurdles in employees' way. It is a time to absorb what current state looks like as opposed to just interpreting it in your mind from a process map, a meeting discussion, or some after-the-fact report showing process outcomes. Reports show numbers, not the actual activity to produce customer requirements. You will never understand the process from a report. The Gemba is where people are accomplishing the work you have asked them to do. It is not a conference room where supervisors come together to communicate the delays, defects, and safety issues manifesting in processes.

Allow me to state my $0.02 with crystal clarity. If you are not Gemba walking on a regular basis, please do not think you are fully behaving as a Servant Leader. You might accept the elements of Lean leadership as the right approach, but if you are not out there directly observing process activity, then your process of leading is inadequate. Not to worry. You can alter your process immediately if you are inclined to drag yourself away from a wasteful meeting or two. Employees are fighting things daily, and you are clueless to this low hanging fruit. Hell, this fruit is on the ground waiting to be picked up! No ladder required. Bring a shovel and a wheelbarrow.

I'm still astounded when people tell me they have been through a formal Green or even Black Belt training program and the term was only touched on superficially. It is certainly the case that these future process improvement practitioners are rarely being taught how to conduct a Gemba walk with experienced coaches, even if the concept is discussed. Such a foundational behavior and it doesn't get front-burner status in training agendas – this is a huge performance gap in my opinion. No amount of numerical data fully prepares a manager to assist with process improvement if they have not seen the process conducted in person. Granted, it is not always practical to observe a process that takes several days, week, or months to complete. Lots of handoffs, waiting for information, or other activity before the task can be finished – I get it. It would be onerous on the walker and the engineer observed to watch an entire software product being developed. There are ways to deal with this, however, rather than the all-or-nothing approach. Long-term processes too time-consuming to physically watch can be Gemba walked where the activity takes place, and the walk becomes an interview with the people who do the work. They can talk through or simulate the various tasks for your digestion. Or, the tasks can be individually observed over time on separate Gemba walks. There is always a way if the Gemba walker is motivated enough to learn what employees are doing, and the struggles they encounter while doing it. I coach people to discard all excuses, and my journey has shown me they can be plentiful when managers are looking for ways to avoid Gemba walking. *"I'm too busy"* was the #1 excuse. I translated the explanations in my head to say, *You are telling me you are too busy to make a commitment to developing your employees and processes to their fullest by reducing wasteful activity all based on VOC.* While I don't say those words directly to an excuse provider, it is always what I want to say.

Before I get too far into this powerful activity every supervisor should learn, I want to clearly differentiate it from what is known as Management by Walking Around (MBWA). Hewlett-Packard is credited with originating this behavior back in the 1970s. The variability in its application is large, but generally speaking, the boss is wandering around talking to employees without a definitive process or scope selected in advance. It's a meet-and-greet and see-what-we-see-by-chance activity. Caution! I think supervisors getting out and about to meet their workforce is a very good thing. You will learn people's names, where they do their work, get to know them as human beings and vice versa, and I highly recommend doing it. But, this is NOT a Gemba walk. Please do not interchange the labels. If you are new to the Gemba walking concepts, the distinction will become extraordinarily clear as I describe it.

Let's start with the four objectives Gemba walking. All equally important and often overlapping.

1. **Gain a firsthand understanding of the value stream**
2. **Identify opportunities for hurdle reduction**
3. **Promote a single value stream mentality across the workforce**
4. **Promote a problem-solving mentality across the workforce**

I will also strive to help you understand how to plan and conduct one properly because a Gemba walk done improperly can quickly shatter the trust between an employee and his/her supervisor. Trust, once damaged, is tough to re-establish. Think about people in your life who have done something to warrant your caution in future interactions. Maybe they lied to you or shared something you asked them to keep in confidence. You never quite trust them the same way you did before the infraction. Their efforts to repair it might make things better, but you still retain a sliver of doubt in your head. It's how human beings are wired. Damaged trust can leave a permanent scar. As such, I would rather bosses never Gemba walk than to do them by instinct alone. *"I got this"* is a process developed by the non-humble manager who thinks longevity in his/her position automatically means they are competent in all things. Such arrogance will not serve you well on a Gemba walk.

Objective #1 - *Gain a firsthand understanding of the Value Stream.* A value stream is all the activity from stem to stern to provide a product or service to a customer. It includes every single morsel of activity – including tasks accomplished by organic employees, contractors, suppliers, transporters, inspectors, and corporate folks in fancy towers – anyone doing anything during the overall process. Value streams can be massive (and overwhelming to digest) if you map them at a low level, but you will capture much of madness people are engaging in. While these maps can be very useful tools (and I highly recommend generating them), they are positively incapable of demonstrating what the workers are physically doing at the Gemba – the hunting and gathering they are forced to do because items are stored all over the place, the confusion they encounter with voluminous instructions written in mind-numbing hieroglyphics, the reaching, the crawling underneath things, the unnatural twisting, the repetitive mouse clicking, the assumptions they are forced to make in the absence of clear deliverable standards and updated information, the inadequate spaces they are forced to work in, the lousy tools they are using, the inadequate training they receive, the things they have to wait on before work can continue, the stressful conditions that crop up, and basically any process frustration they are enduring to produce the product or service for customers. Whew! Talk about opportunities. And if you as their supervisor are living in meetings or spending your days holed up in your office doing paperwork and sending emails because your distorted view of leadership considers this activity valuable, you are missing enormous opportunities to act as a supplier to the only people doing work of real value to the external customers – your employees. While you fill out forms, answer emails, and effectively isolate yourselves from the worker bees, they are left to deal with the madness on their own, or worse, wait for you to finally show up to provide a decision they are not permitted to make or get information you have not made available to them. They don't understand the big picture any better than you do. Their focus is on their little piece of turf, their section of the production floor, their tiny cubicle (I refer to cubicles as timeout rooms), or wherever they hang out during their eight hours of work.

All those supervisors now feeling slight twinges of guilt, place your right hand into the air. I admire you for admitting it. But don't feel too bad, it's not you that sucks, it's your *process* of leading. You're off the hook unless you simply don't care to alter your current state behavior.

Unless you have physically done the work yourself (and recently), including _all_ the upstream and downstream activity throughout the entire value stream, you do not understand it firsthand. I can't sugarcoat this. You don't really know how all the value stream pieces fit together. Period. You might claim you know what happens, and in what order, the multitude of handoffs, but can you honestly say you know the struggles and frustrations *all* the workers (including those external to your company umbrella) are dealing with in order to conduct the process as a single team? Be honest.

Objective #2 – *Identify opportunities for hurdle reduction.* There is a 100% chance employees are struggling with something at the Gemba you can help make easier. Do you know what they are chronically waiting for? Do you know what it takes to accomplish every task? Do you know which ones are using tools that make the job harder than necessary (bulky, slow, confusing, unreliable, heavy, leaking, dangerous)? Do you know what frustrates these workers (lousy software, poor lighting conditions, unreasonable demands, goals without support to achieve them, overly restrictive policies, etc.)? Of course not, and no report on earth is going to enlighten you the way a Gemba walk will. You can look at a movie poster, but you will not completely understand the plot intricacies until you watch the actual movie. Get your popcorn ready. Have a seat. Better yet, actually, take a walk. You are about to witness madness you didn't know existed. Rated G for Great!

I've been on more Gemba walks during my journey than I can recall, but I have never once been on one and not found an opportunity to make conditions better for a worker. Caution. Do NOT start launching countermeasures over the wall like a T-shirt gun when you see obvious opportunities. This is **_not_** an objective of Gemba walking. When you see an opportunity, you must be mindful of getting the employee input by asking why the process has them crawling on their knees to plug in an air hose or climbing on shelves to reach material, or waiting for decisions, material, information, or whatever. You are there to learn and subsequently spark **_their_** problem-solving ideas, not to be the on-the-spot-fixer, as tempting as it will be. This cannot be overemphasized.

Side Story – I was about to teach a class one morning. About 25 employees were seated and ready to go, and I suddenly realized I didn't have the gizmo needed to connect my laptop to the projector mounted in the ceiling. It's called a "1 click button," and it plugs directly into a USB port on the room computer so the computer can talk to the large screen. Typically, these items were located in the conference rooms, but that was not the case in this room. After hunting around the room for a few minutes, I thought I'd ask the person at the front desk. She was always a knowledgeable individual. Perhaps she could help. Unfortunately, she was not there.

A back-up person with 10% awareness of her process said he thought they were kept there in a drawer. The poor lad opened one drawer after another (hunting and gathering because he had no clue where they were stored) and finally came across them. Three of them, just lying in the drawer. He handed me one, and I thought I'd have the projector going in no time. Dream on. I plugged in the gizmo, and it did nothing. By this time, a student shared a nugget of knowledge with me, explaining that the controllers were specifically programmed to a single projector so I might have the wrong one.

Defect!

Back I went to the front desk to get the other two gizmos. On try number three, I was successful and composed myself to teach the class. We were about ten minutes delayed. Completely unacceptable, in my opinion.

When I discussed the problem with the primary front desk person, here are some of the immediate countermeasures she offered up after she explained to me *the back-up person should have known where the items are kept*. Obviously, the back-up person was the cause of this problem. Anyone could see that!

- Train the back-up person on where the gizmos are kept
- Remind the back-up person to ask the instructor which gizmo they need depending on the room they are teaching in (as if the instructor would know which one they needed.)

Notice both of these options do ***nothing*** to the process itself. Instead, they attempt to do something to the worker, and, even if successful, they still include confusion on which one goes with which room, as well as time spent getting and returning them. What if the back-up person is not available either, and someone else is filling in? How will they understand what to do? Should we train everyone that could possibly fill in and hope they all remember?

I asked a silly question at this point.

Why couldn't we store the specific gizmos in the conference rooms they are programmed to – with Velcro stuck right on the monitor itself – kind of like we had in all the other conference rooms? I explained how his was a previously implemented (and successful) idea generated by our co-worker, Daniela Sanders, and would eliminate the front desk staff from the process entirely. No training or reminding anyone of anything ever again.

She was reluctant to do this because of the possibility of people taking the gizmos out of the room. Keep in mind it was virtually useless to anyone because it was programmed to a single projector/screen. When I asked if this had ever happened (that pesky data question), she said no. So basically, a non-problem resulted in a countermeasure adding significant waste to the process, with no apparent benefit. Only more waste was the outcome of the CM.

Notice this process had multiple fault points built into it, each an opportunity for confusion to create delays in scheduled events. All the training in the world would rely on people remembering, plus the insanity of someone having to go to the front desk and *ask* for the silly things. Attack the worker, and mistakes will just be made by different workers. Attack the process, and everyone is positioned for success.

The humorous part of this story – at least to me – is that the gizmos were stored in other conference rooms, but not these three for some reason. Process variability. Why was standardization not in the entire building – or across the enterprise? Did leadership not realize it? Not care? Were they too busy with the problems plaguing their individual silo? All unanswerable questions when you have what I call a non-single value stream mentality. Organizations behaving as separate smaller companies within the larger one. The bigger picture of how people in the value stream are negatively impacted eludes the masses. No wonder attacking people – even if in the form of re-training—becomes so immediate and prevalent. Gemba walking processes can bring these otherwise hidden opportunities forward for improvement. You won't see them on quarterly reports, or in emails from employees hesitant to rock the boat. You have to get out of your office and experience the waste for yourself. Employees are intimately aware of the defects, the delays, and the safety issues encountered every day. Gemba walks will be a regular activity if you are interested in absorbing awareness of these burdens and making life easier for employees.

Objective #3 – *Promote a single value stream mentality across the workforce.* Create a situation where all the players in the process are aware of how they can and do negatively impact one another. Employees need to see the big picture and how all the sub-process elements, especially theirs, fit together. Think about this for a moment. If your company produces a widget, do the engineers in design recognize how they impact the folks in production with delays? Have the engineers ever Gemba walked the downstream process? What about design issues making assembly harder? Do those make it to the upstream radar? Do the people in marketing realize how they can impact the people in the shipping department? Does the supply chain group understand the impact on people storing inventory when vast quantities of it show up because of a volume purchasing decision? Or, as is often the case, do the various players focus on their own world, their own goals and objectives, and the workers downstream will just have to fend for themselves? *I've got my own job to worry about.* This is Siloland. Sub-companies on unique, non-collaborative paths. The larger the company and the more geographically dispersed they are, the tougher it gets to help everyone recognize the negative impacts up and downstream. Gemba walking can help reduce this silo mentality by asking questions of the employees. Do they know what happens when they move the item downstream? Do they know if the downstream recipients ever have issues with the manner or quality in which it is received? And do the downstream employees know if any issues are being communicated to the upstream workers? These types of questions will help employees recognize that they do not operate in a vacuum. As the footprint of Siloland is reduced, you get closer to a Single Value Stream mentality. One team, one mission – increasing the frequency of positive customer experiences and making it easier for every employee to perform tasks.

Side Story – A broken process unfolded right before me one day, which immediately made it clear that a Gemba walk was necessary. A gentleman from the IT department was setting up the room for me prior to a training class. I was going to have about 15 people live in the room, and two remote locations would be attending via video conferencing. The equipment was mind-numbing, to say the least. There were two video screens on wheels, three different remote controls, and an assortment of cords. The fun part was the cords. They were encased in a glass cabinet at the base of the stand supporting the screens, with a locked door. The technician had no key, of course, and was struggling with a quarter to attempt a MacGyver technique for unlocking the door. Good thing he had some change. We could see the cords, but not access them. My curiosity kicked in immediately, and I asked him why the cords were locked up in there. Was there a pesky cord thief in the building?

"Hell, if I know," he said.

"Is there a key for the door somewhere?" I asked.

"Probably," he responded, "but I have no idea where it might be."

And so, the poor lad fought the silly thing unsuccessfully until his frustration sparked a more creative approach than a coin to open the lock. He pried the back of the cabinet open (it was high quality, genuine particle board) and pulled the necessary cords out through the gap he created without breaking the cabinet. Success! Well, almost.

After hooking all these crazy cords to this-and-that (dang things were strung all over the place), he asked me the electronic addresses of the two offices remoting into the training. I explained that I didn't know this information, but we had put them on the online room reservation as required; couldn't he just get the numbers from the system?

"Nope. I don't have access to it," he said.

Several phone calls later hunting-and-gathering, we finally had the information he needed. Next, he picked up a remote control in each hand and began a set of instructions which I couldn't replicate had my life depended on it. He was clicking with both hands. "If you need to do this, click this, or click that unless you want this, then you have to click this, and then. . ." Blah, blah, blah. Fortunately, he was willing to just hang around a few minutes after the class started to make sure everything was working correctly.

Let's recap here. The employee was sent to prep a room for video conferencing without the electronic addresses of the remote locations (because someone upstream in the process didn't take into account he needed this information), no key to get the necessary cords out (because the person locking the doors doesn't realize it will negatively impact the IT guy, and the cabinet didn't have visual management telling anyone where the key is), no access to the electronic reservation page used to select the room so he could find what he needed by himself should he need to check, and no instructions for the speaker to operate the dueling remote controls. Have I adequately described a process full of disjointed silos not caring about the other players in the process? This is the complete opposite of a Single Value Stream mentality. It's more of an every-man-for-himself situation. By chance, have you ever encountered those conditions in your world?

By the way, I asked Mr. IT what the third remote control was for, and he said, "You probably won't need it, but you might." My confidence soared. I'm laughing now with this recount but wasn't at the time the crazy broken process was happening.

Even a traditional manager would have an eye-opening epiphany if he/she were to observe this process play out for the worker. Opportunities abound. But alas, this gentleman is probably destined to repeat this frustrating activity over and over with various other hurdles to plow through. It keeps happening, but no one in leadership seems to care enough to seek out opportunities. They will make all kinds of excuses—I'm too busy, I didn't realize this was occurring, the employee should have told me about these hurdles—but the effect remains the same. Flow stops, and players in the values stream are impacted. It is disrespectful to burden employees with a broken process and provide no support to improve it. Seeing his constraints firsthand could have been enlightening for his supervisor, and Gemba walking is how it happens. Learn it, do it often, and get into supplier mode for your employees. Recognize you as the supervisor work for them, the employees. Not the opposite. They don't exist to justify your position. These are the people doing the actual work. Strive to get everyone in the value stream aware of how their process has the unique ability to wreak havoc on downstream tasks.

Not only is the Gemba walker getting the bigger picture here because they walk processes to the left of the one they manage (their internal supplier) and ones to their right (their internal customer), but the players in the adjoining process are learning these connections as well. The Single Value Stream mentality helps them work more as **one** team with a single objective, a single key performance indicator they all contribute to, rather than a hundred silo teams with multiple, disconnected goals. As various managers of the sub-processes begin discussing the broken elements they find on Gemba walks, these discussions turn into cross-organizational process improvement activity. There's nothing like getting everyone on the same page of music to change the annoying cacophony into a harmonious melody. Sounds good, doesn't it?

Objective #4 – *Promote a problem-solving mentality across the entire workforce.* In a very traditional environment, the boss is doing all the thinking and subsequently tosses his/her decrees over the production (or cubicle) wall to resolve undesirable process outcomes. *"What I want you people to do about this defect we are getting is _____."*

The passive minions wait for the wisdom to show up and become conditioned to suppress any temptation to challenge management directives. Culture dictates this is the safest course of action for the frontline worker. Shut-up-and-color keeps you off the radar while rocking the boat puts the spotlight squarely on you. Unfortunately, the former approach ensures insufficient input is on the table when decisions are made. This dysfunction is common, and the tellers (traditional managers) are missing something they might not even be willing to admit if pointed out to them. You have an entire untapped workforce of SMEs (subject matter experts) with insight and creative ideas. In a different culture, they would be eager to contribute, but Mr. Traditional Manager, incorrectly assuming it would be a display of weakness, rarely asks the simplest of questions: *What do you think?*

Just because your employees don't have titles after their name does not mean they lack powerful awareness. On the contrary, chances are extremely high they possess far more insight than you, the boss, is even capable of. Why? Because these critical players in the value stream are in the trenches doing the actual work on a daily basis. They experience defects, delays, and safety issues; you just hear about them secondhand, if at all. Living inside the broken processes, they absolutely know the software system shortcomings, the information likely to be suspect and/or delayed, the undependable pieces of the value stream, the clunky tools, and the cultural (often wasteful) workarounds to circumvent the difficult process conditions you have established for them to work in.

As an aircraft mechanic on a navy carrier, we would hoard/hide replacement parts because the supply process was painfully long and unreliable. We did it to keep aircraft flying and were not aware of the negative impact. We improvised because management was not helping us succeed. Punishment was the go-to countermeasure if we got caught, and you can imagine the amazingly positive impact this would have on the real problem of procuring parts via the established supply chain process. You as the manager are only marginally privy to such things via reports, hearsay, and osmosis. Even if you performed these tasks before promotion into management, are you doing the work now? Have you done it lately? Employees are informed, current-state participants. To not recognize and seek their valuable input is both disrespectful and narrow-minded. But sadly, it happens with alarming consistency in many companies. Employees have come to expect this pecking order as a normal condition and begrudgingly stay in their designated swim lanes. No wonder so many people dread coming to work and watch the clock all day. TGIF doesn't get proclaimed by worker bees without good reason. I've been in jobs where people started counting down the work-hours to Friday on Monday morning. Wednesday even has its own label. Hump day. Get over it, and the agony is all downhill from there.

Conversely, the highly engaged employee does not anticipate Friday afternoons like an upcoming—if temporary—parole. If your employees view work with sheer dread, perhaps you have an opportunity to improve process conditions for them. My friend Ivan was recently presented a question during a job interview. They asked him, "How do you deal with difficult people?" He responded with a question of his own. "Are they really difficult people or just people who are frustrated because they can't get their problems resolved?" Pretty good answer. Notice how it shifts the discussion to a process flaw and not onto the persons in the process.

Armed with this palpable awareness, the savvy Gemba walker shows up with the intent to spark enthusiasm and continuously nurture problem-solving in the employees. They aren't just doing it to be politically correct or patronizing to subordinates; they positively want and need valuable employee input. They fully accept the workers as more informed and intentionally solicit their contribution. Humility plays an **enormous** part in this activity. The Lean leader has dismounted and put their high horse out to pasture. They *want* employee input. They want them in problem-solving mode. They need them resolving issues without waiting for a decree, or in many cases, without even waiting for the boss' green light to proceed with a process change. Crazy talk, right? Without even getting into the resultant increased engagement levels, the time savings alone is significant. Many a supervisor is the bottleneck to a process flow.

The simplicity of one question can set the stage. *What do* **you** *think?* If we polled all American workers (in non-supervisory jobs) to determine how often their supervisor asks them this question, what do you suppose the results would look like? How many would report they have *never* been asked the question by their current boss? As a boss yourself, what is your inclination to pose the question to employees when process outcomes are less than acceptable? Honest, introspective analysis can be the genesis of shifting closer to the Lean leader label. Unless status quo results are good enough and mediocrity is the company goal, you absolutely need employees seeing themselves as active participants in the problem-solving process and co-owners of the processes they work in. If you disagree, I welcome the opportunity to hear your argument to the contrary.

When is the last time you did a Gemba walk to generate higher levels of problem-solving engagement in your employees? Or do you think getting more engaged is the lone responsibility of the employees themselves? Have you done any research on what it takes to intentionally increase engagement levels? When is the last time you even searched for an article or a book on the topic? Does your company have required training to help supervisors learn how to increase engagement levels? Is anyone coaching you on a regular basis as part of the leadership development model in your company? Does coaching exist for every person of formal authority in your company? Is every supervisor actively coaching someone else less experienced than them?

Allow me to share some corroborating evidence from a book I highly recommend, *Carrots and Sticks Don't Work*, by Paul Marciano. He says: "*The extent to which employees are engaged has a lot less to do with them and a lot more to do with their supervisor and the organizations as a whole.*"

This book will shine the opportunity light for you. Please read it more than once. It is well worth the effort for both managers and employees alike. Buy extra copies and hand them out as required reading for anyone interested in exploring the worker/supervisor dynamic. Human beings are not machines void of emotions, and should you treat them as such, you will fail to benefit from even the most basic of psychological realities.

This author compares employee engagement with ownership behavior. Have you ever gone into a mom & pop store, someplace where the folks placing merchandise on shelves actually produce the product or provide the service? Maybe it's handcrafted furniture, a local breakfast place, an antique shop, or photography or artwork emporium. Or perhaps it's a hair salon, and they own the shop as well as serve customers directly. Now imagine you are in this store and have a question about a particular item or service. How long does it take to get someone's attention? How does this owner respond to your question? What is their demeanor, their tone, their energy level to assist you, their overall interest in giving you the answers to the inquiries you brought up? How patient do they seem? To what extent do they process your understanding of their responses and go the extra mile to make sure you are fully aware of the product's design or capability? How respectful do they seem to your thoughts on the product or service in question? *This* is what engagement looks like!

Now imagine the employees in your charge behaving in this engaged manner with the external customers, the internal customers, with each other, and even closer to home, with you. Imagine they are challenging process shortcomings without hesitation or timid filters to keep them out of trouble. Picture the results your processes could achieve if all the employees were behaving as owners because they are *treated* like process owners. This will not happen spontaneously for most employees, and even the ones pre-wired to be engaged will lose momentum in time if not encouraged to contribute. Engagement gets beaten out of people in suppressive atmospheres. If you can even partially accept this as true, then please also recognize engagement can alternatively be developed and nurtured intentionally by the leadership team.

Gemba walking to energize creative thinking is a reality you can choose to embrace fully, dabble in sporadically when you get around to it, or discard altogether. Whatever your view, I invite you to discuss it with your management peers and then pose the question to them: What do you think? Those with humility will want to learn how to Gemba walk and will try to inspire (and eventually coach) others to do the same. The fully entrenched traditional managers will be disinterested to even give it a try. They will cite all kinds of excuses and model apathy, perhaps because their consuming focus is on their own career, not the trivial frustrations of underlings. Which camp are you in? Your employees are waiting for your assistance to help simplify their processes. Your external customers are waiting as well, and continually comparing your process flow and quality with competitors. Does any of this make the agenda on your staff meetings? Are you waiting for someone else to bring it up? The fog continues to build when status quo remains acceptable.

Ok, now that you have a basic understanding of the powerful objectives associated with Gemba walking and how it should be considered a standard behavior for those who choose to lead versus just manage, I'd like to spend some time describing how to plan and conduct one – the actual mechanics of doing it. After all, dispensing a *what* without the *how* would be positioning you for failure, right? Hopefully, I've adequately described the *why*.

The five basic steps are:
1. **Select a process and scope**
2. **Pre-walk communication**
3. **Coordinate the Gemba walkers**
4. **Conduct the walk**
5. **Post-walk**

All essential steps, each with several opportunities to do things incorrectly, so we'll go through them individually. The cycle time of each will plummet as you gain maturity with the activity.

Select a process and scope. Rather than willy-nilly just showing up where the actual work takes place and randomly deciding on what to look at on a whim, the polished Gemba walker will choose a particular process in advance (e.g., packaging process) and identify a specific start and end point (scope) of this selected process (e.g., the point the product leaves the final assembly task to the point boxes are manually taped shut). Having a defined process and scope in advance is critical for several reasons, not the least of which is preventing employees from freaking out when you show up unannounced. It also positions the walker for success by having a plan to follow. This vital preparation allows you to properly conduct the remaining steps with success.

People often ask me the best place in the value stream to start Gemba walking. There is no hard and fast rule, but having done it from both directions, my preference is to start at the end. If you can observe the final stage, then systematically work backward to the beginning of the process with subsequent Gemba walks, you will understand what each step produces (and the associated dysfunctions) because you will have just seen it. If your first walk is at the start – where designs are happening – you will always be wondering what the next deliverable looks like and how people at that stage have to deal with inadequacies. Not a hard-fast rule, just a recommendation from experience. The flow is easier to compartmentalize in your head if you start at the end and systematically work backward to the first domino.

Alternatively, you might be experiencing a painful bottleneck in your process, and this might be the scope of your first walk. Regardless, you want to pick a specific start/end point for a specific walk and then stick to the scope. I usually advise shooting for a 30-minute time slot so as not to overwhelm the workers. Recognize you being there can have the effect of slowing down the process while you are on-site, so a multi-hour Gemba walk is not a good thing for anyone. Also, the employees are not initially going to be comfortable with you being in their world for long stretches. They are not acclimated to this new behavior yet, so be respectful of monopolizing their time. Whatever you do, don't fall prey to the temptation of expanding the scope during a walk because you get the urge. When those crazy thoughts come into your head (during the planning phase or the walk itself), just recall the Nancy Reagan mantra related to scope creep - *Just say NO*. It will serve you well. Smaller scopes are more palatable to everyone involved.

Pre-walk communication. This is pro-active damage control. Once the scope has been identified, you'll know which employees perform tasks within this portion of the larger process. Their tasks are the ones you will be observing. These people need to be alerted in advance you will be coming, what your intent is, and even more important, what your intent is *not*. This is the time to spell it out for them. If employees are not comfortable with leadership coming around in non-crisis situations, they will assume something negative is simmering. You don't want this. They need to know you are there to **learn**, not teach, preach, inspect, punish, or chastise. Leaving this to chance and assumptions is not going to work. You might have them think about process constraints in advance because this is something you are seeking awareness of. What do they have to wait for? What slows them down? What equipment shortcomings do they experience? What frustrates them about the process? It is critically important they understand you are there to see the process firsthand and to help them. Make sure they know no one is going to get in trouble for sharing anything during the walk. You want to capture all opportunities, not just the ones people think are safe to share with leadership. The employees may not fully believe you, but do the best you can on initial walks. Trust rarely happens instantaneously. Remember, they are learning what this is all about along with you unless they experienced it at some other company. You will briefly repeat this communication when you are at the Gemba, but this planning step is to partially assuage their fears in advance of the walk. The operative word here is *partially*.

Caution! If you have never Gemba walked before, these people are not familiar with you, or they are familiar with you but not used to you being in their workspace, do not expect them to be entirely comfortable just because you communicated your intentions in advance of the walk. To some extent, they will remain suspicious of your motives. Who wouldn't? Accept this reality. Live with it and realize establishing strong trust is going to take time. You do the best you can to convey what this Gemba walking activity is all about and be patient as the trust slowly builds. Put yourself in their shoes. The boss just said he/she wants to observe you performing task X. *Oh my gosh, I'm in some kind of trouble!* It's a normal reaction. One walk, or even a few, won't eliminate it completely. Even if you have a decent relationship with the workers, this behavior is brand new to them. Some apprehension is going to be in the air, so the pre-walk communication is critical to offset it as much as possible. If on the other hand, you currently have a poor reputation with the employees, it's time for a large serving of humble pie. Explain to them you have become aware of your poor leadership techniques and are now motivated to change. Don't sugar coat or dance around it! If your process of supervising sucked, then admit it to them. This can go a long way to them giving you another shot. Everyone can change, even the previously entrenched traditional manager – if they are serious about it. If you try to fake the humility, your disingenuous demeanor will shine through. I've seen this play out, and despite my best coaching efforts, some managers cannot admit to themselves that a gap exists in their process of leadership. Arrogance and longevity in positions of authority are a bad combination.

Coordinate the Gemba walkers. Assuming you are not going on this walk alone, all the walkers need to be on the same page of music. They need to know the Gemba walking rules of engagement. Agree on the process, the scope, the questions permissible to ask, the ones entirely off limits, etc. Just like the pre-walk communication to the employees, this is advance damage control. Just because you are an experienced Gemba walker, taking your friend Homer along and expecting him not to ask a taboo question or do something off-limits can be risky. Trust can be damaged in an instant. You need to brief Homer. Decide on the game plan. I highly recommend having an experienced Gemba walking coach go along with you to help when you encounter a new situation. Not only will they be a safety net when you encounter something you're unsure of how to deal with on-site, but they can give you valuable post-walk feedback on your technique. It beats making and not recognizing mistakes because this can destroy trust between you and the employees. Bad habits become entrenched without you even realizing it if a coach is not there to redirect. A coach can help guide you around the potholes. I don't care where on the leadership ladder you are – first-line supervisor or CEO – if you have not explicitly been trained how to properly Gemba walk, accept the fact you likely do not know how to do it. Be humble enough to learn, and the payoff will be substantial. You don't know how to hang glide either. Would you be likely to strap on a rented kite and go over the cliff without some coaching?

You will also want to carefully decide on how many walkers will participate. There are differing opinions on this given the particular environment where the walk will be conducted (large production floor, a cubicle), but just remember size matters. As the quantity of walkers goes up, so too does the apprehension level of people being observed. A Gemba walk is not a Hollywood tour. It is an intimate opportunity for a leader to learn what current state looks like, to find hurdles in the way of his/her employees, support removal of those hurdles, and generate improvement ownership on the part of the employees. This is a significant agenda. Take an entourage, and things will begin to go south. The boss, maybe an upstream internal supplier to the process, perhaps a downstream internal customer, and a coach. That's about it. This is not a spectator sport. As more looky-loos tag along, it significantly complicates the dynamics of the walk. Even if the space can accommodate them, their opportunity to see the task up-close is limited. Peer pressure can come into play. Recognize there is a lot of psychology associated with a Gemba walk. Also, questions coming from ten different people are going to intimidate even the most confident of employees. I've seen walks done with this many people and I sternly advise against it. Picture eight or ten walkers crowding into a cubicle to watch Jessica perform a task on her computer. She's going to need a Valium and a large glass of wine after it's over. If I were her, I'd consume both before the walkers arrived. Think about the workers nearby seeing this dog and pony show. They will be panicked when it's their turn to be observed on upcoming Gemba walks. Make no mistake about it, employees talk to each other. Negative experiences spread and influence future walks. I'm back to Nancy Reagan's recommendation here again; just say NO to large groups.

Conduct the Walk. All your planning is done, and you show up for the walk. Hopefully, your coach has fully prepared you with the behavioral elements to keep in mind for successful Gemba walks. You will need to maintain a healthy level of the following characteristics:

Humility – Remind yourself you are not the process expert here, the employee is. Show it with your questions, your body language, and your overall demeanor. Nobody likes a pretentious know-it-all, so don't go there. If you are not sure you know how to convey humility, then I recommend you not Gemba walk before you learn and practice humility in other settings. Ask your peers to give you some feedback and tips for leaving your ego at the door. Ego on a Gemba walk is a recipe for failure. Employees will pick up on it quickly, and their tendency to be forthcoming will be shot on this and future walks. If you are already viewed as a pompous person, I recommend you ameliorate this condition first, then try a Gemba walk with a very straightforward coach. Convince yourself the employees are far more valuable in the process than you because they do the actual work. Viewing the employees as your customer is an excellent start in generating this humility. Abandon any projection of an Adult-Child relationship. I'm just being honest here to increase your opportunity for success.

"In a humble state, you learn better." – John Doone

Show Respect for the workers – This includes not attacking them for obviously wasteful activity you observe (trust me, you are going to see some), not trying to teach them their job on the spot, not dispensing fixes just because you know the better way to do something, and not conveying the slightest indication this is an inspection – because it isn't. Listen more than you talk. You are there to learn and empower these employees. You are turning on their creative juices. Ask questions but do so with the intent of picking at the process, not the person performing it. Carefully crafted queries will help an employee see their job in a different light. This is absolutely a learned behavior and why I recommend a coach. If your coach lets you get away with person-attacking questions (e.g., *Why are you making mistakes?* versus *Why does the process produce mistakes here?*), your coach needs coaching. Also, important – to be respectful, use the observed person's name when you address them with questions or comments, but don't overdo it. *"Jack, I noticed you have quite a bit of motion waste. Is this how the process was designed, Jack? Tell me what you think about this, Jack."* See my point? Everything has a balance point. Be sensitive to it. Genuine and overtly contrived are on opposite sides of the demeanor fence. You recognize when someone is speaking disrespectfully to you – use this awareness when you talk to employees on a Gemba walk.

Tone can convey disrespect, so be aware of yours. ***THIS*** *is how you assemble the item??* A question like this can immediately make the employee feel like they are at fault (instead of the process you handed them), so be sensitive to not only what you say, but HOW you say it. If they perceive disrespect, they will immediately put their shields up in defense – and this is exactly the opposite dynamic you want. Again…lots of psychology involved in Gemba walking. You will not excel on your first pass.

Attentive Listening – Phil Logsdon, the gentleman who hired me in the first energy company I worked for was probably better at this than anyone I ever worked for or with. He just had a natural knack for doing it well. I'll be honest, most people struggle with it. Attentive listening is actually a form of showing respect to the workers, but it is so critically important I discuss and coach it individually. A Gemba walker needs to practice it often. Those who do it well are maintaining eye contact with the person speaking. They don't interrupt the speaker, do not finish their sentences, and pause momentarily after the speaker has stopped talking before commenting on what was just said. In this case, the speaker is the employee being observed on a Gemba walk. The listener is the walker.

Attentive listening means you are in the moment. You are not pecking on your cell phone just because it beeped or vibrated. Unless there is a life-or-death situation you need to immediately attend to, the emails, texts, and phone calls must be ignored while you are listening to Julia tell you about the things she has to wait on in her process. Julia gets your full and undivided attention, especially if you don't know her well. Your body language can also convey you are not really listening. Looking away from someone's eyes while they are speaking or leaning away from them seems to imply you are not interested in what they have to say. Taking a deep breath, folding your arms, or nonchalantly lifting a finger or hand signals to the speaker an upcoming interruption is cued up. Many people "listening" to someone speak will actually stop processing the incoming information to formulate their upcoming response. This is NOT listening, certainly not attentive listening. You might as well say, *Julia, I need you to shut up now so I can speak*. Julia is no idiot, and she will probably shut up. The walk will be a moot effort from this point forward. Let the employee talk. Let him/her finish before you respond. If you accidentally interrupt them, immediately apologize, then try harder to avoid doing it again. You want to heap respect on them. If they interrupt you, live with it. Show no sense of being offended or demand attentive listening be a two-way street here. This is Gemba walking, not couples counseling. Allow them to continue until they pause again. This walk is about THEM...and far less about you.

I implore you to practice attentive listening before you go on a Gemba walk. You positively **must** learn how to do this. I'm not remotely suggesting you need to do it in every social interaction with human beings, but on a Gemba walk, it's required behavior. If I am your coach, you will most assuredly hear about an infraction during the post-walk feedback. Bad habits can become entrenched quickly, and you will be inclined to repeat or even inadvertently teach them to others. Sometimes an employee will go on and on. Let them! They will pause at some point, and you can insert your questions or comments then. Don't convey impatience, even with your body language. Remember, you are there to learn and generate comfort on the employee's part to identify broken process elements. Your potential discomfort with their rambling is well worth it. Don't show it. They are exploring new territory the same as you are, but their contributions are vastly more important than your comfort. Please read the last sentence back to yourself out loud.

Open Mindedness – Entering the Gemba with an open mind is key to learning things you were not aware of. If you have preconceived notions of defects occurring due to employees not following the documented instructions to the letter, then you are wasting your time and the precious time of the employee performing the task. This notion will limit your ability to see things conflicting with your suppositions. It's called confirmation bias. Anything aligning with your assumptions is collected as confirming evidence. Activity outside your assumption is discarded if seen at all. Again, you are there to *learn*, not *confirm*. You will fall victim to this occasionally but recognize when it happens, it is a red flag to help you do better the next time. Your Gemba walking process should be improving each time you do it. Get feedback from others and ponder the countermeasures to your gaps.

I recommend taking notes during a walk. Most people have selective memories, and good stuff can be lost or incorrectly remembered if you didn't record it. Just make sure the employees are advised on **why** you are writing things down. How would you feel if your supervisor came to watch you perform a task then started writing things down like a detective at a crime scene? Shields up! You might incorrectly assume negative repercussions are coming and your blood pressure would rise instantly. Steer around this pothole with a clear explanation of your recording intent, assuring Julia the notes are only to help you remember the opportunities she presented. Whatever it takes to convey intent and alleviate apprehension. Humor is very beneficial to offset fear, so embrace and use it to your advantage. Something like, "Julia, I'm writing down opportunities you have identified to me so I can make sure none of them escape my dismal memory." This can also convey humility on your part. Language expressing genuine interest makes all the difference. You are not discussing the weather with a stranger you just met on a bus. Convince yourself you are talking to a customer (which you actually are) and allow this to guide your demeanor.

Very important: You **_must_** avoid the overwhelming temptation to dispense fixes, suggest fixes, or ask the employee to comment on a fix you have been considering. _Julia, do you think it would be better if you had a second computer monitor for this task?_ You just conditioned Julia to wait for your ideas rather than generate her own. These potholes are plentiful, and the temptations are common among the novice Gemba walker. Remember, you are trying to turn the workforce into problem solvers, not compliant drones to marvel at YOUR ideas. A much better question, _What would help reduce some of that excessive mousing you mentioned Julia?_, positions the employee to suggest the fix (a second monitor).

Once while coaching a walk, the supervisor said the following to the employee. "Kyle, I notice the computer in your truck takes a while to boot up when you have to enter the data after performing the inspection task on the valve. Don't you think it would be better if you got the computer going first, and then did the valve inspection?"

Recognizing his process of Gemba walking was flawed, I opted to give him unfiltered feedback after the walk. When I pointed out this infraction, he responded with, "I did that?" He honestly didn't realize it. I explained how it conditions employees to defer to suggestions from the boss rather than suggest some of their own – the exact opposite dynamic to shoot for on a Gemba walk. He appreciated my feedback, and hopefully, it impacted subsequent walks he made in the absence of a coach.

I also coach leaders to seek the negative with the wording of questions. Partway through your meal in a restaurant, the waitperson will often ask, "Is everything ok?", or, "Is everything still good here?" The format is seeking a positive response. I once had a waitress in a plain-Jane burger joint say to me, "Is everything fabulous here?" I'm not sure fabulous is even achievable with a burger and fries, but I admired her energy. With this approach, the customer – unless especially displeased with conditions – will respond with _"Yes, thank you,"_ even if there is something they might wish were different. It's as though we are trained to provide the affirmation being sought. We think it would be interpreted as rude if we ask for a new basket of chips because the current batch is all broken. Recognize this gives the waitperson nothing to improve upon. Broken processes will persist in the absence of opportunity awareness. To offset this tendency, I suggest asking the question to seek the negative. _Julia, what tools do you think are_ *missing in this task which might make it easier to do the task if you had them?* This completely different inquiry is better designed to have an employee offer up ideas. I'm explicitly asking what is missing, so they are nudged to tell me. This is how you tease out opportunities, which is what you are looking for in the first place. If an employee tells you there is nothing deficient or frustrating in their process—not a single thing—they are not being truthful. I don't believe a frustration-free process exists. Recognize this as information; a data point. Culture does this to people, and your post-walk agenda is to find out what drove the employee's hesitation to offer up something deficient in their process. I can guarantee you there is something broken, in every process. They might not all have an impact worthy of addressing, but no process is nirvana from the eyes of the person performing it.

I once coached a supervisor who was reluctant to use this technique. His argument was, "If I ask people what is jacked up in the process, they are going to tell me. Imagine the can of worms it might open up!"

After discussing this further, it became evident he was fearful the employees would be bringing up more things than he would be able to address. I assured him this objection was unfounded. First of all, the intent is not to take on the burden to solve employee problems, but conversely to solicit and support *their* ideas. If employees bring up ten hurdles and you can assist with removing just one, this is one thing made easier in their process. *Score*! You'll accumulate points with the employee and the process outcome. This is why it's called *continuous* improvement. I'm sure my explanation didn't eliminate his fears completely, but he did agree to give it a try. Can't ask for more than this.

Please realize none of this behavioral change happens immediately. It takes learning a new habit before the old one is extinguished. Culture change is a forever journey, so be patient, persistent, and stay on the correct path. Even if the remainder of the enterprise is not following the Lean script, it doesn't mean you have to wait for them or throw in the towel. Influence at your own level, in your own organization, and people will begin to notice. Even if peers don't follow suit, so what? At least you know the respectful way employees should be led, and you are walking the talk. You have my respect as a Leader if you take this bold move.

Of course, no book, including this one, can make you a proficient Gemba walker. I'm giving you the foundational elements here. Only frequent practice and honest, introspective analysis make your technique get better. Critique your Gemba walking and ask for input from your peers. No one is great at anything without doing it over and over. Gemba walking (properly) is not easy. Cut yourself some slack on initial walks and realize competence comes with practice. Lots of it. Your coach (hopefully someone who has actually coached Gemba walks before and not just a person thrown into the role without experience) is there to help you avoid the potholes, so be humble enough to listen to feedback. In time, you should be coaching others on the how-to of Gemba walking. It's part of your forever-development as a leader if you are taking it seriously.

Post-Walk. So, you found all this good stuff on your walk. Julia has to walk 100 feet to get raw materials to do her task, and sometimes the bins are empty. The tool she is provided has to be adjusted every day before she can use it. The system she is handed to capture data takes forever to come up and often freezes or goes down. She waits over an hour for information on X before she can complete a task. Whatever you observed on the walk is an *opportunity*, nothing more at this point. It is absolutely not your job to figure out what the fixes are and dispense them. Even if your fixes make things better for the employee, it reinforces the notion of you being the problem solver. You want *them* to begin taking on this role, so your behavior has to align with the objective. Consequently, the post-walk activity is equally as critical to do correctly.

Opportunities will fall into a few buckets. **JDIs** (just-do-its) are really obvious things which can be inserted immediately because the root cause and countermeasures are no-brainers. Julia identified her cycle time would go down if she was permitted to store her raw material directly next to the task. So, you encourage her to do exactly that. Her idea, her fix, her task to insert unless she needs assistance. This is where your managerial stroke comes in. If she needs materials purchased, make it happen for her. If she doesn't need your help, back off. Let her do it. You determine this by asking her. "What do you need from me, Julia." And by the way…make sure you let Julia know she has your full support moving things around to accommodate her own efficiency. Permission is not required.

Then there are **RIEs** (Rapid Improvement Events). Julia said her computer system goes down unexpectedly and causes her to wait. The impact is worthy of engaging here, but we don't know the root cause, and consequently, we don't know what the countermeasure(s) should be. This is an opportunity to build a team (including Julia) to use structured problem-solving (like the 8-step model) to dig into the whys.

The third bucket of items will be things with unworthy impacts, likely going into the no action required bucket. Maybe Julia mentioned some of the hardware in her bin does not meet the quality standard, but she also says there are sufficient acceptable bolts to keep her process moving. She alerts the supervisor when it happens, but currently, there is no delay. This is an opportunity, but the impact is negligible. It's best to spend precious process improvement resources on things with broader, more impactful consequences. Lower impact issues can take a back seat for a while. Of course, you will explain this to Julia, including the why. Do not leave out the why! If she disagrees with your assessment, listen intently to her argument with an open mind. She might be aware of an impact you are overlooking, and the decision to move forward is back on the table. Remind yourself repeatedly – she understands the constraints in a way you do not – so *listen* to her.

An unacceptable why is, "*Julia, we're not going to address this particular opportunity because I decided not to.*" A far better explanation would be, "*Julia, we decided not to* *address this opportunity because the impact is only $8/month, and the other opportunities you brought forward are far more important at this time."* Notice how this ties credit back to her for the other issues she brought up. You are now showing respect to her. Explaining the "Why" is a change management technique people can get on board with. Saying no because you are just saying no is command/control mode, and disrespectful. It promotes an adult-child relationship. Discard this caveman tendency from your behavioral repertoire. Always keep in mind you are shifting from dictating manager to servant leader. Julia is your customer; you are her supplier.

If you fundamentally disagree with this alignment, your progression from manager to leader will never occur. There is simply no other way to say it.

The last bucket of opportunities are issues requiring more research. More information needs to be gathered before any path forward is even considered. Julia told you the lighting above her workstation goes out often and then comes back on by itself. The impact is a temporary work stoppage while she waits, so this is worthy of attention. It's going to take some inquiry to understand the situation better. Being the diligent Gemba walker you have become, you avoided the temptation to insert the fix immediately coming into your own head (replace the light fixtures). It's tempting because you want the employee to recognize you are in their camp but jumping to conclusions without root causes is the wrong move. Strive to not model wasteful behavior in front of the employees on a Gemba walk. If more research is required, this should be assigned immediately. Get someone (perhaps yourself, but not Julia) moving on this. The employee's job is to perform the task you just Gemba walked, not spend time troubleshooting an intermittent overhead light. Delegate this work to a support person instead of tasking the value-adder to do it.

The most important thing to keep in mind here is to give the employee feedback on the status of opportunities identified during the walk which required your assistance. This is a hard-fast rule of Gemba walking. *You need to provide status updates 100% of the time, and promptly.* If you get busy and don't let Julia know — even if you are diligently researching what is occurring behind the scenes — she might assume you either didn't listen or don't care. This will derail the Gemba walking activity for everyone involved. People's perceptions are their reality. Piss Julia off, and your next walk with her is not going to yield nearly as much fruit as it could. Trust will be damaged. She might now consider your Gemba walking behavior an obligatory goal to check a box. She doesn't really think you are there to help her. *Another worthless manager just wasting my time.* And don't kid yourself into thinking you tarnished only Julia's opinion. Employees talk. She will share this with peers, and the negative perception will spread. It makes perfect sense, and the employee is justified, even if her perception is totally off track. Your Gemba walking process failed. So, regardless of the decisions on opportunities, keep employees informed. If the opportunity is to be abandoned due to low or no impact, explain the WHY to them. Dispense your decision to not pursue something without the why, and your process has failed yet again. I recommend your first choice is to do this in-person (if at all possible), or by phone. If those are not viable options, then by email or text. Do NOT delegate this to someone else like your administrative assistant. The employee will interpret this as disrespectful. Bottom line here, you found some opportunities to help Julia's process become easier to accomplish and at the same time empower her problem-solving skills; don't waste this precious chance to build trust and engagement.

One other thing I'd like to share about my experiences Gemba walking. This stuff is *fun*! I thoroughly enjoy them. Abandoning a day of boring meetings, getting out there watching people perform their jobs at the Gemba, learning how a process plays out, seeing tasks get accomplished by the real experts, helping remove hurdles in the way, leaders gaining capability and value stream awareness they never had before—how can you not enjoy participating in *that*? Leaders I've coached have expressed concern they will not be able to find enough time to Gemba walk, but as they do a few and get the hang of it, they want to do even more. What can be more rewarding? You will begin to prioritize it over other activities once viewed as critical. It becomes the true essence of behaving in supplier-mode.

While coaching a few back-to-back walks one day, a VP in the northeast part of the country said to me, "I was concerned I couldn't find time for this activity but now realize this is what I **should** be doing." *Score*! It warmed my heart just to hear those words from him. I hope he is following through on <u>the</u> most important behavior any supervisor can regularly be doing. Cultures don't improve with emails emanating from corporate towers; they begin shifting with respectful leadership behavior at the Gemba.

The question about how to get supervisors to begin the activity of Gemba walking has come up in discussions. Some would argue setting a specific number of walks in a month is an effective goal/nudge to incentivize the new behavior, but my perspective on this has changed over time. I now believe the more appropriate goal would be to get a collaborative agreement on the number of process hurdles each supervisor will assist in removing/reducing in a period of time. Defining a specific number of walks might initially result in box checking, but actually marching to a number of hurdles removed is targeting the objective of Gemba walking, instead of just the walks themselves. Consider this approach on your companies' new journey of shifting behavior and marching to hurdles reduced as a way to measure the extent your lean needle is moving.

Gemba walking is magical when done correctly. Leaders who have already incorporated it into their standard day know exactly what I'm talking about. Nothing new here to them. Well done, you avid Gemba walkers. My admiration goes out to you for considering your employees and their job conditions more important than your own world demands.

"The growth and development of people is the highest calling of leadership." – Harvey Firestone

Change Management

"I cannot say whether things will get better if we change; what I can say is they must change if they are to get better." - Georg C. Lichtenberg

Let's say you have decided to infuse the magic of the Lean business system into your company. Congratulations! You have made a command decision with the potential to take you to unimaginable levels of excellence, both in customer service and cultural reputation. The wow-factor is awaiting you. That is if you do it properly. So how do you introduce this to the masses and get their buy-in? You need to be proactive and diligent about this with a carefully crafted message, not just at the launch-point, but throughout the journey as new employees come on board. It can't be accomplished with a few impersonal emails, speeches, and some voluntary training classes. Nor can it be delegated to a select few leaders in a transformation office or a director of quality to carry out. Ask the Disney corporation who is responsible for sanitation in their theme parks, and they will tell you every single employee. This is why they are immaculate all-day long. You need to be immersing your entire enterprise with a designed methodology to show people you are serious about Lean, and the option to behave disrespectfully will no longer be excused in this culture. Modeling the behavior constantly is essential, and not just by a few managers. All of them need to be on the Lean bus, so individual contributors don't experience guidance variability or a sense of hypocrisy in their supervisors. Suffice it to say, if your CEO is not leading this charge as the foremost champion, it will have no chance of long-term sustainment. At best, a few pockets of excellence will glow for a while. A passionate, humble champion is absolutely necessary, so this person's buy in must be secured at the onset.

Caution – Be aware of a deep pothole up ahead!

Traditional managers rebelling against the shift—whether in the form of overt refusal to become Lean leaders or just lackadaisical application of the desired behaviors—should not be permitted to stay. No exceptions. Recognize some of them will fake it for a while in the hopes this latest flavor-of-the-day will die out. Some will act like they are on board in public settings, but behavior with their employees will be incongruent with the model. The new behavioral standard needs to be communicated with crystal clarity across your enterprise. If allowed to remain, they will be a debilitating infection, and you can't afford to let them negatively influence your newly planted Lean tree. Those trying to practice the new behaviors will look at their non-compliant peers and wonder what the deal is. The model needs to apply across the board, not just for the ones humble enough to recognize their previous approach was not working to fully engage employees. I simply don't know how to convey this with enough emphasis. I don't care how much seniority the outright resistors have, or how fond of them you might be as friends, they have to genuinely shift or go away. Tough choices, I know, but I will not sugarcoat what I have learned on my Lean journey. Temporary amnesty cannot be perpetual. Should you wonder if a manager is actively changing their traditional behaviors, you need only ask their employees.

Recognize goals and metrics will now need to be aligned with the intent of Lean progressing. Internal VOC gets collected everywhere, turned into performance indicators, and the effort to nurture a single value stream mentality begins. People need to see themselves as one team, with one mission, not twenty. This will allow your workforce to maintain awareness of their collective progress. It stays on a front burner, not some sub-agenda talked about during the last 30 seconds of your quarterly town hall meeting. If you are not willing to use the language in your strategic plan as a company, then plan on confusion and disinterest (or unawareness) from many. Continuous Improvement + Respect for People can't be just a small portion of your strategy on page seven, it needs to **_BE_** the strategy. Anything short of an all-out effort, and you will see the transformation takes far longer than necessary if it happens at all. You just can't throw something over the wall to an audience improperly informed about it (or partially supported) and expect employees to immediately rally around it.

Condition Desired	**What** makes it happen	**How** does it happen	**Why** we are doing it
Process improvement happening daily based on VOC	Widespread desire and respect for employee input on process design	Supervisors soliciting broken process elements constantly	To align with the new vision of empowering employees as valued contributors

People need to understand the various desired conditions the company is shooting for, **what** makes the conditions happen, **how** they will be pursued, and, most important, **why** the condition is being targeted. Leave out the why, and employees will fill in the blanks on their own. They might assume this new activity is a precursor to a reduction in force or something else associated with slashing costs. This will short-circuit your efforts. Honest transparency is your friend to help prevent the need for damage control. I suggest creating a simple table to intuitively communicate the plan elements, then post it everywhere. The table shown has only one element for illustrative purposes. Yours will include more but shouldn't become visually overwhelming. Pile on too much information and your audience will stop processing it. Understand this table will be bare-bones information. The more in-depth communication effort will need to be done in person and include what employees' minimal expected behavior will look like (example: expectation to openly identify wasteful process elements).

Having seen all of this done poorly on more than one occasion and the consequences that followed, I can attest to the value of embracing change management as a critical planning element for planting the tree. Half-hearted efforts yield half-hearted results. More than a year into the "transformation" in my government job, a manager asked me what I thought of the transformation momentum to date. My immediate response to him was, "We have a transformation underway?" I was clueless. Nothing had been communicated formally to the enterprise, certainly not to me. Word of mouth is not your first choice with such a dramatic endeavor. Would you move your family to a different city and not tell them the destination or the vision of why you are all going there?

Understandably, a workforce presented with a dramatic new plan will be contemplating one overriding question in their heads: *What's in it for me?* People are curious by nature, and when we hear the culture is shifting directions, we want to know, with good reason, how we will be impacted. The WIIFM question needs to be addressed without waiting for people to pose it. Don't assume just because you described what a Lean environment looks like and how leadership will be expected to behave the entire workforce will jump for joy and wave rally pennants. Recognize for many of them the language is brand new, let alone the behavioral connections. Do what is necessary to be sensitive and patient to their confusion. If you can tell me the WIIFM of a Lean environment, and I believe you are sincere because I am now seeing tangible examples of your new behavior matching the message, watch me participate. Try to influence me with deception, hypocrisy or cryptic explanations, and I will opt out, perhaps even sabotage the effort. It's just how human beings are wired. Also, be prepared for some to exit. This is a radical shift. Some are too entrenched in command/control methodologies and will be unwilling to acclimate to Lean. Giving up dictatorial authority threatens their sense of importance. Plan on some of this and deal with it swiftly and consistently in alignment with your communication plan. Do not leave this to an improvised reaction.

My sternest recommendation is to get your entire leadership team aligned first. They need to clearly understand what the intended environment will look like, how they contribute as co-champions with conversations with their direct reports, and the consequences of not participating. I'm not suggesting a list of punitive actions here, but rather a comprehension of the undesirable outcomes from a less than all-hands effort. Perhaps you might even enlist the assistance of professional change management persons if the company is large enough. I would also recommend a respected change management model like the Prosci ADKAR to guide the behavioral shift. The acronym steps stand for:

Awareness of the need for change
Desire to support the change
Knowledge of how to change
Ability to demonstrate skills and behaviors
Reinforcement to make the change stick

One year after the launch you shouldn't have a single employee respond to your question with, *"We have a transformation underway? Transformation to what?" Did you send me the memo?"*

I've barely touched on the topic of change management because there is so much to it. Entire books have been devoted to it. Suffice it to say it needs to be formally on your radar before you pull the trigger on any significant change in your company, and most assuredly with a Lean transformation effort. Under the best of circumstances, shifting from traditional management styles to mandatory Lean leadership can be daunting. Having said this, I firmly believe the only thing more difficult than establishing Lean leadership across an enterprise is living with the relentless firefighting of a status quo, traditional environment.

"Change will not come if we wait for some other person or some other time. We are the ones we've been waiting for. We are the change that we seek." - Barack Obama

Polar Extremes Dealing with Workplace Issues

"It's our choices . . . that show what we truly are, far more than our abilities." - J.K. Rowling

Command/Control mode. Self-serving		Servant mode. Is committed to developing employees
Decrees changes to processes without VOC or employee input		and processes to their fullest by continuously reducing waste
Creates an atmosphere of fear and retribution for mistakes		all based on Voice of the Customer (VOC)
Prefers employees who do what they are told without pushback		
Traditional Mgr		Lean Leader

Throughout the recount of my journey of enlightenment, I have talked about the extreme approaches of traditional managers as opposed to Lean leaders. What are the impacts of one style over the other? Again, these labels are at opposite ends of a spectrum, 180 degrees apart (thus the protractor), and not the limit of buckets to categorize behavior. Most people assigned jobs with formal authority behave somewhere in between the extremes and will oscillate back and forth given the situation they are dealing with. But, to help you recognize the dramatic differences, I'd like to share how the behavior varies for those leaning (yes, I said *LEAN*ing) in one direction or its polar opposite. As you digest the disparity of behavioral tendencies, recognize traditional management is costing you money in many different business processes. Every time an employee quits because a traditional manager destroyed their sense of value, the company culture degrades a little bit more.

ISSUE	TRADITIONAL MANAGER	LEAN LEADER
Customer Requirements	Assume, or ask once	Ask, Measure, Ask again
Performance Indicators	Absent, Hidden, or Batched	Posted, Updated, Discussed
Ugly Process	Spin it, Blame others	Embrace the ugly
Employee Input	Unwanted, Tolerated	Actively solicited, Reinforced
Process Performance Gap	Dispense fixes	Support teams to address it
Problem Solving Training	Non-existent	Widespread
Employee Engagement	Hire fresh bodies	Show respect constantly

Customer Requirements. Every customer (internal and external) has requirements for the products and services they seek from suppliers, but this information (VOC) is not necessarily sought out and communicated to employees by Mr. Supplier or given unsolicited by Ms. Customer. Having worked in a lot of job environments during my lifetime, for a slew of managers with varying degrees of care for employees, I was never presented the specific customer requirements up front without asking for them at some point. I came to work and did what I was told. The donuts got made. It was a job. My agenda was to get paid, not improve processes to better meet VOC. Who thinks about this when they accept a job? Culture promotes this demeanor, and I was as clueless as my counterpart minions trying to stay out of trouble and off the bosses' radar. That is until my eyes became open to Lean in 2000.

The traditional manager will make assumptions. (*"Our customers probably want this and will love that other thing because it came to me in a dream during our last staff meeting."*) Even if they do formally ask the questions to customers, it is outside their broken process to return periodically and ask again. Customer requirements change over time, and without advance notice, processes will fall behind. You will be providing X when, in reality, your customer now requires Y. They begrudgingly tolerate X, but only while they seek out a Y supplier. When you do get this awareness—probably from complaints or plummeting sales—the requisite response to update the process will be far more burdensome than if had you known in advance. Firefighting is your go-to approach. Cue the emergency meetings and overtime.

Conversely, the Lean leader keeps this fluid process on their radar constantly. They maintain an intentional dialogue with customers to prevent panic situations. When requirements are about to shift—even if only temporarily—they begin altering processes in preparation without the hair-on-fire reaction of their counterpart traditional managers.

I've had many a student ask me, *So, what do you do if your customer doesn't know what they need or want?* Excellent question. I wish I had tallied the number of times it was posed to me in a classroom setting. Students (and people in general) tend to want organized steps with great specificity. *Tell me exactly what to do.* Unfortunately, it takes some effort to achieve just the right combination of elements to remedy conundrums like this. Typically, I suggest sitting down with customers and explaining what you provide now and the adjusted options you might be able to offer. Critically important, help them differentiate a **need** from a **want**. These are two different things. This will help them analyze their current needs and spark dialogue for alterations on both sides. It might turn out the customer is needing something you are currently incapable of producing. Opportunity! Energize the brilliant minds you have in the company (as opposed to addressing this by yourself) to research the possibilities your customer just sparked. Maybe it's feasible, maybe not, but until you have the discussions with customers, you remain in delayed reactionary mode. Or worse yet, you simply guess their needs and throw things over the wall. Now you're in wish-and-hope-mode. Good luck with that.

And please don't tell your customers, *Sorry, but that just isn't how we do things,* or, *we are not capable of reducing your wait time on the phone to under one minute.* Take the challenge for what it is, set it as your organizational goal to work toward, and start closing the gap a little at a time. Pacman didn't eat every dot on the screen in one giant gulp. Consider this metaphor when you begin to digest the meaning of continuous improvement. Lean leaders do. Even if you never reach this seemingly impossible goal, so what? It's highly likely can you get just a little bit closer to it than you are currently. Your customer has spoken to you. **Listen to them!** Take the opportunity and run with it. If you don't, some competitor eventually will. Traditional managers settle comfortably into the status quo as if the world around them will remain constant. Nice fantasy, but not realistic. The only constant in business is the reality of continuous change. Lean leaders are proactively analyzing shifting tides and respond to continuous change with continuous improvement.

As a consumer of products and services yourself, when is the last time you can recall a provider asking you for inputs on your requirements and preferences? Perhaps a survey or some other method was used after renting a car or using an airline, or even at your local stores and restaurants. Some organizations capture your input as a rule, others by exception when their service has fallen far short of expectations resulting in some ugly feedback. But in either event, do they alter the process with structured problem solving, or just file the survey results away? VOC information without subsequent process improvement effort is just window dressing and a waste of time to collect, but it happens with frequency from providers not immersed in the mentality of continuous improvement.

Something else to consider: to what extent have you communicated this vital information to the employees doing the actual work? Do they know precisely what customer needs are, when these needs are about to change, and the whys associated with both? Or do you just dispense admonishments when desired outcomes are not achieved? The traditional manager will find excuses and justifications for not shifting into alignment with VOC and/or not communicating across the enterprise. How is it possible you are installing conduit throughout a rural neighborhood in preparation for high-speed internet service and your sales department has zero information about it? Status quo is always the easier path but will rarely deliver ever-increasing competitive advantages. The Lean leader knows better. He/she will forever keep this activity on a front burner, seeking customer requirements often, transparently communicating them to employees in the value stream, measuring VOC performance, and then asking again. They support teams to reduce performance gaps and encourage employees to maintain watchful eyes for any waste creeping into the process, so processes are continuously improving to meet VOC more efficiently. This is 180 degrees out from their Fred Flintstone counterpart whose focus is on the next promotion and who they have to schmooze to attain it. Customer requirements are an ever-changing threshold, and the Lean leader is all over it. They view it no differently than preventive maintenance on the car they desperately rely on for transportation. Waiting for it to break down before addressing issues is not a reliable plan. They also recognize promotions will come naturally as they demonstrate true leadership skills by positioning employees for success to meet VOC requirements. Their supplier-customer priorities are straight.

Performance Indicators. Let's go out on a Lean limb and assume you have captured current VOC. Good first step. Take the rest of the day off with pay. But, if you don't turn the information into performance indicators, you will remain unaware of the extent to which you satisfy those captured customer requirements. You might blindly assume all is right with the world until it is not. Recall the car with no gauges in the dashboard. The traditional manager is focused on getting things done, widgets completed, tasks/goals decreed to minions, employees re-trained when mistakes happen, digesting reports, and a plethora of other activities deemed descriptive of their job. But, quantified VOC performance indicators directly measuring how customer requirements are being met is not on their to-do list, let alone making sure employees are aware of the status Or, they have some metrics, but because of batched reviews, process conditions will reach unacceptable levels between review periods. Insert panic mode, overtime and firefighting. Maybe even hire a new batch of employees to get you over the hump, and when the fire is sufficiently tamped down, you can lay them off. It can be a vicious cycle.

The Lean leader model is the complete opposite of this disrespectful insanity. After capturing the VOC requirements, they convene teams composed of people doing the actual work. Then, using a structured process, the team translate the requirements into measurable indicators to continuously highlight performance gaps and trends. Let's say Mr. Customer said they hated your phone menu system when calling in for assistance. But, they believe they could live with it if you were able to 1) connect them to a human being within 60 seconds, 2) ensure the first person they speak with can resolve the issue without transferring them to another "specialist", and 3) keep them (the customer) updated on status of issue resolution without having to call back and tell the story all over again with a new phone person.

Armed with this specific VOC, the team developed performance indicators and began to measure their process. It seems the cycle time to reach a human being can be up to 90 minutes (ranging from 15 – 90 minutes on 2500 data points), reaching the resolution employee initially happened zero times on all 2500 data points, and employees calling customers back with resolution status occurred 35 of 2500 times due to their individual initiative rather than a standard process. Now we know how the car is performing.

The Lean leader (he/she has transformed from the label of manager and now deserves to be called leader) has posted intuitive charts on walls in the work area, keeps them updated, and ensures employees are constantly aware of how their process is doing in alignment with VOC requirements. Daily huddle meetings occur where the information is posted, and there are discussions centered on the process improvement activity to close gaps. Ask any employee how their process is doing, and they can tell you quantifiably on each element of VOC. They can also tell you what is being done to close the gaps because they are on the teams working to do this. The leader acts as a sponsor to the structured problem-solving activity and doesn't dispense his/her own fixes.

Awesome! Now you are on track to improve the customer and the employee experience. Continuous improvement is a reality rather than a propaganda mission. The difference to the workers is profound. Stand ready to witness organizational success resultant from their engagement.

Ugly Process. This can be quite embarrassing to a traditional manager. The daily corporate objective is to remain in good graces with upper management and a disparaging report highlighting some process out of control will need to be spun into a more favorable (or even false) light. Damage control is the agenda here, not actual root cause analysis and countermeasure insertion by a team of subject-matter-experts. No time for such minutiae. Protecting one's reputation is paramount. A meeting composed of only management will be convened, and fixes pulled out of thin air will be the likely deliverables. If the blame can be shifted to someone else or another organization, all the better. This might even add to someone's corporate status. An alternative demeanor is unrealistic. Attacking people versus the process has become the go-to method in the caveman culture. *"Who is responsible for this ugly process? I want names!"* Someone must be held accountable, or we are not doing our jobs as managers. It happens far too often, and people entrench it when they move into positions of higher and higher authority. Dysfunctional, yes, but fortified cultural norms will pressure people to conduct the process as socially acceptable. They will play the game according to whatever rules senior leadership models. Follow the guy in front of you, we are on a mission. The question is, to where?

In 2017, the Navy had just experienced another collision at sea. An ugly process, for sure. The immediate response was to fire the vice admiral of the 7th fleet.[xxi] My heart sank (pun intended) when I learned of this rash decision. Allow me to offer my potentially biased and no doubt only partially informed opinion. The likelihood of this countermeasure (replacing the admiral) eliminating collisions at sea is zero. Zilch. This was purely a punitive action to hold some person accountable, as though it was tied to a root cause and will, therefore, eliminate the undesirable outcome. *Ridiculous* is the kindest word I can muster up for the decision. I'm sure process measures will be considered and implemented, but this Admiral was not sitting around his desk thinking, *"Hmmm. I wonder what I can do to make a couple more ships run into each other?"*

The point is this: The Navy likely had no direct evidence of this Admiral <u>intentionally</u> and with malice doing something specific which led to these collisions. The **_process_** of ships operating in proximity of each other at sea was broken, perhaps is still broken, but they chose to attack the person first. Perhaps a statement was given like, *"Well, if he had been doing his job properly, the accidents would* *not have occurred.*" General assumptions like this are shifting the blame onto a person versus the broken process. It not only addresses the wrong thing, but it creates a conditioned culture of screw-up-and-your-butt-is-fired. Recognize how fear will generate reluctance to try new things. Creativity? Forget that! Continue marching in the safe lane.

I know virtually nothing about this admiral, but I can guess he was acting with the best intentions to create a safe environment for the people under his command. Mind you, his process failed miserably, but I refuse to concede the possibility this man had intentionally contributed to the collisions. No one person can do anything to prevent all the ships in their command from ever having an accident, short of parking all the big grey boats. To blindly think removing one (or more) well-intentioned employees will eliminate any undesirable outcome is caveman management. A similar scenario played out in the Veterans Administration without erasing the original problem of veterans waiting ridiculously long periods of time to see a physician. Firing an individual for malicious behavior is appropriate, but how often is this the case? If it doesn't remove the possibility of the undesirable outcome from occurring again, the countermeasure was ineffective. No other way to say it. And if the person was acting with malicious intent, what does that say about the selection process that put this person in-place?

Side Story - In 1975, as a young lad of 19 years of age in the Navy, I had the unique opportunity to witness a collision at sea first-hand. I was on the USS Saratoga, an aging aircraft carrier designed for a small fraction of the 5000 sailors we had on-board. During a routine refueling process—hoses strung between the two moving ships so we could take on more diesel to propel our floating behemoth through the water—the USS Mississinewa encountered a dramatic malfunction with her steering mechanism. I was walking back from an unappetizing meal and could see the unfolding chaos from the hangar deck opening. A couple of sailors stood on the sponson—a small, porch-like extension from the side of our ship over the water on which people could stand to perform this task. The Mississinewa was violently rising up and down, and on each downward path, it struck the starboard side (that's the RH side for you landlubbers) of the Saratoga. The transfer lines were either disconnected at this point, or ruptured, and fuel was being sprayed all over the place. Nothing like the addition of diesel fuel when massive steel-on-steel collisions are occurring. The fact that we avoided a fire, an explosion, or serious injury to any sailors was sheer luck. The noise alone of the repeated contacts between the ships was terrifying. It was like a scene in a disaster movie. People were scurrying about with chaotic urgency, obviously without pre-trained structure or thought out intent. It was an intense moment, to say the least. I had no idea in the world how to assist in minimizing the horror show. This wasn't even the most dramatic incident I witnessed during my Navy days, but I'll save the fatality stories for another forum.

Now to the point of my story. It's important to recognize the captain of the Mississinewa was not on the bridge saying, *"Hold my beer and watch this!"* It was highly unlikely he had malicious intentions, and also unlikely any single individual was at fault for the collision. On the contrary, multiple ***processes*** failed on this day. Perhaps their maintenance process failed to replace defective steering components because of some unknown root cause. Maybe things in the steering mechanism were put back together incorrectly after the last maintenance action was performed, also with an unknown root cause. I'm making things up here to illustrate my point. Even if it was determined they didn't adhere to periodic maintenance schedules and procedures, the WHYs are still unknown. To stop at a physical cause (the steering pin broke) or a person cause (Chief Bubba decided not to do the maintenance until after this refueling activity) will yield countermeasures attacking preliminary physical components (replace the pin with a stronger unit) or the people element (put Chief Bubba on report, demote him three pay grades, and reduce his alcohol consumption to a 12 pack daily). Note these deficient analyses stopping points will result in correspondingly deficient countermeasures. Nothing has been done to prevent undesirable outcomes in the future because the process itself remains the same. This is caveman problem-solving. I understand it's a 3-credit hour elective management class at UC and comes with an engraved club to discipline malcontents.

Let's follow the people-blaming path here to illustrate there is virtually no place to stop. We could fire the ship's captain because he was in charge at the time. Then we could fire his boss and his boss' boss for selecting these flawed individuals who would allow a collision to occur. Obviously, the Secretary of the Navy needs to be fired, and well, the President of the United States picked the secretary, so he needs to go, too. What about the shipbuilder? If they hadn't built the ships in the first place, none of this would have happened. Perhaps they are at fault for not designing a ship which could sustain collisions without damage. Should we, therefore, go further to the left in the value stream and blame the steel supplier who gave the shipbuilder raw materials? Now we're getting somewhere. I hope you can see the madness of this ridiculous excursion to Peopleland. Without intentional malice, people are not at fault—processes are. Attacking people might make you feel better and satisfy the accountability agenda, but if the situation ever repeats, it is proof-positive your approach was a waste of time. Traditional managers will be repeating the same useless countermeasures for incident #2, and then incident #3. Be thankful Peopleland is not the preferred destination in your company.

The lessons to be learned from sharing this adventure from my Navy days are threefold:

1. Under the best of design conditions and with stringent forethought to prevent negative consequences, some processes will fail. Short of a robust

mistake-proofing process change, or terminating a process completely, undesirable outcomes at some level of impact can eventually occur.

2. If your reaction process to an undesirable outcome is not done correctly, with someone trained in root cause analysis to attack the process, future outcomes will replicate previous undesirable outcomes.

3. Until you recognize your incident investigative process is broken (by virtue of immediately seeking heads to whack), people will behave in self-preservation mode. They will be protecting their job with cautiously answered questions or avoid offering up any insight due to fear of retribution rather than openly challenging broken processes with the proactive intent of making improvements before adverse outcomes manifest again. Now *that's* an ugly process! People who commit crimes will cautiously answer questions from the police to avoid prosecution. Employees in broken process who were just part of an undesirable process outcome should not have to behave this way. If self-preservation is the objective, real discovery of root causes will be exceedingly difficult to achieve.

So how would a Lean leader deal with an ugly process? He/she would embrace it! In a mature Lean environment, it would be seen as an opportunity to improve a *process* and make things better for the workers and customers alike. Punishment isn't even on the radar until it is established someone acted with intentional malice. There exists no decree from on-high to deliver heads on a plate. People don't freak out wondering who will be immediately admonished or fired, so they recognize there is no need to clam up and hide the unfiltered process facts. The Lean leader would have someone generate a strong problem statement, including what process failed, identification of the defect noted in the process, the prevalence of this defect, where the brokenness occurred in the company or process, and what timeframe this brokenness (if ongoing) has been happening. You'll also need a corresponding impact statement (the financial consequences of the broken process including rework and customer degradation, if present), along with the other logical, structured elements populated on an 8-step problem-solving model A3. All activity would focus on improving the *process*, so the undesirable outcome will never happen again or be much less likely to occur. This is accomplished with the subject-matter-experts in the process and not by the manager in isolation. The difference in this world is dramatic. *Processes* are held accountable, and people making mistakes in them are not immediately assumed causal elements to be punished. Outstanding, dedicated workers in a broken process will fall victim to defects, delays, and safety issues because they are operating in processes riddled with opportunities to fail. Even a traditional manager should not be fired until they demonstrate unyielding retention of their dictatorial methodologies. The process of behaving with an ugly management process can be improved when humility and willingness are present.

Employee Input. The most extreme of traditional managers have no need for input from the worker bees. They believe their role as explained to them at UC is to digest problems in isolation from the less advanced on the authority ladder and decree solutions pulled from years of experience, or, in lieu of personal historical data in their work history, pluck one from thin air. Presented with conviction in a public setting, conditioned observers will board the bus to Crazyland without hesitation. It sounds so reasonable, let's do what the boss just said. Of course, when this notion fails to remedy the situation or the undesirable outcome occurs again, bosses stand ready to bark out the next insightful fix to the compliant workers. The process repeats with painful predictability, and the drones stay in their respective swim lanes. There is nary a bold challenger at the table who will offer up, *"Say, boss, can you tell us what root cause this countermeasure is intended to address?"* This would be equivalent to proclaiming the boss has a flawed process. Traditional managers don't want unsolicited input, and they wouldn't consider wasting precious time asking for it or delving into root causes when they can simply spew out a fix and minions will react. Even in the best of situations when the fix does indeed resolve the condition by chance, I claim the manager's process is still dysfunctional in design because it conditions employees to wait for each fix and to not speak up until formally solicited to do so. UC managers will tolerate some input if given unsolicited, but it is seen as coming from the uninformed, and thus not really mixed into the decision-making process. *I listen to your words to be polite in a public setting, but they will have no influence on my decision. I might even thank you for your ideas—all meaningless feedback to make you think I consider you a relevant player in this process.*

Notice the process this boss is utilizing does not define him/her as an uncaring person. They are merely conducting business as usual. Their cultural education has set these rules in stone. Asking employees for input would be equivalent to admitting the boss doesn't have a warehouse of fixes for every malady. This would be a sign of weakness and must be avoided at all costs. *I don't want employees thinking I am a weak leader. It is my job to know what to do and dispense fixes to the workers.* This is the natural order of traditional authority.

Recall my story about the boss who decreed all customer requests for process improvement go through him for authorization to proceed. He positively thought this was the right thing to do. Not only would it solve the assumed problem spontaneously generated from his reasoning process, but it would send a definitive message about who was in charge. Equivalent to a dog peeing on trees, he was marking his turf and displaying authoritative posturing. Let there be no mistake of who the decision maker is. Your input is both unwanted and irrelevant.

I once offered input on the interview process in an organization I worked in, only to be told, *"It is not your place to offer suggestions on the hiring process."* I had ideas on how to structure the interview questions to filter for applicants with more Lean experience than strictly Six Sima backgrounds. Obviously, this unsolicited input was not appreciated. Informal demerits were assigned, and I began shifting closer to saying less and less when I saw broken process elements. This outcome is inevitable, and exactly the opposite of what the Lean leader would reinforce. Notable irony existed in this particular case because the boss was in charge of process improvement. One would expect him/her to behave as a Lean leader.

Assimilation is the outcome of this supervisory demeanor. Employees become programmed to follow orders without challenge. On the surface, you might think this is a good thing. Imagine an entire workforce of people who do what they are told, the first time, and blindly followed without annoying pushback. How awesome would *this* be?! Think of the stress it might prevent. Bosses wouldn't have to sugarcoat things and could avoid the annoying activity of explaining the WHY to employees. The *Because I said so* explanation would work the first time, every time. Everyone would know their place and not stray from their clearly defined swim-lane. Could a work environment possibly get better than this from a boss' perspective?

In the evolved process of Lean leadership, not only is it acceptable to offer up conflicting input, it is an *expectation*. I expect you to challenge my ideas if you think they are half-baked, or still frozen. In fact, I probably won't be offering up fixes at all; I want to shift this onto the workers in the process after I expose them to structured problem-solving training. This empowerment leads to a sense of ownership in the process by the employees and a genuine feeling of being valued. I refuse to be so arrogant as to assume I should be making all the decisions. And, until you feel comfortable speaking up without hesitation or fear of ridicule, I will actively solicit your input. I will ask you specific questions when countermeasures are being considered. *"Marie, what are your thoughts on doing _____?"* Marie might be hesitant at first, but I will give her positive reinforcement in my response as soon as she offers up her thoughts. I do this because I *want* Marie's thoughts. She and the rest of the employees are twenty times more aware and full of insight than I could ever be alone.

The collective genius of the workforce is precisely what I want to tap into as a Lean leader. They will consider things I am incapable of recognizing. My employees should be eager to offer their thoughts, their misgivings about process designs, and their ideas of things to improve, but they won't be if the culture is stifling even the sharing of such thoughts. As Dr. Deming said, *"The Greatest waste in America is failure to use the abilities of people."* It is the Lean leader who understands and fully accepts this reality. His counterpart, the traditional manager, prefers to be a party of one when it comes to adjusting a process. Only you can decide which tendency you lean toward. Once you can put aside the ridiculous notion that only you—the formally authorized individual with a title next to your name—should be empowered to make processes better, the sky becomes the limit.

Process Performance Gap. As I move through these seven issues, please recognize how they overlap with each other. Also, understand they are not the totality of distinct categories to clearly associate a particular behavior with the polar extreme authority figures. In time, the multitude of Lean puzzle pieces will start to come together into a cohesive system your mind. When this epiphany happens at some point in your pursuit of Lean knowledge, it's genuinely a cathartic experience. You'll instantly recognize you only thought you understood the concepts. But please also realize you will never reach the stage of total absorption. The Lean awareness "performance gap" is eternal. The more you digest, the more there is to learn. Only the arrogant individual will claim they have a total picture of Lean behavior. The specific tools alone can be daunting, let alone the psychological and behavioral elements. Your job is to continually close the gap with more listening, coaching, reading, experimentation, and learning what does and doesn't make employees feel valued. Be wary of anyone who proclaims to know all there is to know about Lean (or anything, for that matter). My journey has taught me they are trying to convince themselves.

Whenever I use the term performance gap, realize I am denoting a difference between an organizational goal (some level of process goodness established by a customer or engineering) and the current state of the process. Essentially, it is the quantifiable difference from where a process needs to be and where it is now. Without these two elements, you will be hard pressed to define a gap, except in subjective terms like, *"Our employee morale levels are not where they should be."* I call those gut-metrics—no organizational goal set and no baseline with which to quantifiably compare current state or post-countermeasure insertion state. It just *feels* like we have a gap, or it *feels* like the gap is getting smaller. You probably do have a gap, but the amount you have closed it will be subjective until you actually measure and compare it to a standard.

As touched on earlier, if the traditional manager has not captured VOC and turned the customer requirements into performance indicators, they probably won't be aware of gaps in the first place. But for discussion purposes, let's say they have done these preliminary steps. Assuming a quantified performance gap exists, the traditional manager feels compelled to hand out the fix to close it. They see it as their responsibility, and sometimes, a way to flex their managerial muscles. *Senior leadership is looking at me to correct this undesirable outcome.*

Did you ever work for a boss like this? They love to send emails announcing the new behaviors they expect. Maybe the emails start out with compelling words like, *"From this point forward, it is my expectation that everyone complies with this new process element I have developed. Non-compliance will be dealt with."*

Note the language. It's a dead giveaway the countermeasure was not contributed to by any team. And it's highly unlikely any root cause analysis took place. Maybe employees comply out of culturally established fear, but what is the level of commitment from them? Compliance and commitment are very different behavioral responses. The former might be good enough for the traditional manager, but the latter is what the Lean leader is seeking, and it comes from employees being *part* of the change, not just a recipient of it.

March in this direction now!

Sir, yes, sir!

Not all traditional managers are quite this overt with their decrees, but the effect is the same. Creative juices dry up at the Gemba.

I do make the concession here (in alignment with my position one size does not fit all) a dispensed approach has its place in certain circumstances. There are times when non-compliance could be so negatively impactful a decree from the boss is both necessary and appropriate. An example would be a safety issue of grave importance. To delay a stop-gap countermeasure when someone could die or be seriously injured would be a dereliction of duty. However, I also make the assertion that this approach should be reserved for severe matters and not become the go-to method for every performance gap. Not knowing where a particular employee is all day long does not justify the boss declaring everyone should immediately send wasteful emails about their constant whereabouts and activities. The distinction of impact should not be difficult to recognize.

The Lean alternative approach to dispensing fixes for performance gaps is to rely on employees in the process (subject-matter-experts) to take ownership of the process and the activity to improve it. This is not to say the leader takes a hands-off approach. Quite the contrary. He/she acts as a sponsor (or champion, depending on the label a company selects) for a structured problem-solving event. Employees are indoctrinated to structured problem solving as a rule (hopefully during on-boarding). The folks *in* the process build the problem statement. *They* cite the impact statement, work through root cause analysis, develop and insert countermeasures, re-measure the process after the countermeasures have taken effect, and ultimately establish a method to standardize the process after recognized improvements. Ideally, they are being coached by an experienced person who can provide sanity checks. What does the sponsor do? They are tasked to be a resource for the team and knock down hurdles encountered along the way. These leaders are basically developing their workforce to become an army of problem solvers. Watch engagement levels go up when workers with even rudimentary levels of problem-solving training are empowered to fix their own process. Talk about making a person feel valued. As my sense of feeling valued goes up, so does my amount of discretionary contribution to making processes better. What leadership team would not want this?

Obviously, it can be a huge ask for the traditional manager, to relinquish authority onto teams and then just support the team during the gap reduction activities. I realize this, but nowhere did I ever allude to a shift into Lean leadership being easy. This isn't a minor tweak of current state management; it is a major overhaul.

Difficult shift? Absolutely. Huge payoff potential? Without a doubt. Toyota didn't go from a tiny company to overtaking the big three in the United States by luck or minimal effort.

I have witnessed misguided approaches to Lean transformation, and I want to share my $0.02 here. Some companies have been inclined to build offices of what I call professional problem solvers. They might be organic employees or contracted individuals. These are folks highly trained in problem-solving and completely capable of doing the analysis then dispensing the right fix. They build the current state maps, make the fault point identification, do the root cause analysis . . . well, you get the idea. Now while this might be a reasonable countermeasure for processes completely out of control in companies with no one trained in problem-solving, it must shift at some point. These professionals need to become educators, showing teams how to develop independent capability. They transition into teachers, coaches, and guides. The doer-mode model must be intentionally weaned from the plan. If the experts remain in doer-mode, they build dependency and are nothing more than a substitute for traditional managers who did essentially the same thing.

The Lean leader realizes he needs to provide the workers with fish today so they will be initially fed, but in parallel, we shall teach these workers to fish for themselves. Otherwise, we will need an enormous number of full-time professional fishermen to feed us forever. There's nothing Lean about this model, but it happens when people have not done their homework. Let's make it even worse and put a traditional manager in charge of this professional problem solver department. With an agenda of self-serving advancement and turf protection, he/she will create an empire capable of adding more waste to the company than you can possibly imagine *(I need more black belts!)*, and it will be cloaked in the facade of process improvement. Again, it's not their fault. They were placed into a position their background experience does not support. Broken process. This is why misinformed leaders of process improvement insert bonus programs for employees participating in process improvement activity. It just seemed like the thing to do so they ran with it.

The failed comprehension is the conditioning effect this has. Engaged employees will improve process steps because they feel valued and gain intrinsic reinforcement. Once you start connecting a bonus to process improvement, employees won't want to participate in enhancing anything unless there are financial carrots to be doled out. What then? Increase the bonus amounts? And who gets this money? The person who pointed out the waste? The facilitator, the team lead, the SMEs? Everybody associated with the win? Who will manage this non-valued added process? Imagine the disgruntled reactions of those getting left out of the bonus money despite their participation. This folly will cause the Lean transformation to move at a snail's pace, especially when the focus is on dollars saved, instead of behavioral changes towards the employees. A bonus should be for something above and beyond the expectation. In a Lean world, improving processes is part of everyone's normal duty requirements, not something extra. Everyone does it every day. As for your available experts, the better approach is to embed those professionals in various areas of the enterprise and have them coach/guide those areas towards independence with a singular, aligned voice. This is how the magic spreads. If the coaches reside in your corporate office accessible only sporadically to workers at the Gemba, you are doing it wrong. If the person "in-charge" of the transformation is resistant to understanding Lean and unwilling to be coached, you have a considerable performance gap in placing the right people in the right positions. Management must be practicing servant leadership daily, or they are doing it wrong. They should be the benchmark of excellence for others to emulate.

I want to spend a bit more time on a specific performance gap present in just about every company. It is a gap given very little attention, mostly lip service on corporate wallpaper and town hall meetings but has incredible potential to take a company in positive or negative directions.

The gap I am referring to is employee development to improve their ability to meet customer requirements by continually increasing levels of reliable quality and reduced cycle times.

Imagine a culture where the number one priority of leadership is not to make more money than competitors this year, not to appease shareholders by generating spikes in stock prices, not even to get the latest gadget into the market to spur sales before the next reporting period to the street. All those things are and will be on your radar for eternity, but should any of them really be your number one priority?

No doubt, I have raised some eyebrows with this bold assertion but hang with me while I lay out my argument from a Lean leadership perspective. It doesn't matter what your product or service is. The people in the trenches designing and assembling the latest widget or providing the services you offer like cutting the customers' hair or painting their cars, *these* people make the rubber meet the road. Leaders merely guide the activity, they don't do the value-added work, none of it. If you believe the process to replace worker bees is as simplistic as changing the dwindling roll of paper towels on the wall, you are mistaken. These are the only people who make the wheels turn. A company of only managers produces nothing. What would happen to production if all the bosses left the building at once and were gone for the rest of the day? Now tell me what would happen if the bosses remained at their post and all the workers left for the rest of the day. Just something to imagine as you place value on one over the other.

As you burn through workers within disheartening cultures, the replacement costs become staggering. And don't think your external customers are not feeling the pinch of your cultural shortcomings. Perhaps you are not even tracking this expense. The most amazing strategic plan ever conceived is meaningless without a stable workforce to make it a reality. But how much time is spent developing these people to their maximum potential? For that matter, how much time is spent putting the right people in the right seats to begin with?

Let us walk through a contrived situation for illustration purposes. Shannon arrives for an interview. The job she is applying for is a legal assistant. Shannon doesn't have any actual experience with the gig but seems bright and energetic. She is almost finished with her degree in the field and presents herself well during the interview. Since things have been backing up in the office, the interviewer is satisfied this person will be able to help them out. Congratulations, Shannon, you're hired!

Shannon arrives early on her first day, eager to dig in and make a difference. Her expectations are modest at first, just show me what you want accomplished and what the deliverable looks like. Not unreasonable, but do companies meet even this basic standard? Generally, employees are turned loose to figure things out on their own, ask peers, learn from mistakes (which will happen 100% of the time), and acclimate to the broken processes your company has been unintentionally developing for years now.

Let's assume Shannon manages, for a while, to navigate the unending hurdles and land mines placed in her way. She tries to keep a positive attitude and seems genuinely interested in becoming a more effective employee. She wants to make a difference and feel valued, so she challenges processes not working well for her. Unfortunately, her boss failed attentive listening at his management school and simply dismisses her input. The solid gold opportunity to invest in Shannon's recognition of potential process improvements is missed. She desperately wants to get better at her job. But, what is the company intentionally doing to fill this performance gap? Are they even aware it exists? Do they care?

She continues to make mistakes. Files get lost in the mounds of paper stacked about like barricades for a dug-in army and meeting deadlines at the last-minute increases stress levels for everyone. Tempers are often short in the office, people expecting deliverables just before they are due, and she learns this is an environment of sink-or-swim. Hold your anvil in the deep end and continue to tread water. Life vests are on backorder. Reports are often produced late; re-work and firefighting are the norms of the day. This employee begins to wonder where this company is headed long-term. She requests more training, and one-on-one mentoring, but of course, there never seems to be time available to meet her inquiry. Reacting to the latest crisis gets priority over continuing development of employees. The ship is afloat, but none of the occupants are aware of its destination. Drifting with the tide is the unspoken strategic plan. Plug the big leaks as time permits. No time for the small ones. Someone find the dang sextant when you have a chance.

Fast-forward about a year. Shannon comes to work, but her engagement level has degraded to zero. Sunday night is the catalyst for dread about the next five days. She has stopped asking for training because her boss repeated the same assurances of "when things calm down" one time too many. She feels invisible. The boss is busy fighting fires himself and can barely keep his own head above water. She has ceased to imagine herself working here long-term and has learned to produce at the minimum threshold of productivity to keep from being fired. There is no energy or motivation to go beyond it, and she is actively looking for another ship to board. When one appears, she jumps overboard and swims to what she hopes is a better craft with a culture actively involved in posturing employees for success. Unfortunately, the next situation is not dramatically better than the one she left. A similar script plays out in this next gig, and the cycle continues. Shannon knows something is missing and wonders if it exists anywhere. Head down, she pushes forward to keep the bills paid and lives for Fridays and the occasional sick days she can get away with. Truth be told, they are indeed sick days.

Now multiply this depressing situation by tens of millions of employees across the country on their own dysfunctional ship drifting through the disrespectful fog. All they want is to feel like they are making a difference in their job. They want to get better at doing what they do. They want to feel valued! If you are not currently working in a dismal environment like this, I feel certain you have at one time or another.

To maximize this reasonable expectation of the endless quantity of Shannons, training, mentoring, prompt information updates, and intentional development heaped with respect need to be a cultural standard. It needs to be real, not just empty lingo in the mission statement, embellished descriptions of the culture on your website, or a litany of computer-based classes to check the box. Without structured, designed development, people will tolerate conditions until another ship passes by. Money will only keep some on the hook for so long, because, carrots and sticks really do not work. The most unfortunate of all are the people who have no options to abandon their listing ship. For a variety of reasons, they are stuck in steerage class on the SS Hell with no options. Each day they suffer through their shift and go home. It's a paycheck, but nothing beyond that. No one is taking the time to help them improve or offering development options they are desperately seeking. In most companies, this has become the responsibility of the employee to do on their own. Supervisors will assist if asked and time permits, but they do not view it as a primary role for them. This is both sad and narrow-minded. It's a pervasive, debilitating performance gap. The salient question is, why has it become acceptable from those with the authority to close it?

In contrast, the Lean leader (viewing themselves in supplier-mode) takes an active role of supplying every employee with as much development as they are willing to undertake and supporting them during the endless endeavor. It's a dramatically different process with dramatically different results.

Why do it? Primarily because people deserve it, and also because engagement levels will soar and become contagious. The longevity of employment goes up. Loyalty to the company spreads like wildfire. The best applicants will do whatever is necessary to interview with companies having track records like this. Individual performances will rise, and all of this will directly affect the bottom line for the company. What makes this happen? The Lean leader doesn't see employee development as some side gig when they get around to it. It's their *top priority*, thus the reason I call it supplier-mode. It all falls under the label of empowerment, and it includes making sure every employee fully understands who the customers are, what the requirements are, and how processes are performing against VOC. This leader is perpetually seeking ways to help employees satisfy these requirements easier, faster, and with quality levels competitors cannot keep up with. Perhaps the employee shows interest in furthering their education. The Lean leader assists with this endeavor because the company and the employee will benefit. *This* is the everyday vision of the Lean leader – developing human beings. They recognize the gap is perpetual and continuously work to reduce it by actively seeking what each individual employee needs, then bending over backward to provide it. Organizational success will result from developing these critical people in the value stream—the workers. Lean leaders have their priorities in the right order. **People First!**

Does your company have this performance gap? If yes, what is your current model to reduce it?

Problem Solving Training. The traditional manager sees no need to train the workers in structured problem-solving. Why would they offer training which will never be utilized? I have to give them credit for this approach. It will be a complete waste of time and money to train employees on the 8-step problem-solving model and root cause analysis if the plan is to dispense fixes yourself. The logical decision aligns perfectly with the model.

Seeing the insanity here does not require 20/20 vision. If you limit problem-solving to only the bosses, please recognize the creative potential you are purposely choosing to ignore. Put ten people in a room, let them brainstorm on resolutions to a process fault point, and record all their ideas. Now repeat the process with only the boss generating ideas, the person who never performs the task currently under analysis. Let's compare the two lists. Which do you think will contain a higher level of creativity and applicability? Its simple math. More thinkers (SMEs) = more ideas = greater likelihood of better ideas. To ignore the potential of these ideas is beyond foolish.

Actual training in problem-solving is necessary, not just because employees need to understand *how* to go about addressing a problem, but because often, they don't even know why they *should* address it. The primary objective of problem-solving is not to make more money or increase shareholder earnings. These outcomes will manifest as the natural effect of problem-solving done correctly but are not the focal point to instill in a culture heading down the Lean path. I know, it sounds counterintuitive, but after the comprehension of _real_ Lean seeps into your DNA, it will make perfect sense.

Allow me to repeat for emphasis: problem-solving to make more money cannot be the vision, strategy, tactic, goal, mission, or objective. Pick a noun.

This is not what you are striving for if you are serious about sustained, enterprise-wide continuous improvement through culture change with respect for people. Quick savings are in the playbook of a company hemorrhaging money due to wasteful processes capitulated to for years, or process improvement organizations trying to justify their existence to the C-suite. Some will argue drastic market changes will necessitate slashed budgets to survive. I would then contend these massive changes are probably linked to batched/delayed improvement activity as opposed to continuous improvements made daily based on shifting customer requirements. If data shows customers prefer sport utility vehicles over sedans, why does a huge automobile company suddenly have to close facilities and lay off thousands of employees as opposed to tapering off production of undesirable vehicles and systematically increasing the production of the cars customers do want? Why did vast amounts of time go by without many small changes along the way? What part does wishing and hoping, along with waiting, play in their strategic models? If customers are requesting more bacon on their BLT sandwiches, would a mom-and-pop restaurant put this on their to-do list for the following year or would they make the changes immediately? Do large companies have to have a different cultural model of process improvement than small companies? My Lean journey has taught me excuses for not reacting to undesirable process outcomes are plentiful. Everyone is waiting for someone else to do something. Not-my-job syndrome. As we all wait, the ship continues to take on water below decks, mostly out of sight.

The correct objective of problem-solving should be *Relentless reduction of negative effects in all processes by all employees to increase the frequency of a positive customer experience, while at the same time making the process EASIER and more enjoyable for employees to accomplish.* This is the essence of continuous improvement. Recognize the description of a positive customer experience must be based on the requirements of your customers and their perception of how well you provided them each time your process was turned on. If your problem-solving activities are using a different model or not seeking both of these elements simultaneously, then you will not achieve the maximum potential of your efforts. Of course, this assumes you are trying to improve your processes at all. Some company cultures embrace status quo processes like a warm coat on a bitterly cold day. Their job is just a job, not a mission.

I've encountered too many people who have completed formal Green or even Black belt training and not incorporated this basic concept into their methodologies, not to mention the countless traditional managers driving misguided activity to stellar levels of mediocrity. They work a "project" for some time (several months or even a year), cite savings because something in the process has been altered (often grossly exaggerated and projected over a long period of future time to inflate the wow factor), and then claim success. Wasteful PowerPoint presentations are built, revised multiple times, and widely presented to market the "achievement." The conference room audience sips coffee, applauds, and if all goes according to plan, another large-scope activity will be resourced for the heroes. Release the balloons.

Granted, while these projects are capable (emphasis on the word capable) of improving customer experiences and/or simplifying processes for the workers, this is lightyears from a cultural standard of every employee continuously experimenting and inserting small improvements on a daily basis. Even worse, after these marathon projects, some traditional manager might take the bulk of the credit in order to bolster his/her promotability standing in the company. If you haven't witnessed any of this selfishness in your career, you are most fortunate. I have seen more than my share. These are not the elements of problem-solving modeled and encouraged by Lean leadership. To the untrained audience who doesn't yet comprehend what Lean is all about, they mistakenly label this activity as acceptable. Keep in mind, the occasional home run in baseball is exciting but far less impactful or desirable than a 100 consecutive base hits. Or as Wade Wolfe (a former boss) once told me, "I'd rather have one million projects that save a dollar each, than one project that saved a million dollars". He understood the behavioral shift as the mission.

Consider these questions at the conclusion of your long-duration problem solving "projects." In fact, I encourage you to ask them if you are witness to the presentation of the results. If the person(s) responding to the inquiries recognizes gaps in their approach to problem-solving, perhaps this can become the catalyst for improvement moving forward.

1. What will get better for the external customer (faster flow or better quality), and by how much?
2. Specifically, how will the external customer now have a more positive experience when you turn on the process the next time?
3. Was the savings passed on so they will recognize increased quality at a reduced cost to them?
4. Was the activity intended to make their experience better based on their documented requirements (voice of the customer), or someone's assumed perception?
5. Are the employees performing the tasks doing it with less effort now, or are additional employees working harder with more inspections, more overtime, more inventory, more handoffs, and faster rework to get the product out the door according to specifications?
6. Did the countermeasures reduce process waste (non-value activity) or add more?
7. What root causes are the countermeasures intended to eliminate?
8. Were the employees in the process (the actual subject matter experts) involved in determining the root causes and designing/inserting the countermeasures, or did a well-intentioned manager (or black belt) extract them from their years of experience and decree implementation?
9. Is there a plan to continue closing the remaining performance gap in this process, or will a drastic breakdown of the process be the catalyst to re-engage?
10. Was a simplistic one-page A3 considered for documenting this improvement activity instead of PowerPoint slides?

Problem-solving is sometimes completely missing in companies, and in many others, is turned on retroactively only when processes are completely out of control. Customers are screaming bloody murder because of product inadequacies, late deliveries, unreliable service, an employee was injured or killed, we damaged something expensive, a patient had the wrong limb amputated, etc. Continuous improvement of processes is considered too time-consuming for less dramatic issues, assuming the countless negative outcomes hit the radar at all. Proactively improving process all the time would just be crazy talk at the corporate staff meeting. But in a Lean environment, this type of environmental indoctrination is widespread. Likely it's even part of on-boarding for new employees so they are quickly acclimated to Lean. Everyone understands the basics of Lean and problem solving, then a few who got advanced training are acting as facilitators to guide teams of SMEs through structured problem-solving activities. The boss is acting as a sponsor (or champion) and wouldn't think of suggesting countermeasures. They empower the team to do this, then support the most viable options on the table. This becomes part of developing employees, which generates a sense of worth and ownership in the process, which drives engagement, which drives higher performance of employees, which ultimately drives increased organizational success. Beats the heck out of a corporate goal of *make more money this year.*

Employee Engagement. I begin with the assumption most organizations want this. They realize engaged employees eagerly participate, go the extra mile, think about the company above individualistic motives, seek improvements to process without demanding constant (or financial) credit for themselves, and generate energy in their peers because their excitement is contagious to be around. Engagement in employees requires continuous care and feeding (in the form of rigorous empowerment activity) even after it has been firmly established. A bit of positive reinforcement is all it takes sometimes to keep the flywheel spinning. Policing their activity? Completely unnecessary. Need someone to step up on a challenging project? Mr. or Ms. Engaged employee is at the ready. Engagement is some of the sweetest fruit resultant from a healthy Lean tree. Given all the positives associated with this incredible cultural condition, it would seem a no brainer to develop and nurture it intentionally.

Even the traditional manager wants this behavior in his minions (within limits), but he isn't willing, able, or knowledgeable enough to make it bloom, perhaps because he/she was never shown how and then coached. They just expect the employee to come to work thrilled and display engagement characteristics spontaneously without pause. Some incorrectly assume you can throw enough money at someone and this will sustain engagement. Unfortunately, like many of the caveman assumptions the traditional manager makes, this could not be further from reality. Engagement doesn't soar without intentional intervention. Left untended, it subsides. Disenchantment is not far behind. Cultures will beat engagement out of motivated employees, and when this happens, the traditional manager will deem them no longer worthy. *Get rid of that slacker. I need someone who can get the job done.* Little do they realize their managerial process is the causal element to the degradation. It's easier to blame the employee and then replace them. Good thing hiring and training new employees is free.

Side-story – I was teaching a Green Belt class one week in my federal government job. It was day three of a five-day course. We took a break, and folks were milling around outside in the hallway. A gentleman came up to me during a break to let me know that he was truly loving the class, but that I needed to understand his current work environment. "My boss could care less about all this. I'm to the point where if he tells me to march backward all day long, I'll just do it without objection or even asking why."

Wow. This individual had about twenty years of federal service and was utterly beaten into submission by his boss. I suspect it was probably the cumulative effect of several of them in succession. I had no response beyond, "I'm so sorry to hear that." It was disheartening but not surprising. His condition was not the anomaly data point because I had experienced these toxic conditions myself.

My point is this: He still had the desire to improve processes, to contribute, to share ideas of how to make things better, thus his enrollment and full participation in the class. The energy was still smoldering in his heart. I could see the excitement, hear it in his tone. But it was glaringly evident he would not be engaging with process improvement within his current sub-culture. This unfortunate reality was directly driven by his supervisor's behavior. How sad is this? He worked for a do-as-I-say-without-question type of supervisor. Neither my class nor the employee's behavior was going to change things in his world. It would take a systemic intervention, one that involved superiors above this supervisor to set unyielding expectations of how employees should be treated.

Look at the opposite approach. The Lean leader clearly recognizes the direct connection from his/her behavior to the engagement levels of employees. They know chance is not the reason it does or does not exist long-term. Someone or some training development program (or both) in their past presented the psychological connection, and it stuck. They bought it, they practiced it, and they are notoriously the leaders people want to work for. Lean-minded leaders know companies are successful because of higher employee performance levels. Most larger companies utilize extensive recruiting processes to attract talented individuals. It makes sense. Unfortunately, the structured efforts to build performing teams often stops after the hiring process. Long-term company success is driven from sustained employee engagement levels, which are impacted by the culture people work in, which develops from the two main puzzle pieces of Lean being modeled daily by the leader.

1. **A trained, relentlessly uninhibited, enterprise-wide mentality of <u>continuous improvement</u> of every process by every employee based on VOC.**

2. <u>Respect for people</u> as it applies to the work they are asked to do, and the culture they are asked to do it in.

Note the flow. One thing causes the other in a logical, distinct order. Put the two puzzle pieces at the far left of the process map correctly in place and watch the downstream elements change from undesirable to desirable states. Start somewhere in the middle, and company success might evade you forever, depending of course on how you define success. Most important, recognize that positive outcome from each element is impossible with a preponderance of traditional management. These misguided individuals devote little or no time to empower employees; thus, engagement is not resultant. You might see glimmers of desired results with a few Lean leaders in the shadows tapping cautiously on the drum—I call them pockets of excellence—but you will not have sustainment even there. The majority will dissolve the passion out of the minority. If your culture is laden with these flu germs (traditional managers), your employees will be systemically infected and behave accordingly – minimal or non-existent engagement. As a leader, can you live with that? Are you living with it now? Either way, take responsibility if you are courageous enough. Pioneers have already blazed the trail with a proven formula.

Of course, I have highly simplified these connections. Each of the two major puzzle pieces has an array of potholes you could step in and induce undesirable outcomes downstream even when your intent is genuine. A lifetime of research and practice is necessary to refine the application. This is not easy stuff. If it were, every organization would be good at it.

My advice to leadership teams is this: Instead of trying in isolation to leap to the ultimate goal—company success—recognize it becomes easier when you digest and work on the cause-and-effect connections upstream. Having said this, just because it seems easy to visualize and accept the connections as valid, successful implementation is the hard work. It takes a significant and structured commitment. It also takes patience, with an unequivocal acceptance it doesn't happen overnight. Every supervisor has to be relentless in their activity of empowering employees by remaining in supplier-mode instead of supply-me-mode.

"Highly engaged employees make the customer experience. Disengaged employees break it."
- Timothy R. Clark

"To build a culture of engagement, it is important to incorporate training on intrinsic motivation and employee engagement into management development programs." - Kenneth Thomas

"Paychecks can't buy passion." – Brad Federman

The Cavemen Managers, and the Leaders

"If you could buy traditional managers for what they are worth, then sell them for what they think they are worth, you would be a gazillionaire." – Bill Collins

As I mentioned earlier, entrenched traditional managers are like flu germs. They are everywhere, hard to avoid, quickly replicated, difficult to eradicate, and make hordes of people feel like crap by spreading their infection throughout an enterprise. These folks dispense unilateral countermeasures often without root causes or employee input. I've described managers and leaders at length, but now I want to devote a whole chapter to folks with titles. In this chapter, I will be citing examples of supervisors, both good and bad. The impact of both styles can be powerful in a work environment. The very best barometer of quality comes from asking employees to formally evaluate their boss – a practice all too often absent. If you are a titled supervisor in any capacity, I invite you to honestly reflect and determine if you qualify for the title of Leader, or if your style is only eligible to be deemed a manager.

Side Story - Kenneth (Ken) Sloan – his real name. Ken was indeed a Leader.

I was performing a simple electrical check using an analog multimeter (device to measure voltage, resistance, etc.). Tools were provided to us by the federal government (as opposed to the mechanics owning them), and this particular device was junk, to put it lightly. It would not give me a steady reading, the needle jumped all over the place, making the task very frustrating. Ken came over because I was using colorful language and asked what the problem was. *"Ken, this lousy meter belongs in the trash. Here we are working on multimillion-dollar aircraft with this dime-store tool. How can I be expected to do my job properly with it?"* About 30 minutes later, Ken came back and handed me a brand new, still in the box, Fluke digital meter. It was awesome! If you are not familiar with Fluke meters, suffice it to say they are top-shelf quality. If your objective was to cut down a large tree, it was like going from a pocketknife to a competition chainsaw.

"Ken, where in the heck did you find this?"

"Never mind," he said, *"just enjoy it and tell me what else you need in the future."*

Now, **_this_** is behaving in supplier-mode for your employees! Ken had no clue about the language of Lean. If you quizzed him, I'm confident he wouldn't have known John Krafcik coined the term in 1987, but ignorance to the labels didn't limit Ken's respect for employees and the work they were asked to do. He saw an employee struggling to perform a task, recognized the need for a better tool, and found a way to supply it. He was on the precise leadership mission laid out by Dr. Deming – *"Help people do a better job with less effort."* Doubtful he ever heard of Deming, either. Servant leadership came naturally to him.

Respect for employees was important to Ken, but, unfortunately, Ken Sloan was a rare species in our production jungle.. If you looked at his data point on the behavioral histogram of production supervisors, Ken would be the outlier about 10 miles to the right of the mean. The culture at the time did not reward him for this approach. No doubt he was the subject of ridicule from other bosses for being "too easy" on the mechanics. Irrelevant to Ken. Supplier-mode was his process, and we had enormous respect for him as a result. There was nothing I wouldn't have done to accomplish the goals he set out for us. This man was a Leader, and by now, you recognize I don't hand out the label lightly. Sad to say, the joy was short-lived, as Ken was only my supervisor for about a year.

There were many frustrations in our world. The culture was steeped in git-'er-done mode, and if it took brute force to make it happen, this is what we did. Getting basic information was a daily irritation. Since we had three shifts working around the clock, people needed to know what was done on the previous shift so they could carry on with a task in-work. Dispensing clear information was rare, so we were left to discover the specifics on our own. This was something just short of a Toyota production line—lightyears short of it.

Had I known what standard work was at the time, I would have been keenly aware of how broken my work environment really was. We all just accepted rampant variability and confusion as part of the process. We had no concept that defects, overproduction, waiting, etc. were wastes to be eliminated. There was no mantra of continuous improvement, but we did have a posted slogan of "Excellence in all we do." As mechanics annoyed with the hypocrisy, we re-dubbed it "Excellence in all we re-do." Rework was so common we never expected to get a job done correctly the first time. Lean had not entered our world yet, nor was anyone receptive if we dared bring up issues or hurdles in our way. We lived in a culture of keeping your head down and staying gainfully employed.

I remember the initial uttering of this phrase, stay gainfully employed. May of 1985, my first civil service boss was introducing himself to the new mechanics. He very clearly told us (as a group), "I don't care what you do, just stay gainfully employed." What better way to onboard the new workers? Since he didn't ask if we had any questions, no one requested clarification. What dope wouldn't understand this clear message, right? We just stood there like drones soaking in the government job indoctrination. Later, I asked some of the existing mechanics to explain the phrase, and they told me it just meant, no matter what, when the bosses came around, be doing something. Anything. It didn't matter what the activity was, as long as we always looked busy.

I wasn't dialed into the language of Lean yet, but you can imagine the amount of excess processing and motion waste a message of stay gainfully employed could induce. But what did I know at the time? It was a government job, and I wasn't about to challenge anything—for a while. Fearless identification of waste was waiting on my unplanned horizon. Little did I know what I would evolve into when Lean entered my lexicon, and then my DNA. It would completely transform my perspective of how business should be conducted and how leaders should behave.

Side Story - Many years later, I worked for an interesting boss. We'll call him Joey.

Now many people will say they liked Joey on the surface. He was what you might call a good ol' boy. Joey was quite demonstrative and conveyed confidence when he spoke. The untrained observer would believe he truly knew what he was talking about and accept most of his comments for fact. However, once you got to know him, you realized he was relying on smugness to cloak his extreme lack of factual evidence. Joey had both feet firmly planted in the traditional manager mud. He was a character I will never forget.

When I first met him, he asked me about my background. With the larger than life demeanor he exhibited at the time, I remember feeling like a teenage boy showing up to take his daughter to a movie. It had the air of interrogation with instantaneous red flags. Being cautious and filtering my words, I continued. Without realizing it would be viewed in a negative light, I told him I had just recently completed my graduate degree in psychology at the University of Oklahoma. Oops. Never should have brought that up.

"So, you're one of them there college boys, huh? Never had much respect for folks like you. I've managed to get this far in life without a lot of book learnin' and don't much think it helps a person do his job any better, least of all this job. You'll do well here if you keep that stuff to yourself and just do what I tell ya."

I invite you to imagine yourself in this situation. How would you have responded to his comment? Would you respond at all? Would you try to convey an education is not something to be ashamed of? Would you consciously adjust your facial expression to avoid giving him the subliminal message, *Dude, are you a time traveler from the 1800s?* It was not a great beginning.

Despite my fervent approach to conducting my job with a passion for helping my internal customers get what they needed, Joey never looked at me with a respectful perspective, nor I him. This mutual distrust came to a head during a meeting one day and has forever been an example to share when I teach Lean leadership. While I find it humorous now, at the time it pegged the humiliation needle.

Picture about 15 people sitting at a conference room table. The occupants were mostly my peers, Joey, and a few other formal managers. He was sitting as far away from me as possible at this oval table. The particular topic eludes me after all these years, but I recall having something to add to the discussion. Joey was doing most of the talking—as was his pattern in public settings—and I wanted to contribute a perspective they had not considered. I put my hand into the air to get his attention and said something to the effect of, *"Excuse me, but have we considered . . .?"* The specific contribution is not relevant here, but his response to it was.

After I finished my short question, Joey swung his arm in my direction, aimed his index finger at my face like a gun and said, *"Son, when I want your opinion, I will tell you what it is. Are we clear on that?"*

Quick, put this boss in for a leadership award immediately.

A hush fell over the room while people were processing what to say next, and who would say it. It was probably only fifteen seconds of silence, but it felt like an eternity. Shock was on many of the faces. I can only imagine what my body language looked like. It was apparent even Joey realized he had crossed a line, but given his self-image and smug arrogance, he never offered an apology or even discussed it afterward. Admitting a mistake was never an option for him.

Try to imagine how you would feel in front of your peers and some other managers. I can assure you I spoke not another word in that meeting and offered nothing to him in the future. Regardless of how misguided a behavior or decree from him might have been after this incident, I challenged nothing. He could have been inadvertently entering an elevator shaft, and I would have remained mute. Not surprisingly, my peers in attendance replicated my disengaged behavior from that point forward, as well. It was a powerful moment and taught me the impact managerial behavior can have.

In retrospect, I do not think Joey was intentionally disrespecting me. He was very stressed in a job I believe he was ill-suited for, and perhaps the stress drove him to react without thinking. Leadership development was not on his educational resume. If a person sees themselves burdened to be the sole problem solver in all instances, it can be a daunting mission. It would unduly weigh on anyone eventually. People say stupid things they don't really mean. I'll give him the benefit of the doubt, but not discussing it with me after the meeting was unforgivable. We all cross a line now and then, but leaving it unaddressed is unacceptable. It's pure arrogance. Every employee in the room was affected. The culture was affected, and ultimately, external customers would be affected. Imagine all the good ideas which were never expressed as a consequence. Now imagine this type of manager being replicated in a work environment with a cultural composition of employees conditioned to keep ideas to themselves. These disengaged workers become drones carrying out decrees by the misguided, and processes will remain broken. Let's carry the analysis even further. Imagine the disinclination to speak up being widespread, and these cavemen bosses are actually rewarded for their behavior of keeping people silent and in line. The dysfunction gets replicated by others wanting to reach management positions, and it works for them too. If this is what it takes to get ahead, there are but three options for the employee interested in promotions:

1. Conform and replicate
2. Rebel against the insanity and try to change things
3. Seek an exit ramp

Unfortunately, the first of the three is far too prevalent. Just think about the impact each of these can have on a company overall. Those advocating or showing signs of servant leadership will not be promoted in the first place. It is career suicide if the opposite is revered. Even if they hang around, their repressed inclination to improve conditions will take a toll. Everyone loses. Can you really expect to generate employee loyalty if this exists in your world? Existing managers speaking out in favor of employee input will be ostracized and advance no further. The clear message of shut-up-and-color will be painfully evident to observers of the courageous challenger. Please also realize that if you are a manager and permit your peers to behave as traditional managers by stifling employee input (even if you behave to the contrary), you are enabling the undesirable condition. It is no different from ignoring gender discrimination or any other kind of workplace intimidation. It will persist in the absence of being challenged. And the last choice, exiting the company, ensures only the compliant will remain. The environment will become even more homogeneous. A guaranteed lose-lose situation.

If your company allows this behavior to occur, employees will never reach their full potential, and consequently, the same result is the fate for the company overall. Even if your cultural examples are far less overt than mine, the outcome will be similar. If leadership isn't constantly seeking input from the employees performing the work, they are essentially doing what Joey did during the meeting. Slightly different plot, perhaps without the drama, but the same result. As has been said, "A bad manager can take a good staff and destroy it, causing the best employees to flee and the remainder to lose all motivation." (I wish I knew who said that originally, because they really got it right.)

Now, I ask you to imagine the standard managerial behavior in a company is servant leadership. Imagine if bosses in a company were all in supplier-mode, continually trying to fill gaps in workers' processes so they can more easily and efficiently satisfy customer requirements. Imagine leaders relentlessly developing the potential in every one of their direct reports and selflessly doing it daily. Imagine employees freely and without fear of repercussion offering up opportunities in their processes, then being empowered to determine root causes and countermeasures with support from their supervisors. Imagine processes continuously getting easier to accomplish by the direct labor employees, and at the same time, outcomes are getting better, more reliable, and quicker. Flow is increasing, and your customers are noticing. Imagine employees wanting to seek a formal leadership role, and they intentionally model the behavior of a servant leader because it is the only acceptable pathway. Imagine they are getting constant coaching during their path to a leadership role by leaders who fully understand how to position employees for success, and then after their promotion, they begin to coach others on the same path they just took. Imagine customer satisfaction levels rising to incredible heights because you can now offer a much better process than your competitor, and at a lower cost. Imagine employee loyalty at levels where people wouldn't consider leaving the company just to get more money elsewhere because the elsewhere didn't possess the respectful environment they have come to appreciate. Imagine becoming the company people are dying to work for because they hear stories of how employees are treated with absolute respect for the talents and creative juices they bring to the table.

Depending on the environment you currently work in, this might be impossible to imagine. It's like some fantasy company that couldn't possibly exist. You might think it can't be created in your world because it's a ridiculous pipedream, but my friends, this is precisely the opportunity for a Lean transformation. A wildly different environment from one nurtured by UC grads over many years. Are you courageous enough to be the first to suggest it? If not you, who? Even the longest of journeys started with the first step by a rebel frustrated by status quo stagnation. A necessary disruptor who is convinced a better way is available.

Rebel can be a scary word. It invokes a negative connotation of people wreaking havoc and causing unwanted disruption to established order. The overt display of repugnance or resistance to company policy or process steps is likely to invoke disdain or even punishment from your typical manager, but in my experience in fossilized cultures, respectful rebellion is precisely the behavior you should be encouraging. Allow me to explain.

Something has to spark continuous improvement in any work environment. Employees suggesting tweaks or significant overhauls to process conditions, complaining about a software program not meeting the needs of the user, experimenting with new tools to reduce time and strain on people, repositioning equipment or inventory, challenging a manager's decree in meetings because it hasn't been thought through from a SME perspective, or suggesting elimination of burdensome tasks accomplishing nothing towards increasing a positive customer experience. These are but a smattering of examples when necessary, respectful rebellion is **desperately** needed. Notice I used the word *needed*, and not *tolerated*. To tolerate a behavior is to permit it to occur without actually declaring it as favorable. To desire, promote, reinforce, and even make a behavior an expectation of employment is an entirely different posture.

Respectful rebellion is the lifeblood of continuous improvement maintaining a strong pulse in your company, but it is unlikely to become widespread spontaneously. It cannot get wished into existence. And, you can't rely solely on your millennial extraverts guzzling energy drinks or your outspoken, creative junkies to spark insight you hadn't considered before. What you NEED is an entire workforce of fearless rebels to challenge insanity when they see or hear it. Their firsthand experience with wasteful processes far exceeds the visibility of managers spending most of their day in meetings, with limited exposure to the Gemba. I can promise you there is not a single employee in your company who doesn't perform some stupid, wasteful task on a regular basis (because they were told to), but they refrain in conditioned silence because the culture is non-receptive to challenging the established process. Their repressed objections are lost opportunities with tombstones. "Here lies an idea that lived in this person's mind for 0.5 seconds. Rest in Peace." These ideas go unexplored, and some process element will remain less efficient because rebellion is not a reinforced behavior.

In many cases, the exact opposite of respectful rebellion is the desired, cultural norm – employees who do what they are told and never question the instruction's merit. These unfortunate souls have been beaten into submission, and their misguided manager considers it a good thing. They mistakenly believe a desirable environment equals compliant workers (I call them sheep) always following the guidance of the more astute manager. Those content to shut-up-and-color are then rewarded and promoted. We even label them "team players" because they go along to get along. Rebels, well, they are considered troublemakers and dealt with accordingly. I recall a traditional manager (during my federal government job as a Black Belt) once asked me, *"Must you always bring up the waste you see in processes? It's so annoying."* She much preferred people who followed direction with no questions asked. Even asking, *"Why are we doing this?"* would set her off. Make no mistake, she was unsuccessful at extinguishing my rebellious nature to make processes better.

Think about how dysfunctional this is. Just for a moment, try to imagine how much better processes could be if your company was seeking everyone's respectful pushback on meritless conditions and tasks. Consider the powerful improvements possible if everyone was carefully weighing proposals then fearlessly pushing back if they recognized madness was about to occur. Oh, I know many managers will say, *"I want my employees to tell me whatever they think."* But, do they really mean it? My experience says no. It's lip service until the behavior actually shows up. Send your boss an email and tell them their idea is ridiculous and clearly, respectfully explain why. How will they respond? Will they write back and say, *"Thanks! I guess I really didn't think it through. Please continue to challenge my ideas in the future."* Some will, I suppose. The humble ones. Most cultures are just the opposite. People are incredibly cautious about pushing back, and even when they do, they will highly filter a critique if they think the unvarnished truth will be ill-received. Rebels against process waste are generally not revered. How unfortunate.

Tell me you haven't sat in some meeting listening to a manager describe how a process was to be conducted or read a decree-email from a boss while silently thinking to yourself, *"This is the dumbest thing I've ever heard."* Unfortunately, because of cultural conditioning, you withhold your objection because you know it will degrade your fragile status as a team player. You have fully accepted your role as subordinate. The consequence is another opportunity to improve something gets buried. How did this experience make you feel? Was corporate hierarchy the salient variable in your reluctance to speak up? A non-supervisory level employee challenging the Director? Blasphemy! Retribution would be in order just to remind this employee of their subordinate status. Did this experience increase your respect for the boss or further entrench your loyalty to the company? Did it make you think to yourself, *I never want to leave this place of employment?*

Those of you who are formal managers, when is the last time you asked your employees for examples of process elements frustrating them or encouraged people to challenge things you dispense if they feel a better approach would be more effective? Something like this is necessary to get the feedback ball rolling. If you do ask, and they pause to evaluate the true motive of your inquiry, recognize you have already collected data. If they don't answer immediately with a comfortable, obvious demeanor of negative repercussions being off the table, you have an opportunity to become a better leader. Put your arrogant assumptions aside for a moment and realize your style is officially part of the reason they do not speak freely. Your environment is not as collaborative as it could be. The data is staring you in the face. If you take it as a personal attack when an employee advocates why your idea is less than stellar, your ego is stifling employee development. You are effectively holding the entire company back. Preferring employees blindly follow your dispensed countermeasures without challenge is indicative of your insecurity as a supervisor, but it doesn't have to stay this way. Humility, self-reflection, and coaching can turn things around.

I once had a supervisor inform me (after attending one of my classes) his life would be so much better if his employees would just do what they were told and not question things. He said he was weary of telling people why they had to do something. Their job was just to follow his direction. He was the thinker; they were the doers (his actual words). My reaction at the time was guarded disgust to his approach, but I recognized he was a long way from being receptive to my message of Lean leadership. I suppressed my rebellion, but, in retrospect, I failed myself (and him) by not explaining the stifling potentials of his approach to supervision. If you share his approach in your supervisory process (even if only occasionally), I would argue your company promoted you well before you were ready to lead. The leadership development program has failed you, and your management-by-arrogance approach is negatively impacting your employees. Evaluate their engagement levels if you disagree with my assessment. This is my challenge to your current-state process of being a manager. If you choose to discard the challenge, it should tell you something.

Now, please understand I am not advocating for a workforce of employees chaotically pushing back just for the sake of rebelling. It needs to be culturally understood that pushback must be motivated from an agenda of improving a process (increasing frequency of positive customer experience and/or, making the process easier for the employee to accomplish). This distinction has to be enforced by everyone. Some people just like to hear their own voice in a crowd, and this cannot be the motivation of their input. Pushback is unacceptable if one's agenda is to discredit the person. To do so would be disrespectful. It's the *idea* being discredited, never the submitter thereof. Respect and decorum have to be part of the employee challenge process, so poking a person in the eye is off limits. If the situation turns into an ugly shouting match, you are doing it wrong. Again, you can't just expect this clarification to manifest by chance. Rules of respect for people must be clearly established and communicated so everyone can thrive. This is how you develop a collaborative cultural condition intentionally instead of just admiring the preferred behavior when it occurs by chance.

Lest you think this concept of rebelling comes out of thin air or the land of idealistic nirvana, consider this real-life example. Ray Dalio created a hedge fund company called Bridgewater and wrote the book *Principles*. He advocates for a process of meritocracy—allowing the best ideas to win (based on their **merit**) regardless of the rank or status of the person suggesting it. He describes the critical, empowering elements as *"Radical Truth and Radical Transparency."* This condition encourages employees to freely push back on things they consider less-than-worthy of improving a process. If you feel your idea has more merit, or someone else's lacks merit, you speak up with radical truth and transparency. It exists as the company standard, and position on the corporate ladder has no bearing when it comes to criticizing a process or idea, even if it originated from senior leadership. Can you imagine how liberating this must feel for the employees? No place for egos here. It's all about the best idea being implemented – not the idea from the most powerful person in the room or the loudest voice. Meritocracy is an entrenched part of the culture at Bridgewater and I consider it a breath of fresh air. Imagine the sense of value it would instill in an employee, which is bound to generate increased levels of engagement, which then motivates employees to be even more forthcoming with respectful challenges, which in turn results in opportunities to continuously improve processes for customers and employees alike. I often speak about employee engagement being a powerful condition to nurture in human beings because of what it leads to. My Lean journey has proven this to me more times than I can recall. I've tried to incorporate it into every process improvement and leadership class I've taught over the years.

Mr. Dalio defends his system of meritocracy in this way. "I know that without such a system, we would lose both the best thinking and the best thinkers, and I'd be stuck with either kiss-asses or subversives who kept their disagreements and hidden resentments to themselves. For this all to work, I believed and still believe that we need to be radically truthful and radically transparent with each other."[xxii]

Wow! Don't know about you, but those words give me goosebumps. Who wouldn't want to work their butt off in a company truly valuing rebellion against wasteful processes and ideas without merit? Just imagine how cool it would be for the best idea to win, and everyone was an equal contributor to the end result. Too many employees are mere drones carrying out plans after they were tossed over the wall without the option to challenge any portion of them. Idea submitters might think they have given birth to something marvelous until others poke holes in it. But please understand, the activity of poking holes in it will make for a better idea, and ultimately a better outcome for the process. Isn't this what the objective should be in the first place? I cringe when I think about the insane countermeasures managers have forced on me over the years. Some were so ridiculous you would proclaim I made them up. I laugh now, but at the time, I felt helpless and profoundly disrespected. Fortunately, I learned how not to treat human beings from the plethora of traditional managers I observed along the way.

Ray Dalio also says, "It is more important to have good challengers than good followers." Think about this statement for a moment. Notice how dramatically it diverges from the norm entrenched in the minds of traditional managers. If you believe a "team player" is an employee who does what you say, when you say, and how you say to do something without questioning the merit of your decree, you are as far as humanly possible from developing said employee into the best version of themselves. By instilling fear and subordination, your approach to leadership is stifling opportunities for the tradeoff of making you feel strong and important. How pathetic is this? Does it exist in your company? Are egos and arrogance standing in the way of greater levels of success?

Machines are mindless followers of instructions void of objections or the need to feel valued and respected. This is not the case for human beings. As a titled supervisor, if you reward subordinated sheep and disparage fearless rebels, your dysfunction will eventually drive a company to extinction. At a minimum, it will not be a revered place of employment. Servant leaders clearly understand the distinction.

One of the many individuals I am connected to on LinkedIn created a caricature depiction of the desired relationship rebels are seeking with their bosses. I thank Tanmay Vora for allowing me to share this with you in its entirety. Please take the time to carefully read the nine elements and then discuss it with your peers. The perfect topic for your next staff meeting! Ask each other what the prevailing reaction to rebels is in your company overall, in your smaller organizations, and allow Radical Truth and Radical Transparency to be tested during the discussions. I genuinely believe this will be a valuable exercise. Perhaps it will alter some misperceptions of the rebellious behavior I have been describing, and cultural changes will begin. As I mentioned before, much of the disrespect dispensed onto employees is not intentionally mean spirited. It occurs because the unaware manager is not processing their behavior as disrespectful. That interpretation is absent; thus, their process of leading (not them as a person) is broken. They have some end goal in mind (like, meet the monthly numbers) and workers are just the machines to get it done. They view rebels as slowing down process decrees with annoying questions and challenges. How unfortunate for the creative minds being ignored. Most people truly want to be valued members of their companies, and given the right environmental conditions, they will be. This includes traditional managers who are only replicating the disrespectful behaviors modeled for them when they were value-adding workers. There is hope even for them if humility can overcome arrogance, and if someone is willing to develop them in the direction of Lean leadership. Depending on the level of traditional management entrenchment, this can be an enormous undertaking, but it shouldn't be an excuse to forego trying. Someone needs to be the first to rebel.

Insights from: RebelsatWork.com
Sketchnote by: Tanmay Vora | @tnvora | QAspire.com

Side Story - For a period of about a year, I worked for a traditional manager who wasn't especially mean spirited as much as he was absent. Jack would hand out assignments at the beginning of the shift then retreat to his office. The door would remain closed for the remainder of the day. If we needed his assistance, too bad. Figure it out on your own. If we needed his input on anything, we were out of luck. If something went wrong, deal with it. If the outcome of our unassisted activity was undesirable, there would be a chastising at the beginning of the next shift for guilty parties. All jackass workers must be admonished for poor results. As we finished work tasks, we would knock on his door, and he would open it just enough to hand the completed paperwork through to him. No dialogue, just the transfer of the documents to him. This was how he managed the team. We got used to it for the most part, but it was just weird. Think about this management style (and yours) as you ponder the following questions. Did his process:

1. develop employees to their fullest potential?
2. strive for the empowerment of employees?
3. show employees respect as contributing members of the team?
4. convey VOC requirements to employees?
5. keep employees up to speed on performance levels of their processes?
6. encourage input for improvements?
7. seek hurdles burdening employees?

Now, you might be viewing his management style in a wholly negative light, but please stop and consider a manager who isn't quite *this* absent. The traditional management effect is still present. Perhaps he/she is disinclined to speak to their direct reports, and they spend a good portion of their day holed up in a fancy office (further reinforcing their sense of self-importance) or in wasteful meetings accomplishing nothing of substance to make tasks easier for anyone. They probably prefer emails over direct conversation or even a phone call with employees. Maybe the conversations are batched (they have a 1-on-1 at their convenience every other Tuesday at 9:30, or team meetings once a month) but recognize the tendency toward absentee management is present, nonetheless. Interactions accommodate the supervisor, not the employees. This is disrespectful. It may not be as severe, but they are still unavailable much of the time. If needed, the employee has to hunt this manager down because of whatever excuse the manager comes up with for being gone from the Gemba. Work comes to a halt while we send out the search party for the missing manager.

Bottom line – Infrequently communicative managers are not behaving in supplier-mode for the workers. Probably a culturally developed habit, this style clearly reminds the employee who is the more important person here. If you as a manager are not continually trying to find/reduce hurdles in the way of your direct reports, not talking to them multiple times daily, not actively encouraging their input, not attentively listening when they challenge some portion of a broken process or a countermeasure you dreamt up without a root cause or even a problem associated with it, not frequently hanging out where the real work is getting accomplished, not listening *to* them far more than talking *at* them, then your leadership process is not much better than Jack's was. Feel free to justify your level of absenteeism, but recognize you have a performance gap. You can label this an opportunity to improve, or you can continue the status quo with whatever excuses you can muster up. Your choice, but if you choose the latter path, accept your label of a traditional manager. You've earned it.

This next manager I describe is not a single person, but a compilation of multiple dysfunctional bosses I've worked for directly, been aware of, or had described to me by people working for them. These are not your garden variety traditional manager being disrespectful unintentionally. On the contrary. Their actions are intentional, calculated, willfully implemented, and even mean-spirited in some cases. They are the worst of the worst.

We'll call this collective person Tyran. On the surface, Tyran seems like a decent human being. Well educated, well dressed, probably been with the company for many years, and behaves in public with oral and written political correctness commensurate with his years of practice. Tyran generally displays a corporate demeanor the uninformed observer would interpret as positive. He sports a convincing behavior of faking genuine interest in what you have to say to him. Tyrans have learned the rules of the game very well and play with convincing confidence. Most of them, anyway.

This is the shell of a Tyran. Underneath the façade lies a passive-aggressive, manipulative element rarely displayed in public. These managers will lie to employees, manipulate accounts of issues and conversations, and still remain void of remorse. Their personal agenda of demonstrating complete power over others remains paramount despite the carefully calculated façade they have polished over time. This deceitful behavior has the capability of turning creative thinkers into submissive drones. Employees in his sphere of control will comply for fear of losing their jobs. Not only did Tyran complete a bachelor's degree from the University of Cavemen, but he went to on to acquire an advanced degree in the collegiate discipline of self-serving management. Challenging an idea Tyran throws over the wall will be met with cautious disfavor at first, and ultimately with tactical methods to get you in line or out the door. These all-knowing managers make decisions with steadfast disinterest in employee input and then expect uncontested compliance. Do as they say and you will remain in good favor. Publicly admire their decrees to stroke their significant ego, and you will gain points and perhaps a special stall in their pen of sheep. They admire lackeys who blindly follow, and have no tolerance for anyone trying to alter their carefully designed world. Tyrans know exactly how to play the game and have aspirations of seeking yet higher levels of authority regardless of who gets emotionally damaged along the way. They are self-admiring individuals and view direct reports as tools to be used, controlled, and manipulated. Cross them, and they will embellish something insignificant to paint you in the light of an underperforming employee, regardless of what your actual performance is. Developing you as an employee never hits their radar because there is but one person of importance in their world. Let it never be misunderstood; Tyran is in charge, and you are a pawn to carry out his obstinate vision. Alternatives to Tyran's view are not solicited, and should you boldly offer up nonconforming perspectives, you will be moved into the category of an employee to be 'dealt with.'

On the other hand, the typical Tyran does get things done. Deadlines are met on-time, and goals are accomplished by sheer force of his will. This is what sustains his favor in the eyes of senior leadership. Unfortunately, the employees carrying out his mission are the expendable resource. Arrogance and demonstrative posturing compensate for his shortcomings, and the traditional culture is blind to, or at least downplays, the disrespect shown to employees. Tyrans are polished bureaucrats and navigate the corporate environment with skillful precision. They wield absolute power. People above them in title tend to look the other way when grumblings surface. Managers with this behavioral habit retain a self-evident posture of entitlement, believing their tenure and results will protect all behaviors towards employees. Unfortunately, this is often a reality, further enabling their style. They are dictators with smiles and excel at smoke and mirrors to paint their deficiencies in a positive light.

Tyrans are a cancer in a company. They will systematically subdue initiative not in direct alignment with theirs. Their behavior will keep great ideas from seeing the light of day and will drive good employees to exit if they are unable to live with the subservient demands. Direct reports are warm bodies to a Tyran, and completely dispensable. In fact, employees in their charge will be periodically reminded of this (with passive-aggressive techniques) lest they get a misguided notion to attempt autonomy outside of the master's decreed plan. Taking the initiative without Tyran's prior permission? Don't even think about it. This is their kingdom, and mother-may-I is the required step prior to acting. Autonomous behavior is taboo.

Tyrans consider humility synonymous with weakness. They avoid it with the reliability of muscle memory. If a process outcome was undesirable, some employee is to blame. Tyrans would admit to no contributory role. Three phrases they would never be accused of using are "*I don't know,*" "*I was wrong,*" and "*What do you think?*" These are absent in this manager's vernacular by habit. Tyrans are adept at avoiding HR intervention, and with employees in fear of losing their jobs, formal complaints are unlikely to be initiated. These vindictive managers persist and spread discontent everywhere they set up camp. They use fear as their weapon-of-choice to create compliance because it works.

But perhaps Tyran's most disturbing trait is his self-evaluation. If asked to rate his leadership on a scale of one to ten, Tyran will extend his chest and proudly proclaim himself a strong seven, even as he works diligently at keeping his employees in their "proper place." Tyran absolutely believes he is rocking the characteristics of successful leadership performance. He will cite multiple examples of process conditions that he alone took from failing to stellar. *I'm the guy who can kick ass, take names, and drive the goal condition to reality when others have failed,* or so he has thoroughly convinced himself. In his mind, he is honestly ranking himself objectively. It's not an act. This is perhaps Tyran's saddest characteristic—he is convinced his leadership style is one to be admired, emulated, and rewarded. He honestly does not see the dysfunction. Seven? You decide.

Show of hands, how many of you have worked for or known a Tyran sometime in your career? To what degree did you trust them? If you aren't currently working for a Tyran, are you aware of one or two in your work environment? Anyone want to admit to possessing at least some of their characteristics?

While very few bosses are completely traditional managers all the time, the further they trend toward this extreme condition, the more they contaminate efforts of generating employee engagement. Even void of a Lean transformation underway in a company, they will plunge employees into states of ambivalence toward process improvement. I suppose they could ultimately be convinced to seek and respect employee input, but it seems unlikely. Their years of being rewarded for poor behavior have solidified their broken process of management.

The solution is harsh, but simple: the Tyrans out there will have to be removed if you are to improve your company culture. The people I am describing have already ignored multiple attempts at softening their behavior, and to allow them to remain for whatever excuse you can conjure up (they've been with the company so long they deserve to stay until retirement age, or whatever), is a decision in denial of the negative impact. Rewarded behavior will be repeated behavior. Leadership needs to decide if the positive results Tyrans produce are worth the consequences on the damaged employees left in their wake. Short-term business results pale in comparison to the negative effect Tyrans have on the human spirit of those reporting to them.

I was exposed to many Tyrans during my lifetime, some in my own work situations, others merely observed in stores or restaurants. They all taught me precisely what respectful leadership does not look like. I learned powerful lessons as a result. These individuals will show you the countless ways things are done incorrectly, and I paid attention each time I encountered it. I suspect most people could share stories of intentionally hateful managers they worked for and around.

A friend of mine worked for a traditional manager who would put his hand up (like a stop sign in your face) and announce to the employee, "*I need you to stop talking and just listen to me. I'm not paying you to think, only to do precisely what I tell you to do.*" You can imagine how humiliating and demotivating this could be. No manager on earth would be unaware of how disrespectful this is. This is intentional tyranny. A Tyran is unaffected by the negative impact on the human being. Employees subjected to this disrespectful behavior will be unlikely to contribute beyond the bare minimum to retain their employment status. Imagine an entire company of employees doing no more than absolutely necessary. This, my friends, is a horribly broken management process. Getting replacement employees after the previous ones have run for their lives enables it to continue. Promoting these people to even higher levels of authority spreads the message this is the valued behavior and others will follow suit. This must be addressed if you are ever to have long term loyalty and high levels of engagement from employees.

Paul Marciano talks at length about the negative impacts supervisors are responsible for. In his book *Carrots and Sticks Don't Work*, he says, "*If your employees are failing to meet expectations and goals, it is because you have failed them. Your job is to make your people successful, and you have to take responsibility for setting them up for success. If you believe that the primary reason that people fail to meet goals has more to do with them than you, then you should not be in the business of supervising, developing, or leading people.*"

Paul Marciano and I are on the same page of music. And if this is being rough on managers, label me guilty as charged.

At this point, the traditional managers with egos the size of Texas are crying *Foul!* at my argument. Maybe they have even thrown down the BS flag because they view themselves as accomplished in their career. I can understand this position. If you disbelieve the behavioral connections, you might never be humble enough to process this in a different light. Your flawed understanding of human behaviors is currently set in stone. I get it, but I implore you to step back for just a moment to consider another view, even if only on the outside chance you might not have the causal connections assembled correctly in your mind. If your approach is truly the better of the two, then your employees will be highly respectful of you as a leader. Are they? How is your turnover rate? Have you been courageous enough to collect this data? Are they excited about their job, spontaneously offering up opportunities to improve things, fully engaged with satisfying customer requirements in the most efficient and easiest manner possible, and always going the extra mile to help everyone around them be more successful as well? Do they look forward to coming to work, and would they recommend working there to others inquiring about the cultural environment? If your continued supervisory status was dependent on their thumbs up vote, would you get it? I have often suggested employee input should be a significant consideration for any supervisor retaining their role or being promoted beyond their present title. Until they view employees as valued customers instead of expendable suppliers, disrespectful behavior (intentional or not) will persist.

Consider this concept: The supervisor should be tasked not only with empowering employees, but doing so with the welfare of the employee in mind. In a traditional environment, the employee is blamed wholly when things go south. What responsibility is the supervisor's process taking? Basically none. He/she has decreed the task, and the employee is left to their own devices to make it happen. If the process is fraught with hurdles, delays, and problematic milestones, so be it. Mr. Employee should figure out the workarounds and reach the finish line. This is what they are being paid to do, right? *By golly, back in the day, no one was holding my hand, and I managed to survive. These whiny employees just need to step up, or I'll find someone to replace them.*

Insanity. The cavemen out there are creating havoc with engagement levels of employees and not taking any of the rap themselves. It makes no sense when you break it down. Having said this, I fully recognize few things are one-sided. The employee most certainly has to do their part and take some initiative, but first, they have to be empowered to do so in a safe, respectful environment. They need a culture where it is okay to make mistakes if the process is flawed, but it's not okay to withhold criticism of the process fault points. They need to be trusted. Hurdles need to be removed continuously, and this is the job of leadership because **they have the power to do it.**

One last question. If you possess some of the characteristics of a Tyran, can you honestly say undesirable process outcomes are entirely the result of poor employee performance, and those employees just need to work harder next time? If you responded in the affirmative, then consider the possibility you are blind to the broken elements present in every process. Unfortunately, it is far easier to blame the employee than to pick at the process. Indeed, it's quicker. The boss is tasked with far more important things, like deciding on strategic matters and attending meetings only the more elite thinkers are involved in.

But, as depressing as all this sounds, most traditional managers are not bad people, they are just ill-equipped authoritarians attempting to manipulate others to achieve corporate goals. The boss needs guidance the same as the worker does. Leadership competencies are no more intuitive than assembling a widget according to expectations. I make the claim leadership development programs are failing new managers the same as these managers are failing their employees doing the actual work for the company. Broken processes waiting for rebels to proclaim the opportunity to improve.

What does your company do to prepare employees for leadership roles? Do you have a culture to train them in advance (including engagement generation techniques), and then coach them for the duration of their employment? Or, are they worker bees one day and bosses the next with little or no preparation or subsequent assistance? Do you throw them into the deep end of the pool, hand them an anvil, and metaphorically say, "*Do the best you can. If you screw up, you will be tossed back into the shallow end with the minions where you came from.*"? Does your company declare what acceptable leadership behavior looks like, and then diligently stand behind the documented standards? Or, is unacceptable behavior allowed to exist until overt incidents are impossible to ignore? Do you have a solid awareness of the engagement levels being generated in your company as well as how those levels are influenced by their supervisors, or are you relying on gut feelings?

Most effective leaders do not come by the capability naturally the way Ken Sloan and Phil Logsdon did. For the vast majority of human beings, servant leadership is not innate; rather, it has to be nurtured like any other skillset. This is why leadership development needs to be intentional, continuous (once and done won't cut it), and evaluated according to the employee's perspective. Their behaviors are a direct reflection of the management team over them. Are the managers in your company readers? Do they seek out new methodologies? Do they assist each other in recognizing ineffective techniques, or does everyone just do their own thing? Are the worst of the worst (the Tyrans) allowed to remain, and if so, are you one of the managers looking the other way because you do not consider it your role to get involved with correcting the situation?

If leadership development is the responsibility of the individual manager to do on their own, it will be sporadically engaged in by the curious and the innately humble. The sane alternative is development by structured design. Companies get so wrapped around the axle with day-to-day activities and firefighting because making the numbers is paramount, they sometimes can't justify the time required for developing leaders. Too many other important things to deal with. Customer complaints, screaming shareholders, delayed completion dates, process defects, safety incidents, material backorders, budget balancing, regulatory infractions, union issues, you name it. Activity will be prioritized, but not always with insightful analysis of the long-term impacts on issues not directly associated with immediate financial outcomes.

Just remember that your options are to take what you get by chance, or purposely mold it to a required standard. Shrink the variation. How different would your culture be if traditional managers ceased to exist, and servant leaders piled up at the mean? Reduce the standard deviation to nearly zero and just imagine what could be. The only thing harder than becoming a Servant leader is living with the demoralizing business effects of traditional management.

Side Story - During a portion of my Lean journey, a fairly senior executive offered an assessment of my behavior. He said, *"You are really rough on leaders."* I'm convinced this was not meant to be a compliment, but ultimately, I took it as one. My response to him included concurrence, but with significant clarification because I recognized he was lumping all persons in positions of authority into the Leader bucket. While I profoundly admire and look up to **leaders** in supplier-mode, I am indeed "rough" on **traditional managers** who perhaps unintentionally suck the life spirit out of employees wanting nothing more than to contribute, to present their ideas about process shortcomings, and to feel valued at work. So, yes, I'm rough on self-serving management, especially when they recognize the negative impact they are having on people and processes and then choose to ignore, excuse, or spin it with some justifiable reason. Someone else is at fault in their view. To be something less than rough on them is to look the other way, give them the benefit of the doubt because the culture molded them—effectively reinforcing their behavior—and I am incapable of doing this.

They are not Leaders in my eyes. They are merely the person with the formal title looking out for themselves first and foremost, and I have zero respect for their process. In all actuality, they should be ashamed of themselves, so please don't ask me to not be rough on them. They wouldn't survive one week at Toyota, Honda, Integris, Virginia Mason, Southwest Airlines, or many other companies demanding respect for employees. I only said a fraction of this to the executive offering his critique of my style, but herein you have the full posture I take. Am I too rough? Shouldn't *someone* be rough on them? You decide.

My exemplar, Dr. Deming, was likewise rough on management because he recognized they were the only ones who had the leverage to intentionally shift a culture. Frontline workers are mostly just the recipients of leadership decisions and cannot, on their own, alter cultural conditions. To accomplish this, existing and future supervisors will need considerable training, support, and coaching from their leadership. These are missing elements in a traditional environment. Many supervisors are winging the art of nurturing engagement in others. Deming put the responsibility squarely on the shoulders of management and wanted them to be fully aware of how they alone possessed the ability to move a culture in negative or positive directions via their behavior. I encourage readers to digest some of his literature and videos; you will clearly recognize the genius of the man who was "rough on management."

"A bank that failed last week may have had excellent operations – speed at the tellers' windows with few mistakes; few mistakes in the bank statements; likewise, in the calculation of interest and of penalties and loans. The cause of the failure at the bank was bad management, not operations." – W. Edwards Deming

Without intentionally replicating the path Deming took trying to place final responsibility at the feet of leadership, my Lean journey had transformed me into precisely this mindset. Consequently, I did not feel ashamed when the senior person accused me of being rough on leadership. If a Lean transformation is to be successful, even by modest levels of evaluation, there can exist no excuses for managers not actively seeking constant improvement of their leadership styles. Although we didn't discuss it, his own process – for whatever reasons - was to enable traditional management. It's a systemic problem unalterable by looking the other way. Capitulation to traditional management in a company is equivalent to sitting motionless in a boat, allowing it to drift in whatever direction the wind blows. One must stand up, grab both sides, and fearlessly rock it to alter course. A necessary disruption is required to wake the slumbering managers from their illusion of being leaders. I tried to be this rebellious change agent, but I assure you, it was not well received by those faking Lean under the fictitious guise of a transformation.

I said this before, but it bears repeating: Lean leadership is not a tweak of traditional management, it is a major overhaul. It is also not for everyone. Only those interested in creating an atmosphere of human growth with abundant, genuine respect (emphasis on the word genuine) heaped on every employee should embark on such a journey.

In retrospect, I appreciated the executive sharing his evaluation of my posture toward management. Without specifically saying so, he confirmed I was on the right path. Except for his mistakenly assigning the role of leader to everyone with formal authority in the company, he was correct. Undeterred by the attempted behavior check, I will continue on my mission of helping the world recognize what managerial dysfunction looks like, and the alternative waiting to be unleashed. If I am scoffed at by some for this posture, so be it, and here is why: If just one person shifts from his/her current state into Lean leadership, I will consider my efforts worthwhile. Most supervisors can dramatically improve their process of interacting with employees if they are humble enough to try. The question is, can humility overcome arrogance? It rarely happens without an incentive.

There is one positive thing I want to emphasize about the broken processes traditional managers cling to: They have contributed powerful lessons which I will never forget. Traditional managers demonstrated how to do things wrong and the negative consequences associated with these behaviors. They repeatedly showed me what undeterred arrogance looks like, and each of them was a great—if not intentional—teacher. They would regularly demonstrate how to disrespect employees, and I, their student, would absorb the powerful lesson to not repeat their misguided ways. To this day, I continue to tell my students who share horror stories about the cavemen they have worked for, pay close attention, and learn from these UC grads. They have much to show you. They are modeling the opposite of what to do in a formal leadership position. Even if you cannot change their behaviors, don't miss out on the lessons you can log from those who have failed to evolve from assigned managers into inspirational Leaders.

I especially admire the message Simon Sinek shares about leadership. It perfectly aligns with the model of Lean leadership I have been describing, basically servant leadership on steroids. In a Ted Talk, Mr. Sinek said the following, *"Leadership is a choice. It is not a rank. I know many people at the senior most level of organizations who are absolutely not leaders. They are authorities, and we do what they say because they have authority over us, but we would not follow them. And I know many people who are the bottom of the organizations who have no authority and they are absolutely leaders because they have chosen to look after the person to the left of them, and the person to the right of them. This is what a leader is."*[xxxiii]

It's powerful stuff when you stop to fully digest what he is saying. Individuals with authority who treat employees as a means to their own self-serving end are indeed the furthest thing from leaders. The world has far too many Tyrans.

Quotes of human beings captured over the course of time have always been thought-provoking for me. They teach me things because I ponder the insight they are imparting with a sentence or two from their perspectives. I want to share of few of the ones related to leadership I find particularly insightful. Read and digest these – several times please – then honestly evaluate the culture you work in and contribute to. Are your leaders inspiring people with widespread respect in supplier-mode, or are they systematically motivating workers to seek employment elsewhere? I encourage you to post hard copies in your workspace and generate discussion among your peers. Insight without action is useless.

"No matter how good you think you are as a leader, the people around you will have all kinds of ideas for how you can get better. So, for me, the most fundamental thing about leadership is to have the humility to continue to get feedback and to try to get better – because your job is to try to get everyone else to get better." - Jim Yong Kim

"If you want to be a great leader, remember to treat all people with respect at all times." - Simon Sinek

"Good leaders must communicate vision clearly, creatively, and continually. However, the vision doesn't come alive until the leader models it." - John C. Maxwell

"Life's most urgent question is, what are you doing for others?" - Martin Luther King, Jr.

"True leaders understand that leadership is not about them but about those they serve. It is not about exalting themselves but about lifting others up." - Sheri L. Dew

"The greatest gift you can give someone is the power to be successful" - Ray Dalio

Had Any Useful Training Lately?

"It's not just about teaching, it's about awakening people – turning off their autopilot and seeing a new course of action." – Mark Stewart

Further breaking down the continuous improvement puzzle piece, the humble leader recognizes his/her workforce is not going to learn how to write a good problem statement, document the negative impact, perform root cause analysis, select and insert the best Lean countermeasures, and ultimately improve a process by osmosis.

Quick data collection: Show of hands here for every reader who has experienced an email from leadership or been told directly to *get better* at something. Just once I would have enjoyed hitting reply and asking Mr. or Ms. Manager how they would recommend I do it. Telling an employee to *"get better"* does zip to position a person for success. It's a **what** to a non-empowered worker without the critical **how**, but it sure does make the formal leader feel important. Positioning an employee for failure is disrespectful and happens all the time with ill-equipped managers at the helm.

Employees need to have training related to improving processes, good training! I'm not talking about a mandatory series of computer-based training (CBT) classes to satisfy some misguided requirement. I'm referring to small, logically ordered, palatable chunks dispensed by a passionate subject-matter-expert on process improvement in classroom settings affording questions/answers on the spot. Lean and process improvement need to be taught by someone who has stepped in enough potholes to know how to guide others. You don't get proficient at process improvement just by reading it in a book or hearing someone talk about it in a video. It darn sure doesn't happen because an email showed up in your already cluttered inbox saying, *"You need to do better!"* You have to combine the training with coaching, the actual application, and learning by failures. You have to get out there and actually *do* it. Books are great, and I highly recommend continually reading everything you can get your hands on to spark analysis and augment your current state behaviors, but practical competence comes from doing it, over and over again. Experiencing an instructor-led class, followed by physically engaging in the activity (coaching is critical here) will make the skillset come to life. No substitutions will get you to the land of awareness quicker, or more effectively. Companies serious about turning their entire workforce into critical thinkers will make Lean training part of onboarding, especially the behavioral aspects behind the tools. Allow it to be optional for folks when they have time to attend, and your results will be commensurate with the ineffective, non-serious approach you have chosen.

The training classes should also be evaluated for improvement opportunities every single time they are offered. It's easy to fall victim to assuming your training is all that and a bag of chips just because you built and delivered it. Negative. Ask students what they thought and be prepared to alter the class according to its intended objective. This is VOC. Also evaluate the post-training impact on your culture. Are your certified Green Belts continuing to utilize the skills and increasing flow, or has the training done nothing tangibly recognized by the company? Does the supervisor get involved in supporting on-going improvement activity with their newly certified Green Belt, or has this empowerment died on the vine along with the training?

Caution! Deep pothole up ahead. I'm a strong advocate for training—especially Lean training—being administered by someone who believes in it wholeheartedly, lives it daily, and has significant experience in the topics being presented. Not everyone in process improvement is a SME on every associated topic. To assign this task to someone steeped only in the subjects of Six Sigma and/or lacking the ability to stimulate deep interest in the issue is a recipe for wasted effort. Your Lean transformation will not take root or will be significantly delayed/extended. Students will not get excited about the potentialities of Lean. Not only is it disrespectful to the audience trying to grasp the concepts, perhaps for the very first time, but it is equally disrespectful to the unequipped person asked to teach it. Credentials and certifications mean nothing if the instructor is not striving to energize the room by conveying the psychology associated with process improvement. I've seen this ineffective approach taken and it is a disheartening picture. Tasking the ill-prepared to be the band leaders won't make the music sweet. Everyone has been to a training class at some point in their life and walked away thinking, *I'll never get that hour of my life back*. This is not the visceral reaction you want. People should leave a Lean class thinking, *Oh my gosh, this is incredible stuff. I want to do this. Where do I sign up for more?*

Not everyone is suited to teach, even if they do have the subject knowledge. Round peg in a square hole analogy. Effective teaching is an art form. Ineffective teaching dispenses information like a vending machine – mechanically and without emotion. No amount of coaching or practice will turn just anyone into what you are looking for. Teachers should be passionate, experienced, proficient people who are fully committed to the topic. Get one or two, have others shadow them to learn how it's done, and evaluate their progression via student feedback. And don't turn the newbies loose to solo before their wings are fully developed. This would be disrespectful. Finding people like this cold off the street is difficult to do, so filter your selection process accordingly because the transformation results depend on it. Don't settle on just any credentialed person simply because you need to fill a slot. These are your considerations if you are serious about properly infusing Lean into your culture. The instructors are describing the desired behavior to your employees, so you want it presented correctly. Do they generate excitement in a classroom, apathy, or something in between? Do they live and breathe the material, or view teaching as just a job? A slide-reader is not acceptable. Is it possible you tasked a warm body, and then you blindly assumed delivery was hitting the mark? Selecting and developing trainers should be viewed as a process like any other. Capture VOC and develop metrics, then monitor for gaps, and continuously reduce them with everyone's participation. Instructors need to be positioned for success like everyone else.

Side Story – Before I had any formal Lean training—back when I still thought putting an inspection at the end of a process to catch defects before they went out the door was a great idea—the government sent me to a root cause analysis class. We're probably going back to the late 80s here. Most of us were younger then. I can remember being excited about this topic and going in open-minded. It was indeed an instructor-led class, so we'll give it one point on the positive side. Unfortunately, the positive point total comes to an abrupt stop there.

It contained contrived situations, mishaps, damage to equipment or products, etc. in paragraph form, and then the student was to assign a root cause to the issue. Like all good government processes, they provided the hapless analyst a handy dandy list of causes to pick from. Not only was the brain work done in advance, but a well-intentioned government worker also went the extra mile and assigned a code number to each one. Now all you had to do is insert the code on the standard incident report form and call it a day. Pretty good process, huh?

I recall things like, *"Technician did not follow instruction,"* or *"Lack of communication,"* or my favorite useless root cause of all time, *"Human Error."* Whew! Once you mine jewels of this sparkling clarity, just imagine the subsequent countermeasures people might resort to. *Not following instructions* = Remind Bubba to follow instructions next time, or *Human Error* = Re-train the silly human. No doubt countermeasures of this caliber are destined to absolutely prevent the defect from ever happening again, right? And if by remote chance the defect repeats, we can just trot out the list of causes for some well-intentioned re-work. When I think how ineffective the class was I chuckle now, but at the time, it was dispensed with the same confidence of training kids back in the 50s to get under their desks in the event of a nuclear attack, and I bought into it. What did I have to compare it to? A novice will assume it's the gold standard.

Attention all converts to the belief quantifiable performance indicators are critical to providing you the visibility you need to reduce impactful gaps in your processes: this exact approach should be applied to the training you provide employees. The absence of metrics here may allow less than desirable results to exist. Audiences subjected to ineffective, uninspiring classes will convey the quality gap to their peers, and the energy may dissipate.

Having been to more than my share of totally useless training classes, I realize now how important it is to select and build training with a critical eye to what it needs to accomplish. Design of training is paramount to achieving value. When I start development of any class, there are certain things I have to know in order to produce a useful product. It's a VOC activity.

1. Who is the <u>intended audience</u> of this training? Leadership? Frontline workers? Both?
2. What <u>post-training behavior</u> do we desire from the student? Just awareness? Ability to replicate the skillset or competence to teach it themselves? Something in between?

If you don't have this basic information, your finished product is likely to be less than stellar. You'll need other details, of course, but these two elements are critical. Otherwise, students will not get the bang for the buck you are spending in development and delivery. Re-work and poor results are coming your way, so don't be surprised. The quickest way to turn people off to Lean is to make them endure an ineffective training class. I've been to a few, but this is true for any topic. No matter what the experience of the instructor, or the necessary preparation, defects can happen. But, they have to be viewed in the light of a broken process, not a faulty employee. Measure your training with student feedback, and these opportunities will tell you when it has crossed an unacceptable threshold. Then improve it, and measure again. It's a continuous cycle.

Side Story – I was on the job for barely a week when a certain leader asked me to develop a training class on process improvement. She was well-intentioned, but basically unable to give me definitive answers to my two questions. I gently pushed and probed as much as I felt comfortable doing, but I definitely didn't have enough to go on. I had gads of experience building and delivering training, but I was panicking with the few requirement morsels tossed at me. Regardless, I took an initial stab at the task and presented it for feedback.

She hated it. Okay, I can live with that, but tell me where it falls short of the requirements not given to me. Her feedback included the style was not what she was hoping for. The most specific thing she said to me was she didn't want to use any Lean language because the employees were not yet ready for it. Cue the next round of doomed rework.

Now *there* is a challenge for you! Build a process improvement class and don't mention Lean. And how does an unknowing audience become "ready" for new labels? Are there pills or injections for this eventuality? Might as well ask me to build a class about exciting college football games from the past and not mention my beloved Oklahoma Sooners. It just ain't gonna happen. It would be unnatural.

Desperately seeking useful VOC, I asked the question another way. "What do you envision this training looking like?"

And the answer was, "I'll know it when I see it."

Let's collectively speculate on my projected chances for success given this feedback. I'm not sure how many hours I spent on this material, but the presentation to this boss and some others in the company was nearly the catalyst for my resignation. It was that ugly of an experience.

When I presented the re-worked material yet again in a group setting, she responded with, "No, this is not at all what I want. Obviously, you are not the right person to develop this training."

Ouch!

My spirits immediately sank. I was no longer sure I had picked the right company to share my passion for Lean with, and not a single person came to my defense during this trashing of person and product. Wow. You set me up for guaranteed failure then proclaim to the group I am the cause of the undesired result. My relationship with this individual improved dramatically over the next couple of years, but this was definitely a learning experience of how disrespect impacts the employee, even when it is unintentionally administered.

Side Story – In graduate school, I was required to take one class in computer programming. I don't even recall why, but there was no escaping it. Believe me, I tried. I was a psychology major and saw no earthly scenario where I would be building software programs. The instructor was trying to explain a semester-long assignment given to the entire class. We had to create a simple "guess the right number" program in BASIC. By the way, I do remember what this stood for: Beginner's All-Purpose Symbolic Instruction Code. Wake me at 3:00 am from a dead sleep, and I can explain the acronym. Anyway, after multiple attempts to write code and test it, my program was riddled with errors and infinite loops because of my misapplied "Go To" coding. It was maddening. I remember wondering what kind of human being could find this fun. The instructor tried mightily to explain this and that to me, but his coaching would have had the same result if given with the computer turned off. I knew, and he most assuredly knew, writing computer code was not in the cards for my career choice.

What is my point here? Simple. Forcing an employee to attend a training class not directly, or even indirectly beneficial to improving their ability to perform tasks associated with the job might be an effort in futility. It checks a box but builds zero competencies. **Waste!** Companies do it all the time. The government was notorious for it. I spent 35 years in the world of Uncle Sam—active duty Navy and then 29 years as a civil servant—and the list of worthless classes I attended is as long as an Alaskan winter night. We went to one useless offering after another, and then it was checked off in our personnel records as though we had accomplished something of value. Within a few weeks of starting my job with the Air Force back in 1985, they sent me to a basic hand tools class. Now mind you, I entered employment there with an Airframe and Power plant (A&P) license issued from the FAA and had worked as an aircraft mechanic in general aviation for about 4 years, plus 6 years of aircraft maintenance in the Navy. The instructor was describing a hammer, a screwdriver, a wrench, as though it was required for everyone to begin at this level. Never did they evaluate my mechanical aptitude before assigning me to this multi-hour class. It was on the list, and all must attend. On a side note, imagine the insanity of needing this class for any newly hired mechanics in the first place. Any chance the hiring process might have performance gaps? While many of us found it quite entertaining, it was most assuredly a broken process in need of improvement. A better method would have determined which employees needed it, and which did not. The government, however, was prone to one-size-fits-all. *Send everyone to this class!* Makes the planning process easy but induces incredible waste.

Side Story – Here is one you'll enjoy. I don't even remember the name of it, but many years later, as an aircraft maintenance planner, we had to attend this multi-month class to develop the skill set of measuring cycle time. Seems reasonable enough when you consider part of our job was to evaluate how much labor time to assign to individual tasks the mechanics were performing on the aircraft. I'm fairly certain the course was designed during WW2. The old, poor quality videos they showed us were comically depicting factory workers performing assembly tasks. We had to evaluate if they were working at a normal or increased pace. Completely subjective to establish the fine-line threshold from one label to the other, but this wasn't the really insane portion of this class. The coursework required the student to calculate standard deviation using paper and pencil and the long formula. Excel existed, and we had computers back at our workstations, but in this class, only a calculator was permitted. Cue the furrowed eyebrows and groans.

There were three ridiculous design methodologies at work here.

Ridiculous methodology number **1**. We were calculating standard deviation longhand, over, and over, and over. That's a crapton (actual unit of measure in the government) of in-series calculations with numerous opportunities for one silly mistake along the way to make the final answer wrong. I guess if it's 1958 and Mr. Government Worker is limited to a Big Chief tablet and a #2 pencil, repetition is the way to go. Or, if you just wanted to explain how the formula came to be, it might warrant one or two manual passes at it for the sake of understanding the formula derivation. But to completely abandon how someone would actually determine a standard deviation in the real job situation (by computer) is ludicrous. No telling how much wasted cycle time it added to this class, including the instructor going through every painful calculation on the board for all to digest after we just did it at our own desk. It was torturous, and a mandatory training requirement for our job. Shut-up-and-color.

Ridiculous methodology number **2**. With all the relentless scratching on paper, erasing, and sighing to finally achieve the correct value of standard deviation, and then enduring the same manual calculations repeated step by painful step on the whiteboard, there was not one single moment of explanation of what standard deviation even meant. Just get the right value, and you satisfied the training requirement. No discussion of how it depicts the variability in a data set, how it can be used to compare multiple data sets before and after improvements, or the connection it has to process capability and specification limits. None of that. Just scratch out the right number on your papyrus and cue the ovation. At the end of this mind-numbing class destined to reduce one's IQ by 20 points was a written test. If you got too many wrong, you simply kept guessing at the multiple-choice answers until you miraculously picked enough of the right ones to pass. Failing was an impossible outcome, so students did the walk-of-shame back and forth from their desk to the instructor until the magic percentage of correct answers was eventually achieved. Whew! Just give me the option to be beaten with a club.

Ridiculous methodology number **3**. Planners never actually did time studies on production processes. It was in the documented job description, but the culture had become one of guessing or just asking the mechanic how long a task took. Occasionally, external contractors were hired to do it. So, the entire training was moot. Every planner and every planning supervisor across the Air Force base knew it before sending people to the lengthy class. Didn't matter. The standard set of job training elements was etched on the backside of a fossilized stone tablet, and applicability to the job was not a deciding factor. Every planner followed the same wasteful path and checked the box. That's just how it was. Challenging applicability was not an option.

It was years later when I went through black belt training and made the mental awareness leap to what standard deviation was all about. Not long after, I was asked to teach the class because the sole instructor who had been doing it since prohibition was about to retire and they needed a new drone to parrot the usual drivel to another generation of hapless planners. Initially, it seemed like an intriguing opportunity—I'd always wanted to teach—but when I proposed the dire need of updating the material and exercises to reflect the modern universe, things went south with this gig offer. My challenge to the status quo was seen as disruptive, and I was removed from potential candidates to teach the class. The culture in 2006 was not ready for me yet, but my time was to come. Teaching and coaching would become the most rewarding portion of my Lean journey.

I share these humorous training examples to make a simple point. If the information your organization deems important to expose employees to is not helping them perform their job, is not making it easier or quicker to produce your product or service for customers, or is not advancing critical thinking skills, then evaluate why precious time is devoted to it in the first place. Radical truth and radical transparency need to happen here. What is the merit of the class? Is it just stuff to check training boxes possibly valid in the past, but no longer? Is the driving reason to create a CYA condition in case the employee is involved in a safety incident or other form of defect? *Your honor, we trained that employee! It's not our fault he screwed up.* Does the class exist to justify the instructor's existence? I implore leadership to scrutinize all training and ensure it will absolutely help develop the employee into a more valuable asset for the company or themselves. And if you decide the training is necessary, by all means, measure the impact it is having on the workplace mission. Ask the students what they think about it every single time it's delivered. Do *they* see value in it? Would they recommend it to others? Do they have ideas on how to improve it? Seek this information, use the results to decide if changes need to be made, and then, by all means, *make* the changes. Don't allow training to become stale or irrelevant. If ready-made material is purchased off the shelf, make certain it is thoroughly evaluated by a SME prior to swiping your credit card and installing it on your corporate website for employees. Exit your corporate office now and then, and Gemba walk the classes. Situations change frequently, and just because a course was on-target when it was created does not mean it still is. Your employees' time is too valuable to waste, and your external customer is not willing to pay for it. You are disrespecting an employee by forcing them to suffer through training not capable of helping them better meet VOC requirements or developing them as a person.

If thinking about training in these terms was the standard approach, I speculate the quantity of meaningless classes would plummet, and the quality of training would go up for all of it. But you won't know if you don't measure training in a similar way you would measure your other processes. I remain steadfast in the assertion of a process not continuously critiqued for opportunities is a process destined to perform less efficiently than it can. Training is part of your overall value stream, so please give it commensurate attention.

When companies get the process improvement bug, sending employees to Green and Black Belt training is quite common. It's a logical progression, so you get folks on board with structured problem-solving. It makes sense. My complaint with most of the programs, however, is the enormous emphasis on tools, and little, if any mention of what it takes to make a Lean transformation happen across the enterprise. The cavernous gap is the leadership piece to drive the cultural change. How does the Lean leader behave? What should they do? What are the specific behaviors their traditional predecessors modeled they should now abandon like a worn-out pair of shoes? I don't care how comfortable those shoes were 10 years ago, they are now ill-equipped to serve the competitive needs you have now. You could train/certify every single employee as a Green Belt, but if the company's leadership is not trained to be **Lean leaders**, the momentum will sputter. It's an outdated model inefficiently trying to carry your company forward. Isolated pockets of excellence might glow for a while, but eventually, the spirit of continuous improvement will evaporate.

Worker bees will only do it for so long without passionate leaders supporting them. They will see internal counterpart organizations exiting the Lean bus and challenge why they are still riding on it. The positive reinforcement becomes sporadic. Structured problem solving will dwindle, then vanish. A tendency for reverting back to old behaviors is inevitable. For larger companies, I recommend determining how many employees have attended GB or BB training, and then never engaged in a project beyond the one they used for certification. This will help you determined if your money was well spent. Well, you get the sad picture. At some point, people proclaim the "Lean stuff" just didn't work, and of course, it didn't. Anything done incorrectly with uncommitted executive support won't produce the intended result. You want Lean? You must establish a viable root system to nurture it. No short cuts or fake trees permitted. If leaders are not modeling the behavior themselves, it just won't take hold. If I were king for a day, every Green Belt and Black Belt program would include the leadership piece (including the mechanics of Gemba walking) instead of limiting them to mountains of tools filling every available minute of the class. Students would not be enrolled without a committed supervisor vowing to support the activity post-certification, including the behavioral aspects. Statistics are fine and needed. People need to know about process maps, one-piece flow, Kanbans, 5S, mistake proofing, control charts, root cause analysis, quick changeover, drum-buffer-rope, DOE, Special and Common cause variability, all of that. But leaving out the leadership element is equivalent to teaching me how to calculate a standard deviation and then not telling me what to do with the final number. It will leave me un-empowered. So, don't be shy about challenging the GB/BB programs you pay for your employees to attend. Demand the gaps get filled to meet your need. You are the customer. Speak up. Status quo behavior yields status quo results, and in turn, will bring joy to your Lean-minded competitors.

Art Byrne, the respected CEO of Wiremold and one of my favorite authors on Lean, talks about the tours companies would take at his company so they could witness Lean first hand. When the request for tours became somewhat of a burden, he declared they would only agree to conduct them if the CEO of the requesting company was in attendance. After this rule insertion, the tours dwindled to nothing. Why was this the outcome? Were the CEOs just too busy? Not humble enough to possibly imagine some other company would know something he/she didn't? Hard to say, but the amazing part to me is the pervasive lack of curiosity these managerial giants have. After they reach the leadership summit, does the continuous development part of their brain just turn off? Or does it get delegated? Wouldn't they *want* to learn how to do things easier and get better results at the same time? Do they honestly believe they have everything necessary in their leadership technique? It would be interesting someday to query a representative sample of some of them and build a Pareto chart to display the reasons for resistance. I wonder where "I already do this," and "I'm too busy" would fall.

Side Story – Even with the most refined messages, training can be challenging for the instructor when student pushback occurs. Knowing the topic is one thing, but you have to also be prepared for the unexpected. My approach is to get people's attention with process reality but try to do it as respectfully as I can. Following every Lean class I taught, I'd email the audience with a survey to get their feedback. This was my barometer to understand the current state of the culture at a deeper level. After one particular class, a student populated the open-ended text box on the last survey question with their challenge to my premise all processes were broken to some extent, and all had the opportunity to become better at satisfying customer requirements. *"While the instructor is quite passionate*

213

about this material, he should be cautious about his claim of all our processes having opportunities to improve. Most of our processes are pretty good, and the sky is not falling."

I probably read this a dozen or more times. It spoke volumes to me on several levels.

First, this person was exhibiting a defensive posture, likely from the stance of defending themselves as opposed to the process they worked in. It was my strict intent to model the behavior of attacking processes and not people, but my message was not always received in this manner. Why would they not see the rampant dysfunction all around them? Was it too embarrassing, or did they really believe they were performing at benchmark levels of excellence? My assessment goes back to culture. If the environment you work in is continually peppered with emails from the CEO thanking everyone for their remarkable performance, you tend to believe the language is representative of efficiency across the enterprise, when in fact, this was most certainly not the case. This student interpreted my message as an attack on people instead of the intended attack on processes. They felt insulted, and I totally get that. But I would also challenge a person with this posture to show me a process, any process, void of defects, delays, or safety issues 100% of the time. Every process can be improved and, therefore, is broken to some extent. A large part of teaching Lean is waking the audience from their contented assessment of process performance. Complacency is the mortal enemy of continuous improvement.

Second, the culture of this company was basically void of performance indicators conveying the extent each organization (or the company overall) was satisfying customer requirements, at least as far as I was aware. Perhaps external metrics existed, but I was never exposed to the internal organization's performance indicators. So how could this student possibly know his/her process was performing at a *"pretty good"* level? It might have been excellent, horrible, or somewhere in between; they had no empirical evidence to say. It was based solely on emotion (gut metrics), and my message had clearly struck a chord. The traditional manager might find this survey outcome undesirable, but I found it encouraging. If you fail to strike chords, the music is silent. Said another way by an Air Force pilot, *"If you are not taking flak, you are not over the target."* Passivity in the form of enabling dysfunction is not the catalyst to radical change.

People adapt to their surroundings. No wonder the student felt insulted, or even threatened, by my radical claim of all processes falling short of customer requirements to some extent. In his/her mind, and justifiably, given the environment they assimilated to, their world was functioning just fine. Every indication they had—emails from bosses, gut metrics, lack of complaints, lack of empirical feedback from anyone—bolstered their conclusion of presumed performance within tolerance. I totally get it. I took no personal offense to the survey feedback because I recognize the message I presented was radically different from what they had heard before. This is the point of Lean – unfiltered, non-personal critique of **process** performance based on the customer perspective. Lean is intended to disable the auto-pilot system. For the open-minded, training is an opportunity to experience concepts not previously within one's purview. This, of course, assumes their pre-training posture is to learn.

Third, realizing the enormity of traditional behavior I was surrounded by, I debated how best to react to it. Did I need to adjust the presentation? I pondered this at length. Should I leave out this portion of my message, thus not striking a chord with future students? Soften it to say, *"Perhaps some of your processes MIGHT have opportunities to improve,"* or maybe deflect the dysfunction with examples of other companies not measuring up to customer expectations? With all the traveling I was doing, the airline industry was more than accommodating with examples of broken processes. Maybe I could share those and hope the employees could make the osmosis translation to their own processes.

I could have done any number of things with my future classes, but I opted not to change this message or delivery. I decided if I didn't paint the real, unvarnished picture of how Lean clears the fog away and strives to make every process better, then I was doing the audiences a disservice. Sugarcoating process gaps would not help anyone, and if some individuals negatively labeled me, I was willing to take the heat. People don't spontaneously become Lean-minded. Someone has to show them the x-ray depicting the malignancy surrounding their methods and help them understand status quo behavior will continue to get the same results, or even worse. I wanted them to wake up, and fully embrace the reality of every process having opportunities to better satisfy customer requirements. Anything short of this would only prolong the current state inefficiencies, and I was simply not prepared to compromise what I'd learned to-date on my journey of Lean enlightenment. It was not an easy decision, but I was adamant about giving my students a message of reality, in hopes it would shift behavior, even if only by a few. The trick was making sure they realized I was trashing the flawed process, and not them personally. Admittedly, I was not successful with this student, but the overwhelming majority of my audiences viewed the message as a breath of fresh air. They would remain long after the classes finished to ask questions and share their own stories of opportunities.

Embracing the ugly is not a comfortable behavior, and this seems to be a particularly difficult element to shift toward. When things go south in a process, the traditional culture has conditioned people to downplay it, spin it, or ignore it. But just for a moment, imagine the scene playing out like this.

Employee— *"Boss, I need to report we just negatively impacted a customer. We told them product X would be delivered last week, and we just gave it to them today – with defects they identified immediately. It's going to require re-work to fix it."*

Boss – *"Thank you for bringing that up, Dahlia. Let's build a problem statement and run this through the 8-step problem-solving model to determine the root causes and best countermeasures with the right team of subject-matter-experts so we can prevent it from ever happening again. This is a great opportunity to make our process better, even though this is the first late delivery we've had in 4 months. Really appreciate you bringing this to my attention, Dahlia."*

Notice what this boss did NOT do here. He/she didn't deflect the defect or, more importantly, take on the role of dispensing a fix based on their own level of experience or knowledge of the process. My friend Joyce Hinton shared a quote from one of her Green Belt students. *"Just because you are in supervision does not mean you have super vision."* Pretty catchy phrase and also valid. Why can't supervisors recognize their job is not to immediately dispense the right countermeasure to fix a process? The above supervisor also didn't attack Dahlia as the cause of the defect because this boss accepts that neither Dahlia nor other players in the process orchestrated the defect on purpose. This leader knows the process is flawed, and *it* needs to be addressed, not the employees in the process. And, they know the culture they are trying to promote daily sets employees up to freely identify broken process elements and become critical thinkers instead of waiting for the all-knowing manager with super vision to hand out the fix. When the fear of ridicule is absent, and everyone embraces negative outcomes as opportunities to improve, amazing things can manifest.

People seldom come to work planning to intentionally cause process failures. Outright malice is extremely rare. Instead, they are doing the best they can with the process they have been handed, or the one it has morphed into via rampant variability at the time of the defect. Telling employees to *try harder*, or *stop making mistakes*, or, most ridiculous of all, *you need to meet the goal*, is a message doomed to degrade relationships and the culture overall. It is a caveman management technique void of empowerment. This has always been a consistent message in my Lean training classes. What you are shooting for is an entire workforce fearlessly picking at processes until desired outcomes match actual outcomes 100% of the time, and leaders supporting these people to determine how to adjust the process. And, these employees need to have been exposed to adequate training/coaching on how to do this. The *what* without the *how* is useless.

You simply cannot get this result until you, the leader, model the behavior as a Lean leader yourself. You are the required root system of the Lean tree, and short cuts (more water, more manure) are not going to produce the desired outcome.

I have to say the comments I got from leaders during and after my classes were good indicators the extent we as a nation have ill-prepared people with formal authority positions to effectively inspire employees and garner engagement from them. I contend the big picture process of training them is massively broken, and the problem is not even being considered as a performance gap. Impressive resumes with longevity in management roles do not automatically equal an individual adept at leading people. All their experience and promotions could have been achieved with command/control methods, but we just keep rocking along as though all is well. These people will get hired in company after company and perpetuate disrespect. Are we Lean zealots the only ones seeing this performance gap?

Side Story – I taught my four-hour Basics of Lean Six Sigma class in a New York office. The students, for the most part, were very receptive to the information. It was giving them hope things could be better than the current state, and I found this encouraging. It meant they were pondering the possibilities, and who could ask for more than this on the first pass? After the class, several employees hung around to ask me questions and brought up specific issues of broken processes. When the room finally emptied, a supervisor came back in to speak with me.

"I need to tell you something," he started out. "I listened to all you had to say, and it's important you realize we are not a manufacturing company." This was curious to me because I intentionally have service company examples in every section of the training and emphasize how Lean applies to *any* kind of product or service a company might provide. If tasks are performed, they combine into a process, and opportunities to improve the customer experience are present in every case. Perhaps he had preconceived notions of Lean before coming to the class, but his passion for explaining his position was obvious. The gentleman went on to explain to me how our company provided a service to oil/gas producers, and we were not a manufacturer of widgets. Our business was different, was his argument, and then he summed up his position with, "Stop filling my employees' heads with this Lean crap."

Not the reaction I was shooting for as you can well imagine. I recall considering my responses very quickly while he was still explaining how Lean had no useful place in his world. Should I get back on my soapbox and repeat the two-minute elevator speech about how Lean has taken service companies from mediocre to benchmarks of excellence? Should I point out specific companies like Virginia Mason—a health care *service* provider, not a manufacturer—or Integris Health care, or Southwest Airlines? Was it even possible for me to change his opinion of Lean at this point? My local counterpart, Marie Kelly, was busy reconfiguring the room and didn't hear this conversation, but I was positive I wanted to get her input after this gentleman had departed. She knew these people. I was the outsider from Oklahoma they had not met before. Perhaps she could add some missing information to the conundrum. When he seemed finished presenting his polar extreme position to the applicability of Lean in the company, I decided not to re-challenge it. I thanked him for his input and left it at that. This man's mind was not going to change with any words or examples I could quickly cite in defense. He wanted to vent, so I remained in receiver mode. He simply wasn't ready for the magic yet, so I respected his position by not forcing him to listen to me further.

When he left, Marie and I talked about this at length but were unable to determine his underlying agenda. I never met this supervisor again, and he eventually got caught up in a reduction in force the company enacted some months later. Most unfortunately, so did Marie. It's contraindicated (in my opinion) when companies lay off the process improvement professionals during industry downturns, as this is the time they need them the most. I believe it says something about priorities. While a small fraction of my audiences resisted to one degree or another with similar premises to his, none had quite the polarized stance. Perhaps he had a bad experience with an implementation attempt of Lean in a previous company. I had no way of knowing.

My mission could have been thwarted by this experience, but I did not allow that. I reminded myself that the supervisor wasn't really aware of what Lean was or how it could have improved things for both his employees and the processes he presided over. Misunderstanding what Lean is about is common. People get exposed to bits and pieces here and there, perhaps in a meeting when someone mentions it without clear explanation, and they fill in the blanks themselves. It's not unusual for their puzzle pieces to be misarranged, creating a distorted picture. Add to this the natural inclination for human beings to resist change of any kind, even if it will be beneficial.

Bottom line; training to create Lean awareness and build widespread, independent capability absolutely needs to be done with the leaders, not just the workforce. Ideally, they are in the room for the introduction of the topic so they can immediately become active champions in the presence of their employees. The training needs to be carefully planned and delivered from a SME with passion and courage to speak the unfiltered truth to help audiences recognize a complacent path will never lead to amazing results, certainly not by design. And, it needs to be continually evaluated for effectiveness to ensure quality as reported from the customers—the students. Ultimately, if the behavioral needle (more respectful treatment of employees as it connects to the work they are being asked to perform, more roadblocks removed resultant from Gemba walking, more solicited input from employees, more VOC gaps posted and addressed continuously) is not moving, the training is not accomplishing the intent. I would recommend training be abandoned if A+ delivery and results are not your unrelenting expectation. The last thing you want an instructor conveying is indifference to process flaws, or not touting the distinct behavioral elements necessary. Senior leadership needs to understand the message, model it daily, and demand their peers ride the same supplier-mode bus. Your employees and external customers deserve nothing short of this. Which begs the question, with all the researched evidence available on how to create engaged employees, why are traditional cultural environments Deming described many years ago still pervasive in 2019? When will Lean become the new tradition? I have my own thoughts on this, but what are yours?

"The individual has been crushed by our style of management today." – Dr. Edwards Deming

Put Me In, Coach!

"Today, you've got a decision to make. You're gonna get better, or you're gonna get worse, but you're not gonna stay the same. Which will it be?" - Joe Paterno

Coaching is yet another process. Somewhere along my Lean journey, I began to see everything as a process and associated sub-processes. People do things (a string of tasks) in some order (by intentional design or creative spontaneity), and other things happen as a consequence. It doesn't matter if they are getting ready for work, changing a flat tire on their car, performing open-heart surgery, cooking dinner, ordering material from their supply chain provider or trying to score a touchdown with two minutes left on the clock. It's all just a series of steps. The outcome—desirable, repeatable, or not—is irrelevant to applying the label. It also doesn't have to be documented in specific steps, be on a checklist, or a value stream map. If the work is happening, a process exists. People experiencing undesirable outcomes in their businesses will tell me the reason is that "we don't have a process." Well, in reality, you do. Saying we don't have a process to achieve warp speed in space is a correct statement because it hasn't been done yet. By the way, I hope someone out there is working on that.

When you break down coaching into the most basic of process steps, it matters not the type. Football coach, life coach, or Lean coach, the intent is the same in each case. Someone who has stepped in an incredible number of potholes and learned how to navigate the preferred path to success is guiding others (with a process) in the hopes they absorb the desired capability without stepping in every hole themselves. It is a process to nurture others toward independent capability they do not possess yet. Trial and error without guidance can yield success eventually (school of Hard Knocks), but the unnecessary bruises add up quickly and cycle times are painfully long. Bad habits can become entrenched without you even noticing. Sometimes the learner will discard the activity in the face of confusion and frustration. An experienced coach's job is to offset these undesirable outcomes.

With the right supplier-mode mindset, a coach is absolutely a leader, regardless of a formal title or lack thereof. He/she is imparting guidance with continuous feedback and striving to systematically develop the novice to their maximum potential. Not every student has the same potential, learns in the same manner, or responds to guidance in the same way. Some grasp concepts much quicker than others. Some require patient handholding until the capability develops. The challenge of effective coaching with this guaranteed variability is indeed steep. I contend teaching in a classroom setting has notable challenges, but effective coaching outside the classroom is much tougher. Unfortunately, it is sporadically utilized in the process improvement arena. Even when present, sometimes the coach has been assigned the task without adequate miles in their rear-view mirror or any coaching to assist with their coaching. It takes many years to refine the process, but without a doubt, I view coaching as an inspiring part of my journey. Seeing a student go from clueless to independently capable is indescribable—better than any paycheck. Of course, coaches have to be adequately empowered the same as any other contributor in the process.

Once employees have experienced formal classroom training, they are not ready to solo. Throw them back into the workplace expecting spontaneous performance at high levels, and you will be sadly disappointed. This is a lack of empowerment no matter how you look at it. Performance is likely to be low, or they might discontinue the structured problem-solving endeavor completely. You might even declare the training a failure, and to a great extent, your assessment would be correct. However, it might not be the classroom portion failing here, it may be the condition of stopping the training as students exit the room on the last class day. Handing someone a Green Belt or Black Belt certification is lightyears away from declaring them independently competent to replicate the methodology of structured problem solving, let alone expecting them to efficiently coach others. Unfortunately, it happens. Would you buy your six-year-old a bicycle, show them a video, and turn them loose on their own to ride the thing? Hopefully not. Fresh out of class, students need to be individually coached by people experienced in problem solving and engagement generating techniques. They need a readily available sounding board to pick at problem statements, to give insight on how to deal with a data set or a disgruntled team member. They undoubtedly need help empowering inexperienced team leads and sponsors of rapid improvement events. This is rarely taught. The classroom alone is woefully incapable of fully developing the student on the multitude of elements associated with Lean, especially the behavioral aspects. But companies do it all the time. Students might get some coaching during their formal Green belt or Black belt project, but then it stops cold when they return to the workplace. It would be equivalent to teaching the novice how to fly a jet aircraft in a classroom, including time in a simulator, then shaking their hand on graduation day and telling them to start flying airplanes full of passengers without further guidance or experienced pilots to rely on. Coaches are critical. How many full-time coaches does your company have?

Side Story – When I (and many others) finished the government provided Black Belt training, we were then expected to immediately start coaching students after their Green Belt classes, as well as teaching the GB classes ourselves. The classroom training we had just received discussed neither skillset, teaching classes, nor coaching people. Another caveman process poised for failure, as you might imagine. It was a few years of trial and error before I could honestly say I was any good at coaching, and it was part of my full-time job. The formal classroom teaching piece seemed to come naturally (for reasons I cannot explain), but coaching, well, this was another thing altogether. What progression indicators do you look for in the student you are coaching? When do you let them struggle so they can learn how to guide a team on the construction of a SIPOC, or root cause analysis and when do you insert yourself to rescue them before overwhelming frustration sets in? Where is the fine line between coaching and enabling? Do you rewrite their confusing problem statements for them, or do you ask more questions and hope for self-discovery? None of this was covered at even a surface level during black belt training. We were handed a bucket of tools and sent on our way.

Miraculously, a few of us found the right path eventually and went on to become – in my opinion – very effective at motivating those we guided. But it took years of trial and error with far too many errors. To be clear, empowerment was non-existent. We had some contracted master black belts in our midst, but they were working on projects themselves. Coaching us to become coaches was not on their radar. They were in doer-mode. What a waste of knowledge, and we subsequently learned by making mistakes and refining our process after each novice error. This took far longer than it should have. Many abandoned it completely in frustration. Thankfully I hung on, augmented my technique by reading everything I could on the topic, self-critiquing my process after each student interaction, discussing shortcomings with my peers and eventually, it became a rewarding activity to help new minds shift away from traditional methods of dealing with broken processes. In retrospect, the cycle time could have been slashed had experienced coaches been guiding the fledgling coaches through the minefields of discovery. Imagine the impact we could have recognized if we had wheels on our car at the beginning of the journey.

The point of this story is to avoid the potholes yourself. If you are a leader considering Green Belt training for your employees, ensure they come back to an environment with someone experienced to continue the molding. I'm not talking about someone who simply attained their own GB or BB certification and hasn't actively been coaching others, because the training curriculums are typically void of coaching instruction. I therefore boldly claim a black belt, or even a master black belt certification does not equal an effective coach. Your newly trained students absolutely need expert, ongoing support, or the frustration and confusion they will encounter when trying to utilize the new tools could become the catalyst for developing bad habits and/or giving up. You cannot afford this performance gap. If you don't set these employees up for success (empowerment) with coaching after the classroom experience, many of them will never go on to become change agents and coaches themselves. This is a surefire recipe for waste. Recognize the process of post-classroom support needs to be part of the training strategy – in advance of sending anyone to class.

Fortunately, in the first post-government job I took, the director of process improvement I was working for recognized this. Phil Logsdon was the best. My role quickly became guiding the people the company had sent through GB training, and it was a job I will forever cherish. It was nirvana.

The point I want leadership to grasp is ongoing coaching (unlike once and done) is not a luxury in your Lean transformation, it is a necessity. This activity extends to the leaders as well as the newly certified Green Belt. Their initial exposure to what Lean leadership looks like (in a classroom setting) is not going to fill the entire gap. They need honest, ongoing feedback from a coach who isn't censored or influenced by the reporting structure. They need to be told when they missed an opportunity to provide positive reinforcement to an individual contributor, when they failed to empower a team in light of a widening performance gap, or the folly of forgoing a Gemba walk because some meeting seemed more important to them. They need to be reminded about using the Lean language (correctly) with every public encounter they have with employees, and to actively model the behavior beyond the words. Incongruency will be evident to your workforce, and the coach is there to keep you between the rails. The leader is learning just as the remainder of the enterprise is learning, and osmosis is not a reliable process model. Neither is delegation.

Humility is a massive contributing factor to success here. If an individual sees him/herself in a glorified status as a consequence of their title &/or longevity in the company and is not receptive to someone (a coach) challenging their management style, then behavioral shifting is unlikely. At some point, the coach is going to withhold feedback to avoid the negative repercussions. A coach's job is to recognize behavior not conducive with success and then guide the student in a better direction. Fear or similar catalysts causing the feedback to be filtered gets in the way, so this type of hurdle must be removed if learning is to occur. A supervisor who sees themselves as superior to the coach will probably not be receptive to input from a person beneath their title. Its sad, but hierarchal perceptions will impede the process of learning. Again, this is arrogance winning out over humility.

Imagine if every supervisor in your company was continuously coaching other supervisors on the techniques of Lean leadership as part of their daily routine. Imagine if these coaching supervisors were, at the same time, being coached by even more experienced leaders on how to empower employees for success, how to increase engagement levels, and how to show respect to their direct reports as the number one mission. Imagine a culture where building the capabilities of the people is prioritized over the importance of making monthly numbers or achieving the corner office with the view. Imagine what a company could accomplish if this model was the cultural norm, and traditional management was eradicated. Imagine what your retention rates would be as a consequence of people looking forward to coming to work because they felt valued, safe, trusted, respected, and part of process re-development rather than just a recipient of it from the boss. Sound unachievable? I have just described the cultural norm at a mature Lean company.

Don't take my word for it. Do your own research. Coaching isn't an optional, sporadic activity in their world, it is the standard. To what extent is this happening by design in your company? How many of your newly trained process improvement students have an experienced, full-time, passionate coach at their disposal? If you answered, "all of them," how would the students rate the coaching they are getting? Does the student feel respected by the coach, the same way an employee should feel respected by their supervisor? It's the same process with a different pair of participants. Same dynamics and psychology at work. What percentage of your formal leaders are coaching others on how to treat human beings with respect as it applies to the work they are asking people to do and the environment they are doing it in? Are all the coaches bold enough (and empowered) to disregard corporate hierarchy when they see behavioral deficiencies? Are leaders coached on the multitude of ways employees are unintentionally disrespected by traditional management methods? Are behaviors of supervisors formally evaluated by their employees? If RFP was presented in their leadership development training, is it ongoing and coached after the promotion was handed out? If classroom training were sufficient, college football coaches wouldn't be on the sidelines during the games. Their presence would not be necessary at the Gemba for adjustments and encouragement. Even well-established professional golfers have a coach on-hand to provide objective feedback the player is prone to overlook. Are your employees playing the game without an experienced coach to continue their development? The cost of providing this to all managers in companies is probably the restricting criteria, but what is the cost of not having it?

Just a few things to consider if you want to stand far above your caveman competitors.

"The only person who is educated is the one who has learned how to learn and change."
– Carl Rogers

My Final Thoughts

I cannot possibly report the precise number of Lean classes I have taught and people I've had the honor to coach over the years but suffice it to say the combined student population is well into the thousands. With every single offering, from a forty-five-minute Wasteful Meetings class to my two-hour Leading with Lean message designed to spark the desire for a transformation, all the way to my nine-day, full Green Belt class and everything in between, I always had the same goal in mind; permanently influence at least one person in the room. I wanted to influence them to the extent they grasped the power of Lean and as a result, were inspired to never look at company cultures, process improvement, leadership, and the empowerment of human beings in the same way they did before.

Classroom Training, Coaching, Absorption, Behavioral Shift, then students eventually Coaching others—this is the process flow I strive for. Each step has its own unique hurdles and challenges, and it doesn't always flow in a smooth, linear fashion as illustrated. Re-work is a given, and patience is mandatory. But this remains my high-level process approach to helping individuals transform a company culture into a place everyone is reaching for the same condition of unimagined excellence.

Obviously, I wasn't going to reach everyone in the room every time. Some would discard the message in whole for a variety of reasons, while others would recognize the incredible potential but remain passively inactive in the safety of their cubicle because shifting would be too risky in their corporate environment. Some would noodle on the possibility it might hold and perhaps incorporate a thing or two in their behavioral repertoire, and some—just a few every now and then—would firmly grasp the brass ring for a lifetime and wonder why they ever tolerated traditional conditions before. Those individuals were my paycheck, my oxygen. I could see the transformation on their animated faces, hear it in their anticipatory comments, relished it when they went on to demand respectful behavior from their bosses, and beamed with joy when they took the initiative to challenge broken processes and facilitate rapid improvement events to close performance gaps with a team of SMEs. The ultimate student outcome would be the genesis of a rebellious, empowered change agent determined to forever influence yet more people on what CI +RFP really looked like. A *rebel without a pause*, if you will. They became leaders with or without an assigned title. The only way it could have been better is if I would have achieved an ideal state. This would have me with Pied Piper capabilities - I play the message on my magic Lean flute and the masses follow me from Dysfunction Junction into the world of Continuous Improvement + Respect for People because their immediate absorption of a much better way to behave was indisputable. Nice fantasy, huh? I often ponder how Dr. Deming must have felt when his concepts were initially only embraced in Japan. I imagine what might have been if his home country, the United States of America had listened and absorbed his incredible genius back in the 1950s. I also imagine what the political landscape could look like if elected officials – who claim the title of a public servant—evolved into servant leaders instead of self-serving bureaucrats pontificating for their own benefit. For me, regardless of the numbers boarding the Lean bus after hearing the message, those discarding the habits of traditional management are the folks sustaining my continued mission energy.

I've taken the time to specifically document my mission *why* using the guidance in Simon Sinek's book, *Start with Why*. After several iterations, I came up with the "Why" of my teaching and coaching mission. I do what I do because…

EVERY EMPLOYEE DESERVES TO BE VALUED, RESPECTED, AND INSPIRED TO CONTRIBUTE TO SOMETHING LARGER THAN THEIR ASSIGNED JOB TASKS.

What is the WHY of your mission? Why do you do what you do? I invite you to take the time and discover the words most aligned with *your* why. It is a worthy endeavor to document it and the introspection might surprise you.

I am fully committed to this, and it will remain why I will continue to share the Lean message in any forum, for any interested audience, until I am unable to determine which way is up, and never allow myself to be subjected to traditional management filtration while doing it.

No greater honor can be bestowed upon a teacher than to witness freshly planted seeds grow right before their eyes. It is euphoric and never gets old. Several of those individuals come to mind in no particular order – Bernie Wile, Mike Waits, Danette Beach, Daniela Sanders, Marie Kelly, Mike Cryer, Cameron Hutton, Beau Galloway, Jason Sarakatsannis, Kerri Stewart, Dahlia Rainwater, Michelle LaFluer, Ivan Ortiz, Lucas Hahn, Ryan Mulvania, Brian Jackson, Bryan Robison, Kandi Wilson, Nicholas Christian, Kate Zaychenko, Shawncie Carpenter, Katy Rich, Mari Bagensie, Mike Smith, Jason Schmitz, Melissa McGillen, Rob Johnson, Carter Stokeld, Michelle Holland, Kyle Moore, and many more whose names escape me. I apologize to those countless others I have failed to mention here, but I'm proud of each and every one of you for listening to the message of Lean and shifting even a little bit from your initial view. The energy and excitement receptive students exhibited for Lean sustained and humbled me along my journey. They were a constant reminder what I was doing was worthwhile and to not give up when traditional managers scoffed at my message or tried to manipulate my approach with their traditional command/control methods. I will forever rebel against fake Lean because I know what a properly developed culture can do for human beings, and for a company overall. Subordination and capitulating to dysfunction in order to retain a job should never be burdened upon a person.

With this book, I have intended to cast the Lean net to a much broader audience than I could possibly have done in person. Sharing my experiences would have been too limited had I not undertaken this documentation. I suppose the summation questions I pose to formal and informal leaders are these. Have you settled for the level of leadership competence you possess at this moment in time, and if yes, why? If no, what are you actively doing to improve daily? Reading? Asking peers for unfiltered feedback? Humbling yourself to a coach for guidance? Something else? Wishing your improvement into existence is not going to make it happen. It takes action. Again, unfiltered honesty is critical here. I encourage you to explore the Humble Pie assessment I have provided at the end of the book and determine where your performance gaps are.

In the event you disagreed with most of what I have shared or even took offense to it, can you honestly say with absolute certainty you are treating your employees with the full respect they deserve? Are they as empowered as they could be? Is your environment inspiring them with the motivation to constantly seek improvements to every aspect of their current state tasks, or does your method of managing allow their creative spirit to atrophy? Provide poor lighting and insufficient nurturing to any plant, and its flowers will cease to bloom. In time, the plant will die, and I equate this death to subdued employees beaten into submission and void of any signs of engagement. Once their creativity and sense of value has been destroyed, the company as a whole will suffer. Only your employees can confirm or negate your perception of their work experience. Do they deserve an opportunity to provide this insight? Do you even think their input is necessary in the first place? I challenge you to re-imagine everything you believe about leadership techniques and then decide if you are willing to improve. If you believe improvement is unnecessary, then I have failed to reach any part of you. In this case, I at least can thank you for allowing me the opportunity to present what I have learned. Perhaps in time you might feel differently.

If even a single reader shifts their leadership style as a result of introspective analysis from my journey's lessons, the many months I spent writing this book will not have been in vain. My brutally honest assessment of traditional management is intentionally designed to help people recognize the negative impact it has on human beings, employees who are eager to make a difference but have been demotivated with the broken processes bestowed upon them by their misguided but otherwise well-intentioned supervisors. Most of these bosses do not set out to disrespect people, but I hope they recognize the outcome is equivalent to intentional disrespect. Also, recognize it can be changed. If you are still on this side of the dirt, you have time to shift from a manager to a respectful leader. Perhaps some of you will alter your current process and embrace Lean leadership because you now recognize it will have a positive influence on the people within your charge and ultimately, your organization's success. I also hope you are lucky to work for at least one Phil Logsdon or a Ken Sloan in your lifetime. If so, you will have been given a rare opportunity. These gentlemen both epitomized servant leadership and earned the respect of many during their careers.

Please feel free to share your comments about the book (LinkedIn is one avenue), your own successes with problem-solving, the humorously broken processes you have observed, been subjected to, contributed to yourself, the motivating and demotivating bosses you've worked for, and the engagement levels of employees you personally have helped increase through the magic of empowerment. Strive to continuously accomplish this last element, and you have my respect forever.

Above all, never cease learning more about the behaviors of Lean leadership. No human being has assimilated it all, nor can they. May its wonder permeate your DNA as it has mine.

I close with one last quote because it embodies what I have chosen to devote my life energy to for the past nineteen years. It speaks to what CAN BE when you choose to develop the best version of yourself and the broader environment we all share. Current state, or "pretty good" is never good enough, in my opinion. Only you can decide if it is good enough for you.

"…the people who are crazy enough to think they can change the world are the ones who do." – Steve Jobs

Thanks for reading, and,
BOOMER SOONER!

PS: I always love to hear from people about their own Lean journeys, whether just starting out or well down the path. Feel free to connect with me on LinkedIn or contact me via my website, www.theleanmachinellc.com.

Humble Pie Assessment

Command/Control mode. Self-serving
Decrees changes to processes without VOC or employee input
Creates an atmosphere of fear and retribution for mistakes
Prefers employees who do what they are told without pushback

Traditional Mgr

Lean Leader

Servant mode. Is committed to developing employees
and processes to their fullest by continuously reducing waste
all based on Voice of the Customer (VOC)

Where does your needle land on the Manager – Servant/Lean Leader Protractor?

I've created a brief, two-part, eleven question assessment for managers to evaluate their process of leading others. Please note, this is far from a comprehensive analysis of all things Lean as they relate to your behavioral tendencies, but instead, is just a basic indicator of how your current-state leadership process is doing, and how small or large the performance gaps might be. If you want to know what your reflection in the mirror really looks like, *absolute honesty and unfiltered objectivity is a must*. Anything short of this will be a waste of your time and disrespectful to your employees.

Humble Pie Assessment Instructions (overview):

Part 1, Questions 1-8 are to be answered by individuals in formal management positions, meaning, you have employees reporting directly to you. Then, additional insight comes from comparing the choices you (as a supervisor) selected to these questions with the ones your peers (at least 3 or 4, more if possible) think are most aligned with your actual behaviors. If you are not convinced selected peers will be completely honest with you, please choose someone else. Sycophants are of no use to anyone seeking an assessment of themselves. Any disinclination on their part to be *brutally honest* with you will corrupt the information these questions are intended to discover/measure. To clarify, after you respond to 1-8, you are then asking several individuals above, below, or at your managerial level, *"Which of these answers do you think most represents my behavior?"* If they have zero information with which to provide their observed perception of your behavior, do not prompt them with your antidotal stories – just skip collection of their input on said questions. If they don't know, they don't know. Their guesses are of no value. The only right answer is the one matching your true current state. Comparison of your self-evaluation with how your peers perceive you will add refinements to your actual performance gaps – thus increasing the opportunities to recognize reality and improve accordingly. Sidestepping honesty because you think it will hurt someone's feelings is an example of the filter to avoid. Again, if you and your peers are not 100% honest with the answer selections, this activity will be a waste of time.

Part 2, Questions 9-11 need to be honestly answered by your direct report employees, and additionally, you should speculate on their responses in advance. Share your speculations with each of them **after** they have responded to the 3 questions. This will assist with recognizing differences between how you see yourself, how you think people see you, and how they actually see you. Keep in mind, your employee's perceptions of you are their reality, and this perception is what directly impacts their behavior as an employee. If differences appear between what you speculated they would say, and what they did say, it is likely other discrepancies exist between what you think and what is. This, in turn, should prompt more in-depth digging as appropriate on other leadership issues. The disparity "whys" should be explored with the employees who answered the questions.

Lastly, realize a poor score only indicates your *process* of creating an environment of continuous improvement + respect for people is failing, not necessarily *you* the person in charge of it. That is, unless you, 1) Proclaim you are an entrenched traditional manager and are damn well determined to stay this way, or 2) Call yourself a Lean Leader despite obvious and overt behavior to the contrary and you plan to continue faking it to convince others you are on-board. If either of these two conditions is in place, the just-do-it (JDI) countermeasure should be apparent to the person you report to.

PART 1

Reminder: Questions 1 through 8 are to be answered by individuals in formal management positions and according to the additional instructions given in the overview. This is the ***current*** state – how you behave <u>now</u> - **not** how you intend to behave in the future.

Please read the choices *very carefully* before selection. Adjectives are critical. Compound statements with "and" require your behavior meets <u>all</u> listed elements. If the statement is not a completely accurate description of your behavior, choose the option matching the closest.

1. **Which of these most accurately reflects your approach to process improvement?**

    a. I usually leave a process alone until a customer complains or I am forced to improve it.
    b. I engage with process improvement opportunities if I recognize them and time permits.
    c. I fully engage with process improvement opportunities as they show up.
    d. Regardless of the current state, I relentlessly seek out and act on opportunities to improve a process' ability to satisfy VOC more efficiently.

2. **Which of these customer-related conditions is most accurate for the organization/group you manage?**
(Note: "Downstream" customers include Internal <u>and</u> External customers.)

    a. I do not have documented VOC for downstream customers.
    b. I have documented VOC for downstream customers but have <u>not</u> communicated it to all my direct reports.
    c. I have documented VOC for downstream customers and have communicated it to all my direct reports but have <u>not</u> developed performance indicators to evaluate and act on gaps.
    d. I have documented VOC for downstream customers, have communicated it to all my direct reports, and have posted performance indicators to continuously evaluate and act on gaps.

3. **To what extent are you a Gemba walker?**

    a. I sometimes go to where the actual work is taking place (management by walking around), but I do not formally Gemba walk.

b. I formally Gemba walk, but it is not a regular activity (less than once a week).
c. I formally Gemba walk as a regular activity (at least once a week).
d. I formally Gemba walk daily.

4. Which of these most accurately reflects your pattern as a formally assigned manager?

a. I generally do not <u>solicit</u> input or challenges from subject matter experts (SMEs) on processes.
b. I occasionally <u>solicit</u> input from SMEs but tend to rely on my own instincts about processes.
c. I am open to SMEs occasionally challenging process without my soliciting their input first.
d. I overtly encourage <u>and</u> reinforce SMEs to challenge processes constantly without my soliciting their input first.

5. Which of these most accurately reflects your behavior?

a. If employees cite process hurdles in their way, I typically get annoyed.
b. If employees cite process hurdles in their way, I sometimes get annoyed.
c. If employees cite process hurdles in their way, I don't get annoyed but also don't often make it a priority to help knock down the hurdles.
d. I expect <u>and</u> encourage employees to cite process hurdles in their way, <u>and</u> I make it a high priority to help knock down the hurdles.

6. Which of these most accurately reflects your employee recognition process?

a. I am disinclined to thank an employee for something because I believe it is their job to do the work they are being paid for.
b. I occasionally thank employees for their efforts when they have done something particularly well, but not for everyday successes.
c. I often thank employees for their efforts at batched gatherings or when I remember to do it.
d. I constantly thank employees for their efforts <u>and</u> do everything I can to remind them how valued they are on a <u>daily</u> basis.

7. Which of these most accurately reflects your opinion?

a. People are the cause of most undesirable process outcomes.
b. Undesirable outcomes are caused equally by people and processes.

c. The process is likely the cause of most undesirable outcomes, although I believe people could work harder to prevent some of the defects.

d. In the absence of intentional malice on the employees' part, broken processes are the cause of nearly every undesirable outcome.

8. Which of these most accurately reflects your approach to reading/learning about the techniques of leadership and engagement?

a. I rarely read books or articles related to Servant/Lean leadership or employee engagement (0-1 monthly).

b. I occasionally read books or articles related to Servant/Lean leadership or employee engagement when someone else recommends them to me (1-3 monthly), but I don't seek them out on my own.

c. I occasionally do seek out and read books or articles related to Servant/Lean leadership or employee engagement (1-3 monthly).

d. I continuously seek out books or articles related to Servant/Lean leadership or employee engagement (more than 3 monthly) and continually recommend them to others.

PART 2

NOTE: Questions 9-11 are to be answered by your direct reports. Compare their answers to your speculation of how you thought they would respond.

9. Which of these most accurately reflects how you view your supervisor's demeanor?

    a. (S)he believes/behaves as if they are far more valuable to the process than their direct reports doing the work.

    b. (S)he believes/behaves as if they are equally important to the process as direct reports doing the work.

    c. (S)he believes/behaves as if they are somewhat less valuable to the process than direct reports doing the work.

    d. (S)he believes/behaves as if they are far less valuable to the process than direct reports doing the work.

10. Which of these most accurately reflects how you view your supervisor's efforts to position direct reports for success?
(Positioning for success = Provides the right training, the right equipment, the right support, and clear guidance before, during, <u>and</u> after process execution.)

    a. (S)he <u>never</u> strives to position direct reports for success according to the definition.

    b. (S)he <u>occasionally</u> strives to position direct reports for success according to the definition.

    c. (S)he <u>often</u> strives to position direct reports for success according to the definition.

    d. (S)he <u>always</u> strives to position direct reports for success according to the definition.

11. Which of these statements most accurately reflects how you view your supervisor's behavior according to the two polar extreme definitions?
Traditional Management = Command/Control mode. Self-serving, decrees changes to process without VOC or employee input, creates an atmosphere of fear and retribution for mistakes, prefers employees who do what they are told without pushback.
Servant/Lean Leadership = Servant/Supplier mode. Is committed to developing employees and processes to their fullest by continuously reducing wasteful activity based on VOC.

a.   (S)he leans heavily toward traditional management.
b.   (S)he leans more toward traditional management.
c.   (S)he leans more toward servant/Lean leadership.
d.   (S)he leans heavily toward servant/Lean leadership.

Humble Pie Survey Scoring Process

Award yourself
0 points for each **A** answer
1 point for each **B** answer
2 points for each **C** answer
3 points for each **D** answer

For Part 1, Questions 1-8, the minimum point total is 0 (zero). The maximum point total is 24. Report your total as a fraction of 24. Example: **16/24 points**.

For Part 2, Questions 9-11, the minimum point total is 0 (zero). The maximum possible point total is dependent upon the <u>number of direct reports you have</u>. Each of the three questions will range from 0 (zero) points to 3 points. You can accumulate up to 9 points per employee maximum. Multiply 9 times the number of direct reports, and you have *your* maximum point total possible. Add the cumulative number of points from all direct reports to determine your <u>actual</u> total and report as a fraction of your maximum <u>possible</u>.

Example: If you have 10 direct reports, the minimum possible would be 0 (zero) points. (10 employees, 0 points from each employee on all 3 questions.)

Your maximum possible points would 90. (10 employees, 3 points from each employee max on all 3 questions. 9 x 10 = 90).

If you accumulated 65 points out of a possible 90 total points for your 10 direct reports, your documented result is reported as **65/90 points**.

After direct reports respond on 9-11, check for alignment with your initial speculations of how you thought they would each respond to each of the three questions. This post-survey discussion should be done in-person.

CAUTION! Stay in RECEIVER-mode when you ask employees why they believe the differences exist. Ask for corroborating examples. Typically, you will rate yourself higher than they do. Do **not** challenge their perceptions or attempt to change their minds. Do **not** defend yourself if a difference exists. Their perception is their reality, and a gap in *your* behavior exists. This is the entire intent of the exercise – discovering your behavior gaps perceived by your employees.

For all 11 questions, I encourage you to make a side-by-side comparison of scores with your peers. This is not meant to be a competition, but the leadership pulse of the company overall. I also recommend posting scores for everyone to see and discuss. Share scores as broadly as the culture is willing. This is an opportunity to see what your environment looks like overall. No one should be punished for ugly scores, only encouraged to close the gaps. Repeating the Humble Pie assessment periodically (recommend quarterly) will give perspective on the needle moving or not.

Interpreting Needle Position for Part 1, Questions 1-8:

0-8/24 points. You are very much a traditional manager and need serious intervention if you wish to create engagement in your employees. Your process is currently dramatically failing them. It is time to step up or step away from a formal authority position.

9-11/24 points. Huge performance gap here, but not insurmountable. We call it Sooner Magic in Norman, Oklahoma. Have an energy drink and get started improving with RCA and countermeasure development.

12-15/24 points. Your process is on the path to moderate acceptability, but still lots of work to be done. There is hope for you to become a strong Lean leader if you are humble enough to continue learning and improving.

16-19/24 points. Encouraging signs of Lean leadership are evident in your process. Take the rest of the day off with pay but come back tomorrow with renewed motivation to get even better, because you still have a performance gap.

20-23/24 points. Congratulations. You have evolved beyond a manager into a fairly strong Lean leader. People will want to work for you and would recommend you to others. Now strive to continuously improve your leadership process even more, resist backsliding, and please coach others to help them progress as far as you have.

24/24 points. As my friend, Terri would say, "*Woo Whoo!*" You are a strong, respectful leader capable of coaching others on the proper way to behave towards employees. If you are the CEO of your company, the entire enterprise is poised for greatness.

Interpreting Needle Position for Part 2, Questions 9-11:

ANY response less than 3 on any of these questions from any direct report is a performance gap and should be the catalyst for immediate root cause analysis and countermeasure development. Seek <u>their</u> input on both the RCs and CMs to close the gaps in your management process. Your employees deserve nothing less.

Please do not use an average for any reason whatsoever! An average of these scores is useless because you are searching for gaps. Consider 3 points on each question to be the lower specification limit (a value to never drop below) for that question. The closer you are to the maximum available points, the more you are behaving as a Servant/Lean leader ***from their perspective***. View ***ANY*** employee response short of a 3 on each question as a performance gap with your behavior toward the particular employee. Remember… their perception is their reality. If you attempt to convince them (or yourself) their answers are off-track, you have completely missed the opportunity to evaluate yourself from their eyes.

Next, get input from your employees (collectively) to determine the root causes to <u>your</u> management process gaps and what <u>they</u> believe you need to do to close these gaps. Never stop improving. Status quo will not serve you well.

About the Author

Brian deFonteny found his career passion almost by happenstance—a civil servant on an Air Force base making his way from aircraft mechanic to the process improvement office. He found that his degrees in psychology and human relations provided a good foundation for his new position, and now, as a certified Lean Six Sigma Black Belt, he's spent the last two decades training, coaching, and leading process improvement—particularly as it relates to leadership involvement. He retired from the regular nine to five life in 2018 but has continued to bring his excitement for Lean to organizations to help them find their way to greatness, and has just recently accepted an adjunct position with his alma mater, the University of Oklahoma.

When he's not busy helping people understand and eliminate process waste, he enjoys reading, traveling, the occasional binge-watching of vintage television reruns, and, of course, cheering on his beloved Sooners every football season.

Originally hailing from Pennsylvania, Brian now lives with his wife, Cheri, in Oklahoma. They have one adult son, and various practically feral cats that he helps feed only because Cheri likes them.

Brian welcomes you to connect with him on LinkedIn to discuss any or all of these things (especially the football!), or you can reach him via his website, www.theleanmachinellc.com.

Notes

[i] This quotation is often attributed to John Quincy Adams; I've frequently made that attribution myself. But I believe we've all been taken.

Garson. "If Your Actions Inspire Others To Dream More, Learn More, Do More and Become More, You Are a Leader." Quote Investigator. July 3, 2011. Accessed July 19, 2019. https://quoteinvestigator.com/2011/07/03/inspire-dream-leader/.

Sanders, Katie. "Ivanka Trump Includes Fake John Quincy Adams Quote in Book." @politifact. May 05, 2017. Accessed July 19, 2019. https://www.politifact.com/truth-o-meter/statements/2017/may/05/ivanka-trump-book-john-quincy-adams-quote/.

[ii] "Best Practices from Best Companies, Part 1 of 3: Recruitment." Great Place To Work United States. January 21, 2012. Accessed July 19, 2019. https://www.greatplacetowork.com/resources/blog/best-practices-from-best-companies-part-1-of-3-recruitment.

[iii] "Isao Yoshino Reflects on the Role of Management at Toyota." Planet Lean. September 17, 2018. Accessed July 19, 2019. https://planet-lean.com/interview-with-isao-yoshino-on-management-at-toyota/.

[iv] Ballé, Michael, Roberto Priolo, and Daniel T. Jones. *Lead with Lean*. CreateSpace Independent Publishing Platform, 2016.

[v] Koenigsaecker, George. *Leading the Lean Enterprise Transformation*. Portland, Or.: Productivity, 2013.

[vi] Minshew, Kathryn. "6 Tricks for Better Performance Reviews." Inc.com. July 31, 2012. Accessed July 19, 2019. https://www.inc.com/kathryn-minshew/best-practices-for-performance-reviews.html.

[vii] Marciano, Paul L. *Carrots and Sticks Don't Work: Build a Culture of Employee Engagement with the Principles of Respect*. New York: McGraw-Hill, 2010.

[viii] Deming, W. Edwards, and Joyce Nilsson. Orsini. *The Essential Deming: Leadership Principles from the Father of Quality*. New York: McGraw-Hill, 2013.

[ix] Hunter, John. "The W. Edwards Deming Institute Blog." The W Edwards Deming Institute Blog. March 3, 2016. Accessed July 19, 2019. https://blog.deming.org/2016/03/institute-leadership/.

[x] Liker, Jeffrey K., and George Trachilis. *Developing Lean Leaders at All Levels: A Practical Guide*. Winnipeg: Lean Leadership Institute Publ, 2014.

[xi] Lencioni, Patrick. *The Truth about Employee Engagement: A Fable about Addressing the Three Root Causes of Job Misery*. San Francisco, CA: Jossey-Bass, Wiley, 2016.

[xii] *The Enthusiastic Employee*. Wharton School Pub, 2008.

[xiii] Ballé, Michael, Roberto Priolo, and Daniel T. Jones. *Lead with Lean*. CreateSpace Independent Publishing Platform, 2016.

[xiv] Bradberry, Travis. "9 Bad Manager Mistakes That Make Good People Quit." LinkedIn. January 30, 2017. Accessed July 19, 2019. https://www.linkedin.com/pulse/bad-manager-mistakes-make-good-people-quit-dr-travis-bradberry.

[xv] Richardson, Tracey M., and Ernie Richardson. *The Toyota Engagement Equation How to Understand and Implement Continuous Improvement Thinking in Any Organization*. New York: McGraw-Hill Education, 2017.

[xvi] Byrne, Andrew, and James P. Womack. *The Lean Turnaround: How Business Leaders Use Lean Principles to Create Value and Transform Their Company*. Maidenhead: McGraw-Hill, 2012.

[xvii] Ibid

[xviii] Stoller, Jacob. *The Lean CEO: Building World-class Organizations, One Step at a Time*. New York: McGraw-Hill Education, 2015.

[xix] Prisco, Jacopo. "Why UPS Trucks Never Turn Left." CNN. February 23, 2017. Accessed July 19, 2019. https://www.cnn.com/2017/02/16/world/ups-trucks-no-left-turns/index.html.

[xx] Lott, Jeremy. "New Coke: Anatomy of a Terrible Decision - Jeremy Lott." Michael Hyatt. September 05, 2018. Accessed July 19, 2019. https://michaelhyatt.com/new-coke/.

[xxi] Wetzel, Gary. "The U.S. Navy Faces A Reckoning After Two Disastrous And Embarrassing Collisions At Sea." Foxtrot Alpha. November 02, 2017. Accessed July 19, 2019. https://foxtrotalpha.jalopnik.com/the-u-s-navy-faces-a-reckoning-after-two-disastrous-an-1820067583.

[xxii] Dalio, Ray. Principles: Life and Work. Simon and Schuster, 2017.

[xxiii] Sinek, Simon. "Why Good Leaders Make You Feel Safe." TED, n.d. https://www.ted.com/talks/simon_sinek_why_good_leaders_make_you_feel_safe.

Made in the USA
Coppell, TX
22 November 2019

11704294R00138